Sleeping with
   One Eye Open

Women
Writers
and the
Art of
Survival

Sleeping with
One Eye Open

Edited by
Marilyn Kallet
and
Judith Ortiz Cofer

The
University
of Georgia Press
Athens and
London

© 1999 by the University of Georgia Press
Athens, Georgia 30602
All rights reserved
Designed by Sandra Strother Hudson
Set in Aldus by G&S Typesetters, Inc.
Printed and bound by McNaughton & Gunn
The paper in this book meets the guidelines for permanence and durability
of the Committee on Production Guidelines for Book Longevity of the
Council on Library Resources.
Printed in the United States of America

03   02   01   00   99   C   5   4   3   2   1
03   02   01   00   99   P   5   4   3   2   1

Library of Congress Cataloging-in-Publication Data
Sleeping with one eye open : women writers and the art of survival / edited
by Marilyn Kallet and Judith Ortiz Cofer.
      p.   cm.
ISBN 0-8203-2152-4 (alk. paper). — ISBN 0-8203-2153-2 (pbk. : alk. paper)
1. Women authors, American—20th century—Biography.
2. Authorship—Sex differences.   3. Women—Authorship.
I. Kallet, Marilyn, 1946– .   II. Ortiz Cofer, Judith, 1952– .
PS151.S56   1999
810.9′9287—dc21
[B]   99-23590

British Library Cataloging-in-Publication Data available

Acknowledgments for previously published works appear on pages xv–xvi,
which constitute an extension of the copyright page.

Frontispiece: *My Mother's Garden* © 1993 by Lee Lawson

To my daughter, Heather, whose music is her poetry.

MARILYN KALLET

To my daughter, Tanya, hoping that she will always keep poetry in her life.

JUDITH ORTIZ COFER

The true artist will use her creativity to find a way,

to carve the time, to claim a kitchen table, a library carrel,

if a room of her own is not possible. She will use subterfuge

if necessary, write poems in her recipe book, give up

sleeping time or social time, and write.

JUDITH ORTIZ COFER

"The Woman Who Slept with One Eye Open:

Notes on Being a Writer"

Contents

I. Waking Myths, Waking Words

3. Sounds of Hazard and Survival

4. The Crucible of Family

member of the literary community. Thus I have targeted the encouragement of young writers as a primary concern and volunteer my efforts with the Asian American Writers' Workshop (AAWW).

Like the altar awaiting the tears of repentant girls, each line leads me to tread the double edges of darkness and brightness, to consider the complexities of salvation, even as I stood blinking in the eye of my grandparents' storm. The poem embodies the order and safe ground I so craved in my mother's and stepmother's houses. . . .

Radical politics, dark sexuality, premature death: these three things are, for me, forever connected and intertwined with images of books; and images of books, themselves, are forever connected and intertwined with images of my father.

Acknowledgments

A volume such as this calls for active collaboration. The editors wish to thank each of the authors—most of whom wrote essays specifically for our book, all of whom demonstrated creative insight and rare patience with the process of building the volume. Malcolm Call, senior editor at the University of Georgia Press, helped us to shape the collection and offered trust and encouragement. Karen Orchard, director at the University of Georgia Press, has also been consistent in her support for this project. Prof. Francis Payne Adler, director of Creative Writing and Social Action at California State University, Monterey, offered invaluable suggestions for editing. The Graduate Studies Program in English at the University of Tennessee provided us with a research assistant at the outset of our project; Elaine Oswald was most helpful. Other writers who helped out as needed include Kristen Timberlake, Eileen Joy, JoAngela Edwins, and Jeff Cooper. In the final preparation of the manuscript, the assistance of poets Judy Loest and Victoria Raschke was invaluable. Our copy editor, Gayle Swanson, worked with us to put the finishing touches on this manuscript, and all of us—editors and contributors—are deeply grateful.

Some of the essays and poems in this volume have been published in literary magazines or have appeared in earlier, different versions. Grateful acknowledgments are made to the editors and authors for permission to reprint:

Judith Ortiz Cofer, "Five A.M.: Writing as Ritual," *The Latin Deli: Prose and Poetry* (Athens: University of Georgia Press, 1993), 166–68.

Cofer's "The Woman Who Slept with One Eye Open: Notes on Being a Writer" appeared in *American Voice* 32 (1993): 80–91. Cofer's poem "The Woman Who Was Left at the Altar" is from *Reaching for the Mainland and Selected New Poems,* by Judith Ortiz Cofer (Tempe, AZ: Bilingual Review Press, 1995); copyright, Bilingual Review/Press and Judith Ortiz Cofer.

Julie Checkoway, "The Writer in the Family: Civics Lessons for Kindred Spirits," *Poets & Writers* 26.3 (1998): 54–59.

Lucille Clifton, "Doing What You Will Do: An Interview with Lucille Clifton by Marilyn Kallet," appeared as "Poetry Is a Human Art," *New Millennium Writings* 3.2 (1998–99).

Janice Eidus, "My Father's Legacy, or Why I Write," *American Voice* 30 (1993): 65–71. The essay was also published in a slightly different version in the anthology *Brought to Book* (Penguin) in the United Kingdom in 1992.

An earlier version of Joy Harjo's "Finding the Groove" appeared as "Suspended," copyright Joy Harjo.

Colette Inez, "Sounds of Hazard and Survival," *American Voice* 45 (1998): 80–86.

Marilyn Kallet, "Poetry Began Me," *Entelechy* (1995): 11–21.

Linda Parsons Marion's poem "Rocker" appeared in *Press* in 1996 and then in her collection *Home Fires* (Abington, VA: Sow's Ear Press, 1997).

Colleen J. McElroy's poem "Shelley at Sequim Inlet" appeared in her *Travelling Music* (Ashland, OR: Story Line Press, 1998). Reprinted by permission.

Tillie Olsen, "Excerpts from a Talk by Tillie Olsen," reprinted by permission of Tillie Olsen from *Trellis* 3 (summer 1978): 35–42. Copyright 1978 by Tillie Olsen. All rights reserved.

Katherine Smith's poem "Simmering" appeared in *Now & Then* 15.2 (1998): 35. Reprinted by permission.

Tess Gallagher's "The Pure Place" and Denise Levertov's "The Prime Necessity" appear here for the first time. "The Pure Place" copyright 1999 by Tess Gallagher. "The Prime Necessity" copyright 1999 by the Denise Levertov Literary Trust, Paul A. Lacey, Literary Executor.

Introduction

MARILYN KALLET

The seeds of *Sleeping with One Eye Open* were sown in the fall of 1992 when Judith Ortiz Cofer visited the University of Tennessee as NEA Poet-in-Residence. One afternoon the two of us took time out of a hectic teaching and reading schedule to tape an interview about Cofer's work. We talked extensively about her writing and values, her commitment to "not forgetting" the stories of childhood or cultural traditions. But we had less time to talk about the connection between a writer's life and work, the ways in which Cofer had successfully integrated the roles of professor, writer, wife, and mother. And she was writing not only poetry and fiction but essays and plays as well. Off-tape, we spoke about Cofer's early life as a writer—how she had managed to sustain a full-time teaching job along with mothering a young child, how she began to write by rising each day at 5 A.M. As one who was also juggling multiple roles and tasks, I needed to know more about her skills.

Cofer mentioned that she had written an essay entitled "The Woman Who Slept with One Eye Open," which expanded on her beginnings as a writer, explaining how she had learned from the mythic María Sabida to protect her writing time. We agreed that such an essay could provide an excellent beginning for a book that would be useful to other writers, particularly to women. A few weeks later we began to circulate Cofer's lead essay among women writers and artists. The essays that came to us in response were moving testimonies of how women writers manage to maintain their motivation and inspiration, to thrive in the face of obstacles.

"Waking Myths, Waking Words," the first section of our book, reveals how myth, ritual, poetry, and stories are artistic and personal sources for many women writers. Judith Ortiz Cofer's way of arming herself with courage and beauty for the struggle that a writer's life must take was to wrap herself in the stories she had heard from her grandmother (Mamá) in Puerto Rico. And to turn those stories to account, to reinterpret them in the light of the contemporary woman writer's needs. María Sabida— the woman who slept with one eye open—is both artful and nurturing. She fiercely guards her art. Cofer has chosen a powerful mentor in María Sabida, the one who seized the "macho" on behalf of her life and work.

My own essay, "Poetry Began Me," chronicles the beginnings of a poet's life, telling how words first helped me to shape my destiny. Long before I had a family and a full-time teaching job, I began to build a language for myself that would enable me to explore feelings in a controlled, aesthetic manner. In those days, time was not the enemy; rather, the threat was an intense emotional life that almost drowned me. Poetry was my rescuer, helping me to disentangle myself from the seductive myth of Persephone. Twenty-five years later, as I work at writing, teaching, and raising a family, I feel closer to Demeter than to Persephone— it is Demeter who sleeps with one eye open.

In "Inking In the Myth," Alice Friman also writes about the life of myth in an intimate way, as she recounts her obsession with getting a tattoo. With the image of Pegasus drawn into her back, Friman is the embodiment of the inspired poet. Poetry enables her to grapple with sorrow, with fear and physical pain, with her grief over her father's death, with whatever comes.

Determined to keep writing in the face of censorship, Amy Friedman Fraser turned to creating children's books and myths for young people. "Listening for the Singing Goose" provides an account not only of the artist's motivation and agility but also of the wisdom of children. Here myth is a breathing place for the author, a world in which to survive and to keep writing alive.

While good writing is never easy, sometimes the hardest part is just sitting down to the task. In "Manipulations in the Darkroom," the poet Barbara Goldberg confides in us about the rituals she goes through before writing. She calls these actions "propitiating Eros" and returns to the myth of Psyche and Eros to give a context to ritual tasks in the lives of modern poets and writers.

In "Fire, Wax, Smoke," Sandra Benítez tells us that her own initiation as a writer involved years of hard work at a failed novel before she found her true subject. Like Judith Ortiz Cofer, Benítez writes about the life-enhancing power of family stories that have been passed down by Latina women. Benítez's essay also emphasizes for us the importance of patience and stubbornness in a writer's life. Cofer's "Five A.M.: Writing as Ritual" rounds out this section with its encouragement to women writers, with practical advice on how to get the writing done. The emphasis here is on "writing as an act of will," on not being a victim of our own unfulfilled ambitions to create.

"Writing in No-Time," the second section of our book, tackles the monster that confronts many of us when we try to write—the Monster of No Time. A writer and mother of two young boys who has published several books in the last few years, Lucy Ferriss creates her own myth of "no-time" in her humorous essay. For those of us who are the mothers of young children or of adolescents, it is all the harder to find privacy and quiet time for writing. And for those of us who must also work full-time to make a living, the frustrations of having to piece together our writing time can be intense. Tillie Olsen's *Silences* (1978) is still the best book on this subject of the interrupted lives of artists, particularly of women artists. We are honored to include a talk by Tillie Olsen that was recorded at the first Women's Creative Writing Workshop at the University of California, Santa Cruz, and published in *Trellis* magazine in 1978. Still timely, Olsen's comments speak directly to the struggles of working women who intend to keep writing. She offers the voice of reality, one that keeps breaking silences about women and overwork, expectations and art.

Several other authors provide their viewpoints on trying to write while working as mothers of small children. Amazingly, Lucille Clifton wrote and published her first book of poems while four of her six children were still in diapers. In a recent interview, she talked about the serious motivation that enabled her to accomplish her work. Pamela Walker's "Hedging Bets on Motherhood" deals with the frustrations of trying to write while raising a small child. For many years, the author has lived on the mere hope of writing. Katherine Smith writes from the point of view of a single mother who also needs courage to risk the brief periods of solitude that offer writing time. Elaine Zimmerman, executive director of Connecticut's Commission on Children and the mother of two small children, wrote her essay in the middle of the night, in the only time available for poetry.

In "Writing Fellini," poet Colleen J. McElroy tells us that she ritually gathers images in the imaginatively freed-up state of mind between sleeping and waking. Patricia Clark gathers her images in daylight as she walks her dog each day, making time for the rhythms and surprises of poetry. Denise Levertov's essay, written two years before her death in 1997, emphasizes the "prime necessity" for the poet to be apparently idle, to spend time daydreaming.

"Sounds of Hazard and Survival," our third section, reveals the ways in which several successful authors have overcome obstacles in order to write, as well as how others have created visionary work through sounds, music, and memory. In "Writing the Impossible," Hilda Raz demonstrates for us one writer's way of coping with cancer and shows us the stunning formal possibilities that correspond with the urgency of the subject matter. Lynna Williams contends with "the elephant in her living room" as she tackles the heavy beast of chronic depression. Her essay reminds us that writing itself brings respite rather than darkness. In "Selective Listening and Resistance: A Writer's Capacity to Thrive," Mary Lewis provides invaluable advice about how a writer can tune out damaging messages in favor of those that permit the writing to flourish.

The threat to writing is political in Aleida Rodríguez's experience. In "The Glass Cage," Rodríguez tackles the pernicious effects of cultural and racial stereotyping. Her essay breaks silences in expressing anger over her being pressured to write about certain aspects of ethnicity rather than being encouraged toward freedom of imagination. The power and variety of her poetry is a tribute to her craft and freedom of spirit.

In her inspiring essay, "Sounds of Hazard and Survival," Colette Inez amazes us with her ability to survive difficult circumstances through imagination, by having learned to trust her own sensibilities as a poet. Inez draws connections between her early memories of pleasure in sounds and her vocation as a writer. Joy Harjo also composes her essay, "Finding the Groove," from memories of sounds. She summons up a girlhood moment of revelation, when Coltrane's music and the possibilities of the power of language came to her all at once. She has thrived in a life steeped in music and lyrical language ever since—through her poetry and her playing saxophone and traveling with her band, Poetic Justice.

Our fourth section, "The Crucible of Family," assembles essays in which the family is directly or implicitly a source of art. This section is suffused with the generous spirit of Julie Checkoway, who reminds us to pay attention to our "writerly karma," and of Tess Gallagher, whose interview with her mother the gardener reveals a source of Tess's own skills in shaping words and composing with feeling. Connections between women in the family are also the focus of Amy Ling's essay, "Why Write?" Writing poetry is a way for Ling to explore the differences and the links among generations. Eileen Tabios's "Earning Virginia Woolf's Room" arrives at a similar understanding, for through her writing and editing the poet has made connections with her mother's background and with the wider Asian-American community of letters. Like Julie Checkoway with her ideas of a writer's responsibility, Eileen Tabios also articulates a literary ethic.

The word *salvation* is its own mythology in Southern Baptist culture, but as an adult, Linda Parsons Marion finds that the term has resonance beyond a strict religious definition. She has learned to use poetry as the place for self-rescue and as a home for memory and imagination. Janice Eidus has also transformed memories into art in "My Father's Legacy, or Why I Write." For both Parsons Marion and Eidus, emotionally charged and possibly dangerous situations in family life have provided sources of inspiration for their writing.

We hope that *Sleeping with One Eye Open* will be the beginning of a dialogue about the challenges that women writers face in the twenty-first century. Whether the problem is the struggle with illness, the burden of cultural, political, or family pressures, or the reality of too little time for our own work, we are honest about the obstacles to writing. Like María Sabida, we have developed strategies for surviving as artists. In our writings we are telling positive stories about what we can accomplish, about how we can lead effective lives as women artists—how we can motivate ourselves, be disciplined, and be compassionate toward ourselves when we are less than perfect in our attempts to "do it all."

I

Waking Myths, Waking Words

The Woman Who Slept with One Eye Open

Notes on Being a Writer

JUDITH ORTIZ COFER

As a child caught in that lonely place between two cultures and two languages, I wrapped myself in the magical veil of folktales and fairy tales. The earliest stories I heard were those told by the women of my family in Puerto Rico, some of the tales being versions of Spanish, European, and even ancient Greek and Roman myths that had been translated by time and by each generation's needs into the *cuentos* that I heard. They taught me the power of the word. These cuentos have been surfacing in my poems and my prose since I decided to translate them for myself and to use them as my palette, the primary colors from which all creation begins.

The stories that have become the germinal point for not only my work as a creative artist but also my development as a free woman are those of two women. One is María Sabida, "the smartest woman on the whole island"—who conquered the heart of a villain who would murder his own bride in their wedding bed—and who "slept with one eye open." And the other is María Sabida's opposite, María La Loca: the woman who was left at the altar, the tragic woman who went crazy as a result of a broken heart. Once a beautiful girl, María La Loca ends up, in my grandmother's cuento, a pitiful woman who retreats into insanity because she is shamed by a man, cheated out of the one option she allowed herself to claim: marriage.

The crude and violent tale of María Sabida, which I have found in collections of folktales recorded from the oral tellings of old people at the turn of the century, revealed to me the amazing concept that a woman can have "macho"—that quality that men in certain countries, including my native island, have claimed as a male prerogative. The term *macho*, when divested of gender, to me simply means the arrogance to assume that you belong where you choose to stand, that you are inferior to no one, and that you will defend your domain at whatever cost. In most cases, I do not recommend this mode as the best way to make room for yourself in a crowded world. But I grew up in a place and time where modesty and submissiveness were the qualities a girl was supposed to internalize. So the woman who slept with one eye open intrigued me as a possible model in my formative years as a creative artist. Of course, it would be a long time before I articulated what I knew then instinctively: María Sabida's "macho" was what I myself would need to claim for my art. It is almost bravado to say "I am a writer" in a society where that condition usually means "I am unemployed," "I live on the fringes of civilization," "I am declaring myself better/different," and so forth. I know writers who will put anything else under "occupation" on a passport or job application form rather than call up a red flag of distrust that the word "writer" has come to have for many people.

When I feel that I need a dose of "macho," I follow a woman's voice back to María Sabida. I have come to believe that she was the smartest woman on the island because she learned how to use the power of words to conquer her fears; she knew that this was what gave men their aura of power. They knew how to convince themselves and others that they were brave. Of course, she still had to sleep with one eye open because when you steal secrets, you are never again safe in your bed. María Sabida's message may be entirely different to me from what it was to the generations of women who heard and told the old tale. As a writer I choose to make her my alter ego, my *comadre*. In Catholic cultures two women otherwise unrelated can enter into a sacred bond, usually for the sake of a child, called the *comadrazgo*. One woman swears to stand in for the other as a surrogate mother if the need arises. It is a sacrament that joins them, more sacred than friendship, more binding than blood. And if these women violate the trust of their holy alliance, they will have committed a mortal sin. Their souls are endangered. I feel similarly about my commitment to the mythical María Sabida. My comadre taught me how to defend my art, how to conquer the villain by my wits. If I should ever weaken my resolve, I will become María La Loca, who failed herself, who allowed herself to be left at the altar.

Comadres y compadres, let me tell you the *cuento* of María Sabida, the smartest woman on the whole island.

Once upon a time, there was a widower merchant who had no other children, only a daughter. He often had to leave her alone while he traveled on business to foreign lands. She was called María Sabida because she was smart and daring and knew how to take care of herself. One day, the merchant told her that he would be away on a trip for a long time and left María Sabida in the company of her women friends.

One moonless night when she and her *compañeras* were sitting on the veranda of her father's house talking, María Sabida saw a bright light in the distance. Since the house was far away from the pueblo, she was very curious about what the light could be. She told her friends that they would investigate the source of light the very next morning.

As planned, early the next day, María Sabida and her friends set out through the woods in the direction where they had seen the light. They arrived at a house that seemed to be unoccupied. They went in and peered into each room. It looked like a man's place. But they smelled cooking. So they followed their noses to the kitchen, where an old man was stirring a huge cauldron. He welcomed them and asked them to stay and eat. María Sabida looked in the pot and saw that it was filled with the arms and legs of little children. Then she knew that this was the house of a gang of killers, kidnappers, and thieves that had been terrorizing the countryside for years. Sickened by the sight, María Sabida picked up the pot and threw its contents out of the window. The old man screamed at her: "You will pay for this, woman! When my master comes home, he will kill you and your compañeras!" Then at gunpoint he led them upstairs where he locked them up.

When the leader of the thieves arrived with his gang, María Sabida heard him conspiring with his men to trick the women. Bearing a tray of *higos de sueño,* sleep-inducing figs, the *jefe* came up to the bedroom where the women were being kept. In a charming voice he persuaded the women to eat the fruit. María Sabida watched her friends fall deeply asleep one by one. She helped the jefe settle them in beds as she planned. Then she pretended to eat a fig and lay down yawning. To test how well the potion in the fruit had worked, the jefe of the thieves lit a candle and dripped a few drops of hot wax on the women's faces. María Sabida bore the pain without making a sound.

Certain now that the women were deeply asleep, the jefe went to the second-floor veranda and whistled for his comrades to come into the house.

María Sabida leaped from the bed as he was leaning over the rail, and she pushed him off. While his men were tending to their injured leader, María Sabida awakened the women and they followed her to safety.

When María Sabida's father returned from his journey days later, she told him that she had decided to marry the leader of the thieves. The father sent a letter to the man asking him if he would marry his daughter. The jefe responded immediately that he had been unable to forget the smart and brave María Sabida. Yes, he would marry her. The wedding took place with a great fiesta. Everyone in the pueblo hoped that María Sabida would reform this criminal and they could stop fearing his gang. But as soon as the couple had arrived at the thieves' house, the new husband told his bride that now she would pay for having humiliated him in front of his men. He told her to go to the bedroom and wait for him. María Sabida knew that he was going to murder her. She had an idea. She asked her husband if he would let her take some honey to eat before she went to bed. He agreed. And while he drank his rum and celebrated her death with his gang, María Sabida worked in the kitchen making a life-size honey-doll out of burlap sacks. She filled the doll with honey, cutting off some of her own hair to glue on its head. She even tied a string to its neck so that she could make the doll move from where she planned to hide under the marriage bed. She took the honey-doll upstairs and placed it on the bed. Then she slid underneath the bed where she could see the door.

It was not long before the husband came in drunk and ready for blood. He struck the honey-doll, thinking that it was María Sabida. He insulted her and asked if she thought she was smart now. Then he plunged a dagger into the doll's heart. A stream of honey hit him on the face. Tasting the sweetness on his mouth and tongue, the assassin exclaimed: "María Sabida, how sweet you are in death, how bitter in life. If I had known your blood contained such sweetness, I would not have killed you!"

María Sabida then came out from under the bed. In awe that María Sabida had outsmarted him again, the leader of the thieves begged her to forgive him. María Sabida embraced her husband. They lived happily together, so they say. But on that night of her wedding, and every other night, María Sabida slept with one eye open.

I have translated the tale of María Sabida several times for different purposes, and each time the story yields new meanings. Time and again the words I use to roughly equate the powerful Spanish change meanings subtly as if the story were a Ouija board, drawing letters out of my mind to form new patterns. This is not hocus-pocus. It is the untapped power of creativity. When a writer abandons herself to its call, amazing things happen. On the surface the cuento of María Sabida may be interpreted as a parable of how a good woman conquers and tames a bad man. In the Spanish cultures, with their Holy Mother Mary mystique, the role of the woman as spiritual center and guide in a marriage is a central one. Men were born to sin; women, to redeem. But as a writer, I choose to interpret the tale of the woman who outmaneuvers the killer, who marries him so that she does not have to fear him, as a metaphor for the woman/creator. The assassin is the destroyer of ambition, drive, and talent—the killer of dreams. It does not have to be a man. It is anything or anyone who keeps the artist from her work. The smartest woman on the island knows that she must trap the assassin so that he/she/it does not deprive her of her creative power. To marry the killer means to me that the artist has wedded the negative forces in her life that would keep her from fulfilling her mission and, furthermore, that she has made the negative forces work for her instead of against her.

Her sweetness is the vision of beauty that the artist carries within her, that few see unless she sacrifices herself. Does she have to be destroyed, or destroy herself so that the world can taste her sweet blood? Woolf, Plath, Sexton may have thought so. I would rather believe that the sweetness may be shared without total annihilation, but not without pain or sacrifice: that is part of the formula for the honey-filled burlap sack that will save your life. The transaction that took place between María Sabida and her assassin-husband was a trade-off on macho. She took on his macho. He understood that. So they embraced. The artist and the world struck a compromise, albeit an uneasy one on her part. She had to sleep with one eye open and watch what was offered her to eat. Remember the sleep-inducing figs.

Some women eat sleep-inducing figs early in their lives. At first they are unwitting victims of this feminine appetizer. Later they reach for the plate. It is easier to sleep while life happens around you. Better to dream while others *do*. The writer recognizes the poisoned fruit. She may pretend to sleep and bear the pain of hot wax as she prepares herself for battle. But she knows what is happening around her at all times. And when she is ready, she will act. Occasionally my comadre will try to save other women who have eaten the higos de sueño. She will try to rouse them, to wake them up. And sometimes, the sleepers will rise and follow her to freedom. But very often, they choose to remain unconscious. They rise briefly, look around them. They see that the world goes on without them. They eat another fig and go back to sleep.

There is another kind of woman that my comadre cannot save: María La Loca, the woman who was left at the altar. I first heard my grandmother tell this cuento when I was a child in Puerto Rico. Later I wrote this poem:

The Woman Who Was Left at the Altar

She calls her shadow Juan,
looking back often as she walks.
She has grown fat, breasts huge
as reservoirs. She once opened her blouse
in church to show the silent town
what a plentiful mother she could be.
Since her old mother died, buried in black,
she lives alone. Out of the lace
she made curtains for her room,
doilies out of the veil. They are now
yellow as malaria.
She hangs live chickens from her waist to sell,
walks to the silent town swinging her skirts of flesh.
She doesn't speak to anyone. Dogs follow
the scent of blood to be shed. In their hungry,
yellow eyes she sees his face.
She takes him to the knife time after time.

Again this is a tale that is on the surface about the harsh lessons of love. But even my Mamá knew that it had a subtext. It was about failing oneself and blaming it on another. In my book *Silent Dancing*, I wrote around my Mamá's cuento, showing how she taught me about the power of storytelling through the tale of María La Loca. Mamá told it as a parable to teach her daughters how love can defeat you, if you are weak enough to let it.

There is a woman who comes to my comadre and complains that she knows that she has talent, that she has poetry in her, but that her life is too hard, too busy; her husband, her children, are too demanding. She is a moral, responsible person and cannot in good conscience allow herself the luxury of practicing art. My comadre takes the time to tell this woman that she can choose to "learn to sleep with one eye open," to conjure up some female macho and claim the right to be an artist. But the woman is always prepared with an arsenal of reasons, all bigger than her needs, as to why she will die an unfulfilled woman, yearning to express herself in lyrical lines. She will, if pressed, imply that my comadre cannot possibly be a nurturing mother or caring partner, if she can find the time to write. In my culture, this type of woman who has perfected one art—that of self-abnegation, sometimes even martyrdom—is called *la sufrida*, the suffering one. There is much more admiration and respect for la sufrida in our society than there is for the artist.

The artist, too, suffers—but selfishly. She suffers mainly because the need to create torments her. If she is not fortunate enough to be truly selfish (or doesn't have enough macho in her to do as men have always done and claim the right, the time, and the space she needs), then she is doomed to do a balancing act, to walk the proverbial line that is drawn taut between the demands of her life—which may include choices that were made *before* she discovered her calling, such as marriage and children, and her art. The true artist will use her creativity to find a way, to carve the time, to claim a kitchen table, a library carrel, if a room of her own is not possible. She will use subterfuge if necessary, write poems in her recipe book, give up sleeping time or social time, and write.

Once I was asked to teach an evening writing class for a group of working-class Latinas who had taken the initiative to ask a community arts organization for a workshop they could attend. These women toiled at mind-numbing jobs eight or more hours each day, and most of them had several small children and a tired husband at home waiting for them to cook at the end of the workday. Yet somehow the women had found one another as artists. Perhaps on a lunch break one of them had dared to mention that she wrote poems or kept a journal. In any case, I met a determined group of tired women that first night, many nervously watching the clock, since they had had to make complex arrangements to leave their homes on a weeknight. Perceiving that the needs of this class would be different from those of my usual writing students, I asked these women to write down their most pressing artistic problem. I read the slips of paper during the break and confirmed my intuition about them. Almost unanimously they had said that their main problem was no time and no place to write. When we came together again, I told them about my method of writing: how I had developed it because, by the time I knew I had to write, I was a young mother and wife and was teaching full-time. At the end of the day, after giving my child all the attention I *wanted* to give her, grading papers, and doing the normal tasks involved with family life, I was done for. I could not summon a thought into my head, much less try to create. After trying various ways of finding time for myself, short of leaving everyone I loved behind for the sake of *Art*, I decided on the sacrifice I had to make—and there is always one: I had to give up some of my precious sleep-time. In order to give myself what I needed, I had to stop eating the delicious sleep-inducing figs that also make you good at finding excuses for not becoming who you need to be. I started going to bed when my daughter did and rising at 5:00 A.M. And in the two hours before the household came alive and the demands on me began, I wrote and I wrote and I wrote. Actually, I usually had just enough time, after drinking coffee and bringing order to the chaos in my head, to write a few lines of a poem, or one or two pages on my novel— which took me, at that pace, three and one half years to complete. But I was working, at a rate that many unencumbered writers would probably find laughably slow. But I wrote, and I write. And I am not left at the altar. Each line that I lay on a page points me toward my comadre María Sabida and takes me farther away from falling into the role of la sufrida.

The first assignment I gave that group of women was this: to go home and create a place to write for themselves. It had to be a place that could be cordoned off somehow, a place where books and notes could be left without fear of someone disturbing them and ruining a thought left unfinished; and, also important, a place where no one would feel free to read a work-in-progress—to ridicule and perhaps inhibit the writer. Their second assignment: to come up with a plan to make time to write every day.

As I expected, this latter injunction caused an uproar. Each of them claimed that her situation was impossible: no room, no privacy, no time, no time, no time. But I remained firm. They were going to write their version of Virginia Woolf's *A Room of One's Own* to fit their individual lives.

Two evenings later I met them again. I recall the faces of those weary women on that night. They were tired but not beaten, as they were used to challenges and to dealing with nearly impossible odds. I had dared them to use the strength of character that allowed them to survive in a harsh world of barrio and factory and their endless *lucha*. The struggle for survival was familiar to them. One by one they read their cuentos of how they had made a writing corner for themselves, the most fortunate among them having a guest room which her mother-in-law often occupied. She turned it into her study and bought a lock; permission for other uses would have to be requested. Others had appropriated a corner here and there, set up table and chair, and screened off a space for themselves. The *No Trespassing* rules had been discussed with family members; even mild threats had been issued to nosy teenage children: you mess with my papers, I'll make free with your things. It was a celebration, minor declarations of independence by women used to yielding their private territory to others.

That night I saw that the act of claiming a bit of space and time for themselves was the beginning of something important for some of these women. Of course, not all of them would succeed against the thief of time. Some would find it easier to revert to the less fatiguing norm of the usual daily struggle. It takes a fierce devotion to defend your artistic space, and eternal vigilance over it because the needs of others will grow like vines in your little plot and claim it back for the jungle. Finally, we came to the last writer in the circle. This was a young woman who always looked harried and disheveled in her old jeans and man's shirt. She had two sons, little hellions, both under six years of age, and an absent husband. The story she had brought to class the first night had made us cry and laugh. She had the gift, no doubt about it, but had been almost angry about the writing space and time assignment. She lived in a cramped apartment where the only table had to be used to store groceries, change babies, iron. The story she had read to us had been written during a hospital stay. What was she to do, cut her wrists so that she could find time to write? We waited in respectful silence for her to begin reading. She surprised us by standing up and announcing that she had brought her writing place with her that night. Out of the back pocket of her jeans she pulled out a handmade notebook. It had a sturdy cardboard covering, and within it was paper cut to fit and stitched together. There was also a small pencil that fit just right in the groove. She flipped the notebook open and began to read her essay. She had nearly given up trying to find a place to write. Everywhere she laid down her papers the kids had gotten to them. It became a game for them. At first she had been angry, but then she had decided to use her imagination to devise a way to write that was childproof. So she had come up with the idea of a portable room of her own. Since she could not leave her children and lock herself up in a room to write, she constructed a notebook that fit her jeans pocket precisely. It had a hard back so that she could write on it while she went around the house or took the kids to the park, or even while grocery shopping. No one thought anything of it because it just looked like a housewife making a laundry list. She had even written this essay on her son's head while he leaned on her knees, watching television.

Again there was laughter and tears. We had all learned a lesson that night about the will to create. I often think about this woman carrying her writing room with her wherever she went, and I have told her story often to other women who claim that the world keeps them from giving themselves to art. And I have put this young woman, who knew the meaning of *being* an artist, in my little pantheon of women who sleep with one eye open, the clapboard temple where I visit my storytelling comadre, María Sabida, to seek her counsel.

There are no altars in this holy place, nor women who were left at one.

Poetry Began Me

MARILYN KALLET

Poetry began me, gave me a place where I could imagine and shape my life, my voice, my way of being both in language and in the world. A life. Poetry was a form of survival, a way out of prison, a breathing place. In my early twenties when poetry grabbed hold, I was a graduate student in the comparative literature program at Rutgers. In the background of my privileged life in New Brunswick, the bombings in Cambodia were going on. The days spent protesting those bombings were tense on campus. In my private life I existed in a dry and suffocating marriage, living out/dying in my mother's dream. Poetry, a wisp, a thread in space gave me a beginning: I took every risk to know it, leaned over the edge of a conventional life and reached for language as my lifeline, the beginning of a weaving. A life's work.

I craved the beauty in my life, in my own hands, that had given me pleasure and courage in the work of others: Adrienne Rich's poetry was a major influence in the 1970s. Her work helped me to discard the role of victim and become active toward my destiny. It is true, as Linda Hogan says, that poetry is *not* bread. But it does answer a deeply felt hunger with meaning and music: "Hearts starve as well as bodies / Give us bread but give us roses" (from "Bread and Roses").

The first poem in my first book had no title—how could I know what I would become? Where the language would go? All I could see were faint traces of a path in my hands. Until my personal genesis in poetry everyone else had determined my life:

trace of web when I swallow.
barely a lifeline in the palm.
every character narrates
but the heroine.
(*Devils Live So Near*, 1977)

I was not a capital "I" but rather a beginner at selfhood and poetry.

As an undergraduate I had loved the poems of Yeats, Pound, and Baudelaire. In those days I imitated their work, lived in their music. Reading these poets clinched my destiny as one who would always love poetry. I had excellent teachers, too—among them Marcia Stubbs and X. J. Kennedy, who has remained a friend over these thirty years.

In Pound's work I first experienced the elation of consciousness made musical and precise. One of my first poems, a response to Pound's *Pisan Cantos*, brought me closer to my own voice. For the first time, I felt that a poem had been "given"—it seemed to happen through me, without conscious effort. The rhythm had a life of its own, pulling images along with it on the waves. That first "real" poem was beginner's luck, and it was enough to keep me going as an apprentice writer. At the end of the poem I refer to myself, the poet, as "he." I had been imitating Pound, so in a sense I was "he." That was in 1968, before consciousness that the poet could be "she" (or me)!

All of my professors in graduate school were men. (There was for a short time a woman instructor, but her contract was not renewed.) All of the books we studied were by men. On my own I read Nin and Sarton, Woolf and Levertov and Rich. I began writing poetry in earnest as a way of keeping my sanity. Though I spent my days in academia, I was not an academic poet. In my writing I was tearing down walls. My poetry began in a naive and naked place where I discovered my emotions intact. Amazing, since the daily life in graduate school required a false sophistication, an intellectual snobbery that left me cold.

When I started to write, I had to shape the tools to take me to the depths of my feelings. Such work was like trying to build the diving bell and diving at the same time. Rich's *Diving into the Wreck* later became a metaphor for many of us. But even in my first poems, with their stutter, their baby talk, I was able to probe, to see more than in routine life. Poetry was in advance of my life and pulled my actions along with it. There I saw a true mirror of my marriage. The poem presented the symptoms and the diagnosis:

dizzy she embraces
what's concrete

prison.

It prescribed the antidote:

step one: climb
don't ski into the sucking
fear of being
alone/
     her long eyes have to fight.

Poetry helped teach me how to live alone. Taught me the distinction between loneliness and solitude.

At twenty-four I began psychotherapy. The combination of therapy and poetry helped to pry me out of that marriage. It is not true, as many believe, that madness is necessary for poetry. Confronting my demons not only gave me more material for poetry, it also freed up my energy and my imagination for writing.

I moved into my own apartment, wrote more often, according to my own schedule and moods. Having a "room of one's own" does make the discovery of one's own language more possible. From a hotel room in San Francisco, on a job search, delirious with my new freedom I wrote "a room of my own":

from here the landscape of love hums
like a Mondrian roadmap.
the window overlooks the city of senses,
lights the base of the spine.
the city is wine,
"she is coming, my dove, my dear," on streetcars,
footsteps on Vallejo Street, eyes
on the Golden Gate, throat of steel.
my life, my fate, she is near.

❧

In my early work, love and anger mingled in primary colors and in incandescent black. I dreamed often about Persephone and wrote a chapter of poems for her. But I did not give way to the lure of Persephone, to the luxury of "going under." Poetry permitted anger against voicelessness and powerlessness, against anyone who took away strength. Poetry taught me to face my own complicity in being a victim: "I raped myself by defying my dreams." Poetry was my way of telling my professors that they could not control my language or my body. The term "sexual harassment" had not been invented yet. One of my teachers, a poet, thought he was being romantic when he said, "Be quiet so that I can invent you." I wrote "Vampire" as a spell to keep away the Takers:

> you bled me for images
> to feed your image.
> I have been your poem for so long
> I lost my own songs.

This poem from *Devils Live So Near* was written at least a year later than the book's first poem. I had begun to use the capital "I," to see myself as the authority where personal life and feelings were concerned. As the shaper of my reality through language.

Historically, the emergent women's movement gave me permission to express anger in poetry. There was a chorus of angry voices at that time—we were waking up. Since then, many of us have moved beyond rage, though I hope we still know how to call upon anger when we need it. Unfortunately in the last two decades there has been a literary back-lash—it's harder to find a publisher for an angry poem than for a neatly contained one. But like Sharon Olds, talking and tricking her way out of the music box with its pretty ballerina, we have to get out of the confined spaces imagined for us by others.

I learned then to distance myself from those whose language and/or whose treatment of me would not permit me to survive and to grow. In *Devils* I grappled with rage and with danger, with terrific loss and risk:

> Shoot the bear.
> Shoot the mother.
> Shoot the stars.

For me then, poetry was self-creation beginning over and over in dark-ness in chaos in my own heart and skin.

The danger was real throughout the writing of that first book. The suicides of Sylvia Plath and Anne Sexton provided proof of how strong the undertow of emotional life could be for poets. Confrontation with the contents of my unconscious life was frightening; it tore at me as I struggled to order emotion and make it musical. Contrary and powerful feelings erupted, and my skills as a poet were new. I dreamed of lava in the backyard of my childhood home—could see in these images the force of what had been unexpressed and could see as well the young self who was threatened:

lava drums a warning,
the body is a volcano and cannot leave
the dream is a volcano that has split its seams
the surface of the sea seems still
but waves wait to bury her like a village.

Would my new language save me? Could it contain, could it sing, could it even name the dangers I faced, much less help me to survive them?

As Adrienne Rich eloquently expresses it in "Transcendental Etude," at the moment of waking up to our own lives we need language immediately as an ally. But we haven't had a chance to learn the language that would describe us, protect us. Rich reminds us:

No one ever told us we had to study our lives,
make of our lives a study, as if learning natural history
or music. . . .
(*The Dream of a Common Language*, 73)

We are plunged into the thick of our lives and emotions at birth; "forced to begin / in the midst of the hardest movement," we scramble to find a language that will help us to know and to shape our world.

I had learned nothing in graduate school about my life as a woman writer. Luckily, among my graduate student colleagues there were many poets. We formed a strong bond through our love of language. We encouraged one another, gave each other books, wrote love poems to each other. Who were my true teachers? My friends—especially poets Bill Wolack, Kathy Stein, Miguel Algarin, Jim Krell, Elton Anglada. Alicia Ostriker in the English Department at Rutgers encouraged me, as did Kate Ellis, who reviewed my first book of poems. Anthropologist Nathaniel Tarn gave me books and encouraged my reading in ethnopoetics. Serge Sobolevitch helped me to translate Paul Eluard's last love poems. I was asked to give poetry readings, with other graduate students and with Ostriker, Penelope Scambley Schott, and Cleopatra Matthis, among other fine writers who have since achieved renown as poets. My women friends nurtured me through the most difficult days.

My first publications were in local magazines. Fellow grad student Bill Wolack started *Dream Helmet,* a surrealist magazine, and published several of my poems and translations. A few of my students and I published two issues of a magazine called *Salamander.*

I wrote to other writers and poets and found teachers and friends that way. Anaïs Nin encouraged me in my poetry writing—I treasure the letters from her. Clayton Eshleman, editor of *Sulfur,* was kind and generous with his letters though he did not publish my work for thirteen years! He told me that like the painters whom I loved—Van Gogh, Cézanne—I had to hone my tools, my words, by writing every day. I went to museums and galleries regularly and held quiet dialogues with Cézanne and Picasso, Courbet and Gauguin. Those paintings spoke to me in a deeper way than the chatter around me. Day after day I sat with Cézanne's *The Black Clock,* a still life that held movement for me. That painting offered a contained image for anger, for mortality and loneliness, for the shape of beauty in time. One chapter of *Devils* is titled "The Black Clock," and several of the poems there spring from my dialogue with that painting. *Woman with Bangs,* a Picasso blue painting, revealed a portrait of the creative imagination in sadness, depression contained in color and form. *Woman with Mango,* Gauguin's sensual painting, provided a contrasting portrait of the delicious joys of perception.

I loved that image of a woman luxuriating in her body. I wanted to provide such an ambiance for myself. No one was going to give me that portrait of myself—I had to paint it myself, and I did so in the brighter poems in *Devils.* My body became my best teacher. I learned to listen to it as a source of poetry:

> between sleeping & waking
> I rattled the poem in my ear
> I was a dancer inside the maracas
> a baby inside the rattle
> a woman listening to the dark house of cells.

The poet's mind orders what the body reveals to give the song its measure. Not until my mid-forties did I start to write passionate love poems again. It took me many years to come home to the body.

❧

When did I first want language so badly that it made me sick not to write? As an undergraduate I fell in love with a young Greek poet whose gift for language astonished and seduced me. Poetry used him as its medium. He became for me the *animus* figure that Jung wrote about, the Muse who embodied the traits that I craved for myself. Often this relationship with the Muse can be confusing—do we love the poet or his poetry? To "have" the poetry, do we try to "possess" the poet? As Yeats puts it in "Leda and the Swan," "Did she put on his knowledge with his power / Before the indifferent beak could let her drop?" The short answer is *no!*

As a graduate student, living alone in my own apartment, before the threat of AIDS, I lived a more passionate life than I had ever known. And this freedom to express love in the body was the source of many of my poems. Yet these relationships were confusing too, often the trigger for depression and sorrow. I was learning to turn to myself as the Muse, as the reliable source of my own music.

Relationships with other poets give us the charged atmosphere, the intimate dialogue, the intensity, the desire to share a language that will touch the other. Erotic love pressures us to speak an inspired tongue. But over the years I have found work itself to be a faithful love, the way to a language that is sustaining. Many other subjects besides romance call to me now. My relationship with my daughter, Heather, has been a wonderful source for writing. Now I am closer to the role of Demeter than to Persephone—sleeping with one eye open, I want to protect my daughter from harm, and I want my writing to inspire her strengths.

Work at writing creates in the worker a sense of dignity. I love my ongoing relationship with the blank page, with the rhythms of thought greeting the world. Though I still fall in love with the Muse in person, that yearning is the background music of my life. These romantic encounters, fully imagined but not acted upon, nevertheless compel me to write, teach me about myself and about being a woman aging in this culture. "Mental things alone are real," Blake said. In poetry that's true.

❧

In 1977, during my first year at teaching at Hobart and William Smith Colleges in Geneva, New York, I drove over to Ithaca to visit with Baxter Hathaway, the editor at Ithaca House Press. I took with me a chapbook of my poems—*woman with bangs/woman with mango*—which a friend of mine had published in New Brunswick. I asked Baxter if he would consider publishing my poems at Ithaca House, which was in those days one of the finest small presses in the United States. He stood there and read the chapbook right in front of me. On the spot he accepted the manuscript. *Devils Live So Near* came out in 1977, in a beautiful handpress edition of four hundred copies.

Baxter Hathaway changed my life. Along with other Ithaca House poets, I gave many readings in upstate New York. Not only did I have a new book, but I had also gained a new community, a family of other poets. Writing is solitary activity, a lonely business, but that published work took me out of my solitude.

❧

Like stand-up comedians, most poets hunger for approval. When I was in the first grade, I read "Goldilocks and the Three Bears" aloud to our class. Miss Howe, our teacher, gave me a big hug after my reading. That hug was decisive. It is still in the air as I write this, and I return it with thanks to those who love language and reading and who encourage writing and its writers.

Inking In the Myth

ALICE FRIMAN

In two days I will be going in for surgery, surgery that I have been dancing around for nine months—although "dancing" is the wrong metaphor here since it is back surgery I will be having, and I can hardly walk,
let alone dance. I want to tell you the story of my back, not of the operation and the three-inch vertical scar soon to be there. There are many
scars on my body, each another story for another time. I want to talk
about myth and the tattoo on my back. It's a Pegasus designed for me by
the "Tattooer of the Stars." At least that's what the newspapers called
him—Kevin Brady, tattoo artist of Mellencamp and McQueen, who
lived in southern Indiana for a while before the county fathers made life
more than difficult for him in the name of "family values" or Indiana
virtue or whatever epithet they use down there for rigidity. But that, too,
is another story.

Nowadays, many young women get tattooed. A bud on the inside of
an ankle, a butterfly on the breast, a well-placed shoulder rose for kisses.
Tattooing has become such a fashion statement that women are buying
false ones—rub-ons, like the ones boys used to apply with spit to shock
their mothers. But I am sixty now, fifty-one when I had it done, and in
my family there was no such thing as tattoos. I was a child of the Great
Depression, WW II, savings bonds, ration books, saved balls of tinfoil
peeled from the inner wrappings of cast-off cigarette packs, all for the
war effort. In college they called us the "silent generation": take good
notes, keep your mouth shut, graduate, marry in short order, and decorate your living room in pinks and grays. (Colors to my dismay I see
coming back in vogue. Look in any doctor's office or hospital waiting

room—the colors of death.) Back in the late 1940s and early 1950s, there were no tattoos, not in my circles anyway. We were the "good" ones— responsible, well-behaved.

I can remember when the realization came to me that I wanted a tattoo. At first I figured it was a joke my subconscious was playing on me, a variation of its old trick of *I want I want*, but this time the *I want* was for the inconceivable. It was as if at the age of forty-nine, I had suddenly found myself expectant. I tried to dismiss it, an obsession surely beyond the adolescent's wish to shock Mama. You must understand, the idea was as incongruous to me as running away to join the circus.

I am a lover of mythology, have been since that day in sixth grade when I looked over the shoulder of Maye Critzas and saw a picture of a flying horse in her Greek mythology book and knew that whatever that was, it was mine. I've hiked Olympus, wandered the ruins of Knossos, sat hours under the oak at Dodona planted in the same holy spot where twenty-five hundred years ago the sacred oak of Zeus whispered the garbled message of the god. And I have made my pilgrimage to Delphi. I've taught mythology and thought I knew it; I've used it in my own poetry for years. But except for the times Aphrodite picked me up by the scruff of the neck and slammed me against the wall, I never felt or experienced the power of myth as strongly as I did those three years before I finally got the tattoo. And I am convinced that's what the obsession was: something struggling to be born and inked in. But what? And why?

I went to the library, read about tattooing in Japan, scarification in the South Pacific, the three lines tattooed on a girl's chin at puberty by the Native Americans in southern California. I had stumbled on the sacred—I with my trimmed lawn and *New York Times* crossword puzzles. I had stumbled on the sacred, or it, in a weird form, had stumbled on me.

I looked in the yellow pages for the address of Indianapolis's local "parlor." Heart hammering, I went. Understand, this was not easy. I knew I was going for information but did not know how to begin. What should I ask? I am close to fifty years old and want to know why I want a tattoo? I couldn't even say those words to my dearest friends.

Don's Tattooing Studio consisted of two rooms, the larger containing a selection of sample tattoos that papered the walls from ceiling to floor; the smaller, an inner room from which I heard the ominous buzz of an electric needle. No one appeared, although I was sure I could be heard.

No one acknowledged my presence. How could I ask my question to an empty room? I felt invisible, the same feeling I used to get in a garage or barbershop or used-car lot—male bastions where the unspoken message was *Women, keep out*. Girlie magazines, a lot of hiking up of pants and spitting going on. If this is all foreign to you, you're either very lucky or very young. For me, such places go with the history—that is, the days before men discovered that money from a purse is just as green as the cash in a man's pocket.

I examined the walls. There was what you'd expect: hearts pierced with swords, naked women, Mother, and initials twined with snakes. There were roses and dragons and stuff so misogynist and hateful, I'll let you imagine it.

The needle kept up its steady buzz from the inner room, but no one came out. I wanted to leave but couldn't, still waiting for what was supposed to happen there. Finally, after what seemed an eternity of re-examining the samples on the wall yet one more time, I approached the door of the inner sanctum. A middle-aged man, stripped to the waist, was gripping the armrests of what looked like an old dentist's chair. He was getting what's called in the trade a "body tattoo." The man plying the needle never looked up. Only the customer in the chair. Silence. "Does it hurt?" I finally asked.

"Nah," he answered. What else did I think he'd say?

I stood there, stuck in a doorway. In desperation I mumbled something inane. "Don't worry. It's all right. I'll just see myself out," I said, slowly backing out the door. The rest of the day passed in a dream.

Once more I took up my inner dialogue. "Do you still want to go through with this?" *Yes. But not with him.* "But this is the only place in town!" *I don't care, not him.*

Since my desire for a tattoo was so strange and alien to me, in order to clarify my own thinking, I'd ask people what they thought of the practice in general. Then I'd weigh their reactions to try to discern what I felt in relation to what they had said.

Reactions ranged from amusement to horror. "That's disgusting." "Secretly I always wanted one." "You've got to be sick in the head to deface your own body." But nothing people said seemed to make a difference.

Three years went by, and I came to the conclusion that this strange desire for a tattoo had a life of its own and that if I just waited, it would eventually tell me what it wanted me to do. Understand, I am not into omens or portents. I do not believe in spirits of any kind although I often wish I did. And although I've had my share of what are labeled extrasensory phenomena, I always thought I was too rational a creature to reach out in any way to some purported shadowy otherworld. The world of the daily newspaper I find shadowy enough. So I dropped it. Or rather, I let it alone and waited.

June 1985. A Sunday morning. Imagine. Quiet in the house except for Mozart, I think, on the radio. Coffee. The Sunday papers. I turned the page. There it was—"Kevin Brady: Tattooer of the Stars." His picture and a feature article. The absurdity of such a headline in the *Indianapolis Star*—the conservative rag of the universe—never struck me. There *he* was, weight on one foot, hands in his pockets, looking out at me and waiting. The messenger, the deliverer of the gift, had come. So I yanked on some clothes and went outside to mow the lawn. Of course, this was the time to mow the lawn. Maybe if I'm lucky there will be vacuuming to do. Ironing. Thank you ironing for always being there, for holding me with board and cord to what's sane. Sane. I mowed furiously, up and back, up and back, the neat lines. I am fifty-one years old, I said. Fifty-one. Fifty-one. I stopped the mower and let the handle drop, there in the middle of the back lawn, in the middle of the month, in the middle of the year, in the middle of my good, "good girl" life, and I went inside to make the call.

Do not imagine I knew what to say. My years of articulation—forty-two semesters of studied commentary, students hanging on every word— kicked away like a crutch. I heard his voice, and somewhere in the speech center of my brain a door cracked open, letting out a flood of babble. "Hello, you don't know me and why should you but I'm a middle-aged woman and you'll think I'm silly but I'm a poet and I want, that is I think I want, I've thought about it for three years so I guess I do want a tattoo, that is, yes, I saw your picture in the papers and I. . . . Look, can I just make an appointment to see you?" Silence.

"What picture do you want?"

That stopped me. For a moment all words failed. Then, "I don't know, I never thought, perhaps, yes, a flying horse, Pegasus. Yes."

"When you come, bring a picture."

"I don't have a picture."

"Then get one," he ordered gently. We made an appointment for the next day. I never finished mowing the lawn.

He was shy, this tall man, and impeccably clean, this man the Indiana fathers wanted out. His studio in a pleasant house on a tree-shaded street in Bloomington, Indiana, the inside as spare and sparkling as an operating room, a degree from an east-coast art school framed on the wall. I gave him the small picture of Pegasus I'd found in the children's section of the Indianapolis Public Library. It was just like the picture in Maye Critzas's mythology book, with great wings and a luminous, breathless quality. My heart was steady in my chest. I never asked how much it would cost. I didn't care. All I wanted was for it to be beautiful.

Wednesday, June 19, 1985. The day of the tattoo. It was one of those heavy days in an Indiana summer that take their sweet time stacking up clouds, the kind you make pictures of lying on your back in the grass. All day I kept my eye on them as if they were an alphabet of signs, e-mail on a blue screen. I went through my sundry chores as if I were marking time. There was no turning back now. I had bought my ticket, boarded the train. Everything funneled down to 4:00 P.M., when I'd start the hour's drive to that shaded street and house of my appointment. I told no one I was going. It was not to talk about.

The drive south was glorious, the clouds building their baroque palaces familiar as a Rubens painting, sky of angels and mythical beasts. Bending over the steering wheel as I drove, peering out the windows, "Send me a sign," I begged, "give me a sign." And there, out the right window, I swear, curving up at a 45-degree angle, was a horse, carrying the afternoon sun on its wings.

I arrived five minutes early. Kevin was not alone. My heart fell. A man, Hawaiian shirt, porkpie hat, hiking up his pants that insisted on slipping beneath his belly. I imagine he and Kevin had business dealings, for the man was determined to stay. "What ya got goin' this afternoon?" Kevin waved vaguely in my direction. I was invisible again, one hundred and forty-five pounds of invisible.

"I'm doing a tattoo."

"Well," said the visitor adjusting his crotch and then wiping his face with a hanky, "we can talk while you're doing it."

I stood stunned. Suddenly something else was in the room—a *No*. A *No* such as was never seen or heard before. A *No* for three years of searching. A *No* for me, for *no more*, for a *Yes* for this thing that wanted to be born, now, this day. The man looked at me in horror—when the earth speaks, Vesuvius roars—then backed out. Kevin locked the door after him. "Thank you," he said in his soft way, and we began.

The tattoo is on my back. Why did I put it there? Maybe because it was always at my back, nudging me for three years, pushing. Behind me, the tattoo is more presence than decoration, its visibility always a surprise—a flash in my bathroom mirror, more beautiful than I could have imagined. And being on my back, the tattoo is private—only mine, to age with me, and when I die, just think, it will be the one thing from this world I can take.

I have been writing poetry for thirty years, teaching myself, alone, without benefit of teacher or program. And suddenly in the exact middle of my life, this urge, this visitation. Roberto Calasso in *The Marriage of Cadmus and Harmony*—surely the finest work of and about mythology since Ovid's *Metamorphoses*—speaks of the "mythical gesture" that, when it comes, breaks like a wave and assumes a shape. Why was it that for me the shape it took was a flying horse? I like to think the answer lies in the ancient story itself. Pegasus rose fully grown from the blood of Medusa, the slain Gorgon, and flew immediately to Mount Helicon, home of the nine Muses. There he kicked a hole in the side of the mountain to release the gushing waters of the Hippocrene (*hippos*, "horse" + *krene*, "fountain"), the fountain of poetic inspiration. Only by accident and two years after I got the tattoo did I discover that.

Calasso says, "We enter the mythical when we enter the realm of risk, and myth is the enchantment we generate in ourselves at such moments. More than a belief, it is a magical bond that tightens around us. It is a spell the soul casts on itself." At the end of the twentieth century, it is hard to imagine that the old myths are still out there waiting for us. But what else could that urge for what I conceived of as inconceivable have been? I have never had the desire for another tattoo. It is difficult to imagine now that I ever did. Whatever it was, it is finished, done. The mark of it flies on my back. But sometimes I like to remind myself that the ancients used to say only a poet can ride Pegasus.

The operation I face in two days is on the fifth lumbar disc. That means even though I will be out like a light, my horse will be soaring over the incision and later the scar. I am ready. When I look in a double mirror and breathe deeply, I can see the flexing of its incredible wings.

Two years have passed, and the scar on my back is tamed from the raw line it was to a pale reminder. I still have back problems, but daily exercises keep the beast at bay. One doesn't get over back surgery. Enough to say I can walk, and I am grateful. Pegasus is still there despite one doctor's admonition to get rid of the thing and how he was the man to do it. Funny that about men, how they meddle so, wanting always the credit for effecting change, whether you want it or not. But I have not gotten rid of it, nor will I. The tattoo seems an intricate part of me now, not the Other, not even a sign of the visitation of the Other, which it was at the beginning. And it has gotten smaller—not actually, of course, but still, smaller, the way things incorporated into your everyday life seem to shrink, take up less room.

In the meantime, life has gone on. I took early retirement, wanting more time to write and having enough of papers and faculty meetings. My too-young husband and I wandered for six wonderful weeks through Italy. My daughter plans for her wedding. My father, who has given me nothing but grief, died at ninety, and I, holding his two cold hands, forgiving nothing, forgetting nothing, wept on his chest all my old tears. Funny that there were still so many. And just this morning I found out I won a state grant for poetry. My husband claps his hands and celebrates, but he's young, and I have become a stoic in my age. Not that I can't use the money. I need a few crowns, and dentists are expensive nowadays.

This year, the application from the Indiana Arts Commission was different, more complicated than it used to be, asking for a statement of philosophy, a detailed account of how I view my work, how my "artistic style has evolved over time and why." I did the usual whining and postponing before finally sitting down to write, and I discovered, once I got going, that I was on new ground, never having really thought objectively about my work. In retrospect, I am sure my answers were not that extraordinary. Perhaps many grant proposals ask the same or similar questions. But when it asked what my most valued artistic accomplishments were and why—a cinch, I said. The prizes, the new book, the teaching stint in Australia. Easy! The high points of my little career diced up and dried, just enough to fit into the five-line allotted space.

But what *are* they, my "most valued artistic accomplishments"? A few prizes? In one hundred years what will they matter? In one hundred years everyone you and I know will be gone. Think of it. And if they're lucky, a whole new set of people like us who love words and are addicted to struggling with language will be filling out grant proposals, roasting a chicken, trying to make sense of *their* little allotment of time between the two great yawns of nothing.

So why do we do it, this poetry, this "bubble work," as Edwin Arlington Robinson said, "that only fools pursue"? I sit in my chair rewriting the same eight lines over and over, trying to make them right. All the time recognizing the paradox. That, first of all, it doesn't matter. That except for a few exceptions I can count on one hand, no one cares. That my work will all be lost, along with (cold comfort) 99 percent of everything else being written today. That, in a time of mindlessness, reported attention spans of ten minutes, television and the fifteen-second sound bite, whether I write on a given day or not write for a year doesn't matter. At the same time, I am convinced that writing and rewriting my eight lines for as long a time as it takes to get them right is the most important thing in the world. For if I can just get *these* words right, then there is one thing—albeit small, I grant you—but still, one thing that *can* be made right.

What is my greatest accomplishment? Given my childhood and all that has happened to me—divorce, deaths, disappointments, betrayals—I still get up in the morning and, since I have stopped teaching full-time, straighten up, pack a lunch, and walk the ten minutes to my studio, where I sit in a green chair all day trying to put one word after the other as if my life depended on it.

My mother calls that being stubborn. Strange how those old epithets stick. And maybe she's right. My sister, in psychotherapy for over a decade, once told me that the writing stemmed from repressed sexuality, and she had Freud to back her up. Perhaps that too is true, except that my sexuality, that bright ribbon humming through all my days, never seemed a problem. And if I think about it too long, well—I digress. My first husband said the writing scared him. Poor dead dear. It probably didn't frighten him as much as I did when I discovered I had it in me.

But in the final analysis, what does it matter? A few years ago I got a tattoo, and since then, there is this chair, this pen, this paper, and my eight lines. There is this poetry at my back, this pushing. Why or how, how much or how long has nothing to do with it.

Listening for the Singing Goose

AMY FRIEDMAN FRASER

Several years ago the newspaper for which I had written a column for five years censored me. The particulars of the circumstances require another essay altogether—a story of prison life, about which I have yet to find my voice. But for five years I had, once each week, provided for the newspaper, for my community, and for myself a two-thousand-word essay. The job was a dream, except that every moment of my life turned into one excuse or another for writing an essay. I often laughed remembering a friend who also wrote a weekly column. One day he was kicked in the head by his horse. As he wrote, his first thought was "Am I dead?"—followed swiftly by "Can I turn this into a column?" The vagaries of everyday life were swallowed by the drive to tell. And then one day I decided to visit one of the area prisons.

The city in which I live is surrounded by prisons, but I had never been inside of one. My father had been a prisoner of war during World War II, my ancestors prisoners of Nazi concentration camps, my grandfather an exile to Siberia in World War I. I needed to know what prisons are. The trouble was, I discovered what they are, and the town where I live—which brims with employees of the Correctional Service, as the prison system is so euphemistically dubbed—had no interest in hearing the perspective of those who live inside those walls. Too quickly for prison officials' taste, I came to recognize that prisons are evil, dangerous institutions designed to destroy, often more than they are to be successful in their efforts. No, I could not be permitted to write about prisons, and when I balked and fought my censorship, the publisher fired me. I know I had a perfect court case: wrongful dismissal. The problem was, by that time I had also come to love a man who lived behind those walls, and his very life depended upon my silence. And so, after years of speaking openly, forthrightly, boldly, and brashly (and sometimes, perhaps, unwisely), I was silenced.

To find some way to tell the stories that I knew, I returned to fiction, to fairy tales and myths and legends. Like Zola, who wrote children's stories upon his exile from France following the Dreyfuss trial, I realized that I did not have to remain silent. I could speak truths, and I could continue with this drive to say things to people, to communicate somehow in a world rife with avenues for communication but far too often frightened of what we might hear or see or know.

Some months after I began writing fairy tales, I took to telling them in large gymnasiums packed with sweltering students. One day in March, as wintry winds howled outside, I stood before a group of children and their parents and teachers, hearty souls all, who sat on bleachers and on blankets spread across a cold, hard floor, listening to us storytellers tell our tales.

As Scheherazade knows, there's nothing like a story to take us out of ourselves, out of this world into another, one full of possibility. I stood up in front of my fellow travelers and began. I told them the story I had written of a pig and a goose who met one day at river's edge and fell in love. The pig, prior to finding love, had been a whiny, self-pitying, miserable fellow, forever dismissing every possibility for joy, especially after his own family disowned him. They had told him that the things he believed and felt and desired were wrong and untrue. They forbade him to speak, closing their eyes and ears when he began. At last, after months of misery, he met a goose who not only listened but loved him. He loved her in return, and the love they felt for each other created in each of them new talents, ideas, and abilities. Their imaginations soared, and at the same time, so did their powers. They imagined greatness, and in imagining, they created just that.

When the story session ended, I felt just like my pig who learned to fly. I floated down the hallway, oblivious to the throngs surrounding me. Suddenly one of the children grabbed my sleeve, jolting me out of solitude and reverie. "Hey," he said, "I have to tell you something."

I looked down at this nine-year-old wearing frosty eyeglasses and a filthy parka. "Sure," I said. "What's up?"

"The story you told isn't true," he said accusingly.

"How do you know?" I asked. His words stung.

He squared his shoulders. "I just know. You lied. My mom says people shouldn't lie."

"There's a difference between lying and telling a story," I said.

"No, sir," he snapped. "Same thing."

The metaphysics stymied me. I scrambled to find something to say. "Well, not exactly. I mean as far as I'm concerned, the story about the pig and goose is absolutely true in its way. It's filled with little truths, if not precisely facts. If you use your imagination, you'll understand what I'm trying to say, and what I'm trying to say is true. . . ." I noticed he was scowling, so I stopped short.

"Explain yourself," he demanded in the space of that silence.

Remembering Scheherazade, I inhaled. "Listen," I said softly, "you realize, of course, that neither you nor I know for certain that there isn't a pig out there somewhere who loves a goose, and neither of us knows that there isn't a pig who can fly. And nobody can tell me that he or she knows absolutely that pigs don't dream about traveling the world, or finding love, or changing their circumstances.

"And honestly, you and I can't possibly know for certain that pigs and geese don't talk to each other. Do you know that it's impossible for that story ever to have happened? I mean, think of the things people once thought were impossible. A man walking on the moon? Think of the things people thought were facts. People thought the world was flat, for heaven's sake. Can you look me in the eye and tell me, truthfully, that the story I told wasn't true?"

He shuffled his feet and pawed his parka. "Yeah, well, OK. I know there's a lot we don't know, but. . . ."

I jumped at the advantage. "What exactly do you know?" I challenged him.

He looked down at the scuffed linoleum, then into my eyes. "I don't know a lot of things," he whispered, "but I know a few things. And I know one thing for sure. The story you told isn't true."

I shrugged and turned to leave, but he grabbed my arm again. "It isn't right to tell people stories that aren't true."

"That depends on the story," I said.

He thought for a moment, cocking his head to one side. "Some people might have believed you. Some people might think you were telling the truth, and if people believe things, then lots of times those things turn into truth, and other people believe something that isn't true and everyone becomes confused."

"That's true," I said, and I realized I'd met a wise young man, and I remembered then a card I had received just days before from a friend. Her card said, "When the mind is ready, a teacher appears." My mind was ready, so I relaxed and said, "Listen, I'm ready and willing to hear truth. You sound like you might have a handle on that. Maybe you can tell me what truth is."

This child was nine, and I blushed to think someone might overhear our conversation. I could hardly expect a nine-year-old to explain what truth was when, as far as I knew, no one else had managed to do so. Still, he had offered, and he seemed wiser than many adults I know. So I bent my knees and asked, "Will you tell me what truth is?"

"Truth is what I believe," he said firmly.

"True enough, and you don't believe a pig can fly."

"That's not the part I don't believe."

"Was it the whining? Do you think that pigs don't whine?"

"No!" he said. "Pigs whine just like everyone. That's not the problem. I never said a pig couldn't whine."

"But you don't believe that my pig whined?"

"I didn't say that," he snapped.

True enough. By then we were so deeply engrossed in our conversation, we didn't notice the stream of students heading into the gymnasium for the next session of the school day festival. Without saying a word, in unison we leaned against the wall outside the gym, and still in unison, we slid to the floor, crossed our legs, and went on talking.

"OK, so what isn't true? Was it the singing goose that threw you?"

He shook his head and stared straight ahead as people walking past glanced down at us. I followed his lead and stared ahead too, remaining silent, ignoring stares. Clearly he didn't mean to reveal his truths to just anyone. This was between us.

At last the hall emptied. Silence enveloped us two. The only sound came from behind the closed gymnasium doors, where musicians were warming up, tuning their instruments. The boy and I relaxed.

"This is killing me," I said. "You're going to tell me which part wasn't true, aren't you?"

He nodded, but his lips remained pursed.

"Well?" I urged. He put his fingers to his lips.

"Shh," he said, "I'm thinking."

"Was it the part about the goose family taking the lonely pig into their family that you didn't believe?"

"No," he said, "I can imagine a family of geese loving a pig who's all alone in the world. Even if you made that up, it's nice to think it could happen. I'm sure it does."

I smiled. "Yeah, but you know what? I made that part up. Or, let me put it this way, it sort of came to me one night in a dream."

"Dreams are true," he said with such serenity I felt every muscle in my body relax.

I nodded. "Yeah, I know."

"And things that come from dreams are true too. So that part's true. In a way."

Again I nodded.

"You don't really know anything, do you?"

"You're probably right," I admitted. "I mean, every time I think I understand something or, as you put it, know something, something even stranger than those things I dream happens, and I realize I don't know much at all. But you promised you would tell me what truth is."

He glared at me. "I didn't say that. I only said your story wasn't true. Now listen," he said, and his voice grew soft, "no one knows exactly what is true, but people believe things, so you have to be careful about what you say."

"Tell me," I said, touching his arm, "why did you come up to tell me my story wasn't true?"

He gripped my arm. "It's a good story," he said. "I guess I wanted you to tell me I was wrong. I guess I wanted you to tell me it was true after all."

I grinned. "But it is!" I nearly shouted. "You see, originally I invented the pig and the goose, but after awhile they were real, and now I know them almost better than I know myself, and now you know them too which makes them even more real."

The boy nodded. Suddenly he turned his head toward the gymnasium doors. "Listen!"

I listened, and I could hear the faint sounds of a woodwind trio as the notes drifted out of those doors.

"Do you hear that? It's the singing goose," he said.

I leaned forward to listen harder. "It could be," I said skeptically.

"It is!" he beamed. "It's your singing goose."

I didn't tell the boy, but I heard only a flute and an oboe and a clarinet, but I knew that he could hear the singing goose, the goose I had almost begun to doubt. F. Gonzalez-Crussi writes in his book *The Five Senses* about a particular moment in time when people are apt to receive the impression that they are hearing voices. This, he says, happens most often during a segment of life in which time does not exist—when neither past, present, nor future exists. Nathaniel Hawthorne called this time the intermediate space, a spot where Father Time, when he thinks nobody is watching him, sits down by the wayside to take a breath.

Some people think the air is charged with spirits and intelligences. Others, of a more rational bent, disagree. Many physicians, for instance, say that to hear voices is simply to misrepresent one's own thoughts.

But we all know doctors don't know everything, and that child and I had just determined that very few people, if any, know precisely what truth is. And thinking that, I too began to hear the goose singing her song.

"I hear her," I whispered to the child. He smiled and closed his eyes, and together we sat and listened awhile longer, traveling together, listening to the singing goose.

And I knew I would somehow find a way to keep writing, to keep aiming for some kinds of truths, if only to help create them.

Manipulations in the Darkroom

BARBARA GOLDBERG

Recently I had the happy task of choosing cover art for my book *Marvelous Pursuits*. I wanted an image that would be a visual metaphor of my work. Finally I discovered a photograph of a naked woman with enormous wings suspended over a ripple of water. In the background, a mildly cloudy sky.

It felt right. Those immense wings, forceful, realistically depicted down to each feather. How did they spring so naturally from between the woman's shoulder blades? And her miraculous suspension between water and air—was she rising out of the water, ascending to the sky? Was she falling from the sky, soon to be immersed in that calm lake? The image, by photographer Jerry Uelsmann, was "marvelous" in the way I meant the word, true to the old French *merveille*.

"Unsettling," "enchanting," "magical," and "oddly melancholic" is how critics describe Uelsmann's work. He is considered a master of photomontage. Working from an "image bank of negatives," he arrives at a linkage, a persistence of vision, by assembling, fitting together, or superimposing one image on another. In short, by manipulations in the darkroom.

For me, all art—art worth its salt, so to speak—occurs by manipulations in the darkroom. In that darkroom we come to our own image bank of negatives.

Yeats called that darkroom the "foul rag and bone shop of the heart." In *The Wild Iris*, Louise Gluck writes:

At the end of my suffering
there was a door. . . .
It is terrible to survive
as consciousness
buried in the dark earth.

Maurya Simon writes:

The room glows like a mad hornet:
it doesn't let anyone else in.

And Robert Hass:

Not to go in
stupidly holding out dark as some
wrong promise of fidelity, but to go in
as one can, empty or worshipping.

Empty or worshipping. That's how I enter my darkroom, which I locate somewhere between stomach and heart. There, light and reason are banished; primitive feelings collide and collude; chaos is both contained and roams free.

Some artists have gone to inconvenient extremes to gain admittance to their darkroom, performing a sort of "rite of entry," an outward and visible ceremonial that reflects their desire to bring the order of art to the unruly world of the imagination:

Schiller kept a rotting apple under the lid of his desk to help him enter his darkroom.
Wagner needed to surround himself with soft fabrics, feathers, and perfumes. People speculated that he indulged in transvestism because he owed such exorbitant sums to a Viennese dressmaker.
Stravinsky's study was meticulously arranged. Writes a biographer, "His writing desk resembled a surgeon's instrument case. Bottles of different colored inks in their hierarchy . . . blue, green, red, two kinds of black (ordinary and chinese), each having its purpose, its meaning, its special use: one for notes, another for text, a third for translation, one for titles, another for musical direction."
Cocteau believed inspiration resulted from profound indolence. "By a

thousand ruses [an artist] prevents nocturnal work from coming to the light of day. The poet is at the disposal of his night. His role is to be humble. He must clean house and await its due visitation."

Tess Gallagher—poet, essayist, short story writer—awaits with pen in hand: "the same Montblanc pen I've had since 1976." Eventually, she hits the typewriter, then scribbles all over the typed copy, moving elements around. This process goes on for weeks, even months. Like a painter, "I just keep brushing on layers."

Cynthia Ozick also arms herself with a pen: "For many years I was devoted to a fountain pen (until I made the technological ascension to the dollar-and-a-half Expresso, a throwaway pen with a most supple, seductive, luxurious writing point). Next, I transfer what is generally illegible onto a very old, first-generation, Smith Corona electric typewriter."

Maxine Hong Kingston underwent hypnosis in an attempt to salvage material contained in her only copy of a 156-page manuscript destroyed by fire. Hong Kingston visualized herself collecting a vial of special water and sprinkling it onto her papers, pencils, even her computer. "Wherever I put the water, it was wet, golden, and shiny, and then I called for my characters who had burned in the other book, and they all appeared."

Here's how I do it. It is early morning, before speech. I'm in my nightgown, still rumpled from sleep. First I dust the surfaces around me, inhaling the scent of lemons. Then I straighten the shelves, line up books, pull out some at random—on psychology, on the thirty-six Chinese stratagems, on proverbs or folk sayings. Always the Heritage dictionary, which contains the roots of words. If I'm lucky, I'll remember a dream and start recording it in my journal. If not, I smoke. Or go shopping—that is, scan pages, hunting for a word that resonates. It might be *bracelet:*

> Then a fairhaired boy
> gave me a bracelet
> of hammered gold and aquamarine.
> He spoke of fish that glowed
> phosphorescent.
> (from "Erendira Remembers")

Or *ample:*

> Narrow
> the bed we lie in, ample our need.
> (from "What Is Served")

It might be a phrase from the newspaper, like *fell from the fifty-third floor:*

> There for the grace of god there
> for the grace there for the window
> the housekeeper carelessly left
> ajar for the five-year-old boy
> who fell from the fifty-third
> floor.
> (from "There for the Grace")

Then I'll start writing as fast as I can, trying to ignore those demons hissing, "Crap! It's all crap!" This is the creation of that precious first draft.

Many artists feel that the work comes from a force outside themselves, such as the Muse or the White Goddess. As Cocteau says, "We believe that this work comes to us from beyond and is offered us by the gods."

I like to think that all the machinations, time-consuming rituals, delaying tactics, are propitiations to the god Eros, whom we must appease before gaining admittance to the darkroom. Eros resides in the darkroom—Eros, born of Chaos, always hearkening back to his origins.

But, as in the myth, wherever Eros dwells, Psyche can also be found. And wherever Psyche is, wounding, reflection, and insight are inevitable. For she eventually comes with her lamp.

That's why Uelsmann's photograph so appealed: the half-woman, half-angel reminded me of Psyche midway on her journey to immortality.

To review the myth: Psyche is the most beautiful of mortal women. Aphrodite, the divine goddess of beauty, is jealous of Psyche's charms. She instructs her son Eros to wound her with one of his arrows. But Eros sees Psyche and falls for her himself. He commands a wind to carry her to his sumptuous palace. By day she is surrounded by luxury and delicacies. At night, she is led to a dark room where Eros enfolds her in a rapturous embrace and makes her his bride. By first dawn, he vanishes, only to return at nightfall. Thus time passes. Both Eros and Psyche are content in their dark paradise.

Every paradise has its serpent, here represented by Psyche's sisters. Learning that she is pregnant, they pique Psyche's curiosity about the husband she has never seen. What if the father of her unborn child is a monster?

As in the Bible, heeding the snake leads to expulsion from Paradise. It also leads to higher consciousness. Psyche is fearful about the true identity of her husband. In fear begins wisdom. Armed with a knife and a lamp, Psyche approaches her lover. In the light she recognizes her husband as the god Eros. She accidentally pricks her finger on one of his arrows and bleeds. She is overcome by love. As she stoops to kiss him, a drop of scalding oil from her lantern falls onto one of Eros's wings and wounds him.

The myth implies that all love is a wounding. But suffering from a physical or a psychic wound can lead to an initiation, to a change in the structure of consciousness. Eros, enraged, flies off to his mother. Psyche will not reunite with him until she successfully completes four tasks. I believe these tasks correspond to the stages of creation, the voyage of a work of art from inception to completion. If successful, the work will represent the union of a creative, liberated Eros and an awakened Psyche.

Psyche's first task is to sort out a hopeless muddle of seeds. A promiscuity of seeds. Barley, millet, poppy seeds, peas, lentils, beans. I liken this to the first draft with all its prodigality, inconsistencies, and tumult.

Psyche is aided by the common ant. The instincts of this tiny earthborn creature embody the principles of selecting, sifting, correlating, evaluating, and thus revealing an order amid confusion. My first drafts are uniformly dreadful—clumsy, chock-full of adjectives, too many details, not the right details. After that first impulsive rush, I too apply the ant's skills, rearranging, cutting, getting rid of deadwood. The ant is earthy, industrious, never highfalutin.

Psyche's second task is to gather a hank of wool from the "shining golden sheep." She is advised by whispering water reeds not to go among these wild sheep until the sun has set. Once the sun goes down, they are "disarmed." I take this to mean not to expose newborn creation to too much light—a sun that will devour and destroy. Wait. Be patient. Don't rush to completion. It is not always high noon. I've learned to resist the urge to call my best friend, who will say what I have written is great. Or my worst enemy, who will say, "Not bad, a B— poem." Both responses can nip a poem in the bud. A poem needs to hibernate. At this early stage, neither poet nor poem can withstand the glare.

The third task: Aphrodite sends Psyche to fill a crystal vase with the waters that feed the streams of the underworld. Likewise, an artist must tap into those streams. The work must somehow contain the uncontainable energy of the unconscious. How to encompass this power without being shattered by it? Here the eagle, an airborne creature, helps Psyche by holding the vessel.

Let it go. The poem, I mean. Let it fly—allow the fingers of the unconscious to hold the vessel.

In fact, for me, a poem gets worked out through my fingers, perhaps a remnant from my piano-practicing childhood. I must type and retype the fledgling poem over and over, varying line break, sequence, words here and there. My fingers tapping the keyboard are making music. My mind is elsewhere.

I am grateful when my fingers make a "mistake." I regard mistakes, jokes, and puns as messages from the unconscious. For instance, once my fingers intended to type "much" and typed "muck" instead, a far more robust choice:

> that time in the bistro
> I bit your sister and squealed on the porter
> and who pulled you out of the muck of intention
> who sang hosannas for spunk and risk.
> (from "Ballad of the Id")

Another time I mistyped "ludicrous" for "furious." The poem begins with an image of Aida and Rhadames locked in an airless crypt. By singing of their love for each other, they use up available oxygen and hasten their own demise. Here's how the poem concludes:

> The day before my mother's lover died
> he seized her hair and tried to mount her
> from behind. Your father

at eighty-four stripped himself naked
and made obscene gestures.
A ludicrous passion survives. Nobody
tells us this. No consoling arias.
(from "Heroics")

When I saw the mistake, I shivered. Always a good sign. Is passion ludicrous? Checking my *Heritage*, I found the root of *ludicrous* is "game."
The word also echoes the word "lute." That clinched it. If I had "tried"
to tap into the stream, I doubt I would have succeeded. I give thanks to
the blessed accident.

Psyche's fourth task is to journey to the underworld and return with
Persephone's jar of beauty ointment, unopened. That is, to carry something concealed beneath the earth out into the world. In effect, to die
and be reborn. She is expressly forbidden to help the donkey driver, the
corpse, and the weaving women she will meet on the way down. This
seems harsh—to resist pity, not to be tempted by the distraction of re-
latedness. But in art, the laws to obey are for the sake of art, not for the
sake of humanity. All too often, helping leads to being possessed by the
one who is helped.

It takes an act of will not to be sucked into other people's dramas. I
don't always succeed. I have not always been the most available mother
or dutiful daughter. It is always a balancing act between striving for perfection of life versus perfection of art. There is guilt to contend with. But
not during working hours.

Contrary to instructions, Psyche opens the jar and is overcome by a
deathlike sleep. All seems lost. Can this mean that by choosing death
(see Freud essay "The Theme of the Three Caskets" for more on this
subject), she defeats it? Or that she is willing to risk all to make herself
pleasing to Eros? Eros will be unable to resist a Psyche anointed with
divine beauty.

Unless we are overwhelmed by beauty, a terrible beauty perhaps, that
surpasses understanding, the work of art may as well be stone soup.

Going back to ludicrous/furious. The whole poem changed by closing
on a "foolish" (ludicrous) note as opposed to an "angry" (furious) one.
Now the poem was tragic in a way I didn't understand. The artist doesn't

have to understand. When I feel my heart skip a beat, it's because I've crossed a threshold. There's some aspect of human nature or perception I'm unveiling. Even if it's ugly, if it's "true," it assumes a divine beauty.

> Father, I know now we are imperfect
> inventions . . . I too have struck
> my own children and not repented.
> Where does it end, this impulse
> to wipe their milky faces clean
> of adoration, this refusal
> to suffer unblemished trust?
> (from "Land of the Dead")

The truth is, I rarely struck my children. If I did, it was a swat across the backside. I certainly was sorry. But in this poem I wanted to reach the "underbelly"—why we sometimes want to hurt those we love. Perhaps it's harder to tolerate an adoring gaze than a disdainful one. We know how unworthy we are. If you confuse the poet with the poem, this is not a pretty view of Barbara Goldberg. But I didn't hesitate for a second— it's the right closure for the poem. I never knowingly betray a poem.

Here's the happy ending to the Psyche and Eros myth: Psyche is awakened by a kiss from Eros, who has freed himself from incestuous mother love. Through Psyche's labors, Eros, the divine boy/lover, grows up. Aphrodite forgives Psyche. Psyche is deified.

Take Psyche's acts as devotion, and we can see the kinship between her struggles and the struggles of the artist.

And let us not forget that the child born unto Psyche and Eros, or the work of art resulting from their union, is called Pleasure. Pleasure not in its shallow sense—art as entertainment—but as the poet Jack Gilbert puts it: "Pleasure as fruit and pleasure as ambush."

Sources

Bolick, Katie. "A Conversation with Tess Gallagher." *Atlantic Unbound* (Web version of the *Atlantic Monthly*), July 10, 1997 [http://www.theatlantic.com/ unbound/factfict/gallaghe.htm].

———. "The Many Faces of Cynthia Ozick." *Atlantic Unbound,* May 15, 1997 [http://www.theatlantic.com/unbound/factfict/ozick.htm].

Freud, Sigmund. *On Creativity and the Unconscious*. New York: Harper and Row, 1958.

Ghiselin, Brewster. *The Creative Process*. New York: New American Library, 1952.

Gibbons, Reginald, ed. *The Poet's Work*. Chicago: University of Chicago Press, 1979.

Gilbert, Jack. *The Great Fires*. New York: Alfred A. Knopf, 1994.

Gluck, Louise. *The Wild Iris*. Hopewell, NJ: Ecco Press, 1992.

Goldberg, Barbara. *Cautionary Tales*. Takoma Park, MD: Dryad Press, 1990.

———. *Marvelous Pursuits*. Valdosta, GA: Snake Nation Press, 1995.

Graves, Robert. *The White Goddess*. New York: Farrar, Strauss and Giroux, 1948.

Hass, Robert. *Praise*. New York: Ecco Press, 1979.

Hillman, James. *The Myth of Analysis*. New York: Harper Perennial, 1972.

Kris, Ernst. *Psychoanalytic Explorations in Art*. New York: Schocken Books, 1952.

Mandelbaum, Paul. "Rising from the Ashes: A Profile of Maxine Hong Kingston." *Poets & Writers* 26.3 (May–June 1998): 46.

Neumann, Erich. *Amor and Psyche: The Psychic Development of the Feminine*. Princeton: Princeton University Press, 1971.

Simon, Maurya. *The Enchanted Room*. Port Townsend, WA: Copper Canyon Press, 1986.

Storr, Anthony. *The Dynamics of Creation*. New York: Ballantine Books, 1972.

Uelsmann, Jerry. *Jerry Uelsmann: Photo Synthesis*. Gainesville: University Press of Florida, 1992.

Yeats, W. B. *The Collected Poetry*. New York: Macmillan, 1956.

Fire, Wax, Smoke

SANDRA BENÍTEZ

I came to writing late. I was thirty-nine before I gathered enough courage to begin. When I hear other writers talk about their work, or read what they have to say about their life, I'm amazed by those who profess they always knew they would be writers. In the 1940s and 1950s, when I was a girl growing up in Mexico and El Salvador, it was a doctor I dreamed of being. Still, when I was young, my favorite pastime was reading, and so, early on, I was linked to writing and to the spell that stories cast. My favorite book was *Las mil y una noches*—*A Thousand and One Nights*, sometimes called *The Arabian Nights*. The book relates the tale of Scheherazade and of how it was that her stories, night after night, kept the caliph's scimitar in its scabbard and away from her dewy neck. Oh, but the power explicit in this: stories can save our lives.

Back in the 1950s in El Salvador, there was only one library in the capital: la Biblioteca Nacional, an imposing wooden structure that took up an entire downtown block. When stepping through the huge double doors, you were enveloped by a distinctive smell: burnished wood, paper, glue, ink—the redolence of stories. Stories shelved high and low along narrow aisles that creaked when you walked along them.

In la Biblioteca Nacional, I'd slip between the stacks for a visit with the characters living between the covers of *Las mil y una noches*. The book was thick, gold-edged, and richly illuminated. I can still see its magnificent illustrations, all protected by vellum as delicate as dragonfly wings. I had to stand on tiptoe to pull the book off the shelf. I'd plop down, right in the aisle, although the light there was dim. Caught in the spell of stories, I would turn the pages slowly. I never checked the book out. I believed its proper home was the library.

When I was fourteen, la Biblioteca Nacional burned to the ground. We lived on the outskirts of town, but I could see the plumes of smoke rising high into the atmosphere. In those clouds, churning from white to a pitch black, I saw Ali Baba and the forty thieves, Aladdin and the enchanted lamp, Sinbad, the sailor, with his wide belly-sash. And I glimpsed Scheherazade herself soaring into the sky. Back then, I watched stories and smoke commingling.

The heart. It's where stories come to rest. Where stories reside, if we allow them entrance. John V. Hicks, in his marvelous little book *Side Glances: Notes on the Writer's Craft,* says that to be a writer, to be "the kind of person to whom ideas come, you need inside you a soft-wax area that will take an impression the moment something touches down on it." When I was growing up in Latin America, it was the women working in my house who left inside my heart their deep impressions. Yet it took almost a lifetime for me to discover this.

Allow me to explain.

Fortunately for me, my life represents a cultural mélange. My mother is Puerto Rican. My father is from Missouri. I was born in Washington, D.C.; my younger sister, in Mexico. We lived in the capital for several years until we moved to El Salvador. In 1955, when I was fourteen, and as a way to Americanize me, my father packed me off to his parents' farm in northeast Missouri to attend three years of high school. In Missouri, I was Americanized, all right. I had moved from a house staffed with servants, with three bathrooms and three bidets, to a dairy farm manned by Grandma and Grandpa themselves, to a farm house with no running water but with a sturdy outhouse only steps from the back porch. The outhouse was a two-holer, the extra seat one of the prides of Grandma's life.

In 1980, after earning a B.S. and an M.A. degree, after the birth of two sons, a failed marriage, a teaching career, a move to Minnesota, after a new career in the corporate world and a second marriage, I decided to try my hand at writing and signed up for an evening writing class. There were ten of us in the class, all over thirty, all raw beginners, but we each had pent-up stories to express, which, after some prompting, came tumbling out. Our teacher was a nurturing mother hen who gathered us patiently under her wing, clucking approval and encouragement, teaching us how to get our stories down, how to revise them till they shone.

In class, my teacher told me I was a good writer. Her praise emboldened me. I set aside the slice-of-life vignettes I weekly wrote and plunged headlong into a novel. It took place in the mid-1950s, a murder mystery set in Missouri. It was the story of a fifteen-year-old girl who witnesses a murder and who, through a tangle of circumstances, is out to find the body of the victim and to bring the murderer to justice. The murderer, of course, is out to get the girl before she can incriminate him by finding the body he has so cleverly hidden.

I spent three years writing the book. A year into it, my husband urged me to resign from my corporate position so I could devote full time to writing. He volunteered to support me financially until I finished the book and searched for a publisher. I've often thought that it's only second husbands, eager to foster their own second marriages, who might do a thing like that. Had he known then that it would take thirteen years for a publishing contract to come in, I wonder, would he have made such a big-hearted offer?

When I finished the book, I sent part of the manuscript off to a prestigious writers' conference in Vermont. When I was accepted, I was sure I was on my way to fame and fortune: I would attend the conference where agents and publishers would discover me. My three years of toil would be acknowledged. My husband's generosity would be repaid.

But things turned out differently than I had dreamed. At the conference, my critiquer said, in so many words, that my novel merited a flushing. At the end of a devastating critique session, he flashed me a smile and said, "I hope I haven't been too easy on you."

I flew home and went to bed. For two weeks, I stumbled around in my pajamas, dazed by the realization that my book would not be published, that as a writer I was simply no good. I toyed with the idea of going back to work. Real work, the kind that brought in a paycheck, but neither my husband nor the writing class would allow me to quit.

Without a novel to work on, without a real job, I had time for plenty of thinking. Lying on my bed in rumpled pajamas, I finally realized that the critiquer had been right. In truth, my novel was not very good. But contrary to his advice, I would not flush it down the toilet. My book deserved a better fate. Hadn't it taught me the discipline of keeping faith each day with the empty page? Hadn't it shown me that the true writing method was placing one word after another, one sentence, one paragraph, one chapter after another, until you wrote "the end"?

I decided to give my book a proper burial. For its coffin, I purchased a durable storage box, lit a candle, laid the manuscript, all my notebooks filled with scribblings and sketches, inside the box and closed the lid. I said prayers over the defunct. Thank you, little book, I said. Thank you for throwing a light on the writing path. I slid the box under my side of the bed where it's rested ever since.

For days after the ritual, while I was languishing in bed, my failed novel beneath me, the most important thought I've ever had about writing came to me like manna: *Write only about what's precious to you.* Write about what truly matters. Clearly, for me at least, a murder mystery set in Missouri hardly constituted precious material. But the stories recounted by the women in my house certainly did. The realization prompted impressions set down in soft wax to rise up to astound me.

Here are two memories that, back then, showed themselves so powerfully.

In 1944, when I was three and my sister, Anita, was half that age, she and I, in the company of María Luisa, our nursemaid, left Mexico for northeastern Missouri and Grandma and Grandpa's farm. We stayed four months, while Mother followed Dad, who was busy earning his air force wings at various bases in the southwest. At the farm, Grandma and Grandpa spoke no Spanish, and María Luisa spoke nothing but that. At the farm, my baby sister preferred the pointing method for making her wishes known. I, on the other hand, spoke both English and Spanish. Because I did, I became the family's official go-between.

More important, at the tender age of three, I was the keeper of María Luisa's mother tongue. I was the only keeper of her concerns, and she had many: the nuggets of copal incense she'd brought with her from home to help her to remember were fast running out; the single Catholic church we could attend, with its soothing Latin mass and pungent rituals, was miles and miles away; the relentless drudgery of fieldwork and twice-a-day milking frequently kept my grandparents from driving us to attend. Thus it went, for four months, María Luisa saving herself by pressing story after story down against soft wax.

Here's yet another memory, equally formidable.

In El Salvador, the women working in my house could not read or write. The women had left villages and towns; they'd left children and families to come to the capital to work for people like Mom and Dad. When I was older, and was attending school, the women would ask me to write letters home, to read letters for them they received in return. Back in the 1950s, I would sit at the kitchen table, my writing tablet filling up with homesick women's words.

Each letter began with the selfsame phrase: *Espero que al recibir ésta, todos se encuentren muy bien de salud*—"I hope when you receive this, all find themselves in very good health." As they dictated, the women would sit ramrod in their chairs, their hands bunched stiffly in their laps as if their fingers might fly off. Soon, when storytelling overtook formulaic expressions, the women's posture softened as they opened their hearts and thereby saved their lives.

I took the stories down, not knowing that in the very act, I was becoming a writer, that I was, way back then, starting to save even myself.

And so it happened that fourteen years ago, when I was forty-two and languishing upon a bed under which rested a book that would never see print, but which would always sustain me, I turned myself over to precious material and to telling the stories that most mattered to me. To do it, I took the surname Benítez, my mother's maiden name. To do it, I reclaimed my Latina self and climbed on the slow-moving bus named "Paciencia," though, at the time, I did not know the ride toward publication would take so long a time.

No matter. The world is filled with stories impressed on people's hearts. We have only to speak out to set the stories free. Like smoke from burning candles, stories rise up. In the vast collective unconscious, stories amass; they bump against each other, calling out to us.

Here's a final story for proof.

A few years ago, when my Dad came to visit, we took a ride to the public library to get an armful of books. In the car, I brought up the subject of that long-ago Salvadoran fire. "Remember, Dad," I said, "when I was fourteen, just before I left home for Missouri? Remember how terrible it was when la Biblioteca Nacional burned down?"

Dad frowned. "What are you talking about?"

"In 1955, in San Salvador. Remember when the library burned to the ground?"

Dad answered, "That wasn't the library. It was the post office. It was el Correo Nacional that went up in smoke."

I was dumbfounded. "Are you sure?" I asked.

"Of course. It was the post office in 1955."

I could only shake my head. All those years I had thought one thing, when something very different had taken place. It's not important. When I was a girl, something had been burning and smoky clouds had billowed up. In them, I saw stories. The stories, as I later learned, a world of letters had contained.

When all is said and done, I believe this: if we are open to it, true stories impress themselves on the soft-wax area of our hearts. It is the fire of remembering that sets the wax to melting. We have only to take up a pen, or set fingers to keys. We have only to trust and stories will come: like sacred smoke rising up to restore and preserve us.

Five A.M.

Writing as Ritual

JUDITH ORTIZ COFER

An act of will that changed my life from that of a frustrated artist, waiting to have a room of my own and an independent income before getting down to business, to that of a working writer: I decided to get up two hours before my usual time, to set my alarm for 5:00 A.M.

When people ask me how I started writing, I find myself describing the urgent need that I felt to work with language as a search; I did not know for a long time what I was looking for. Although I married at nineteen, had a child at twenty-one—all the while going through college and graduate school *and* working part-time—it was not enough. There was something missing in my life that I came close to only when I turned to my writing, when I took a break from my thesis research to write a poem or an idea for a story on the flip side of an index card. It wasn't until I traced this feeling to its source that I discovered both the cause and the answer to my frustration: I needed to write. I showed my first efforts to a woman, a "literary" colleague, who encouraged me to mail them out. One poem was accepted for publication, and I was hooked. This bit of success is really the point where my problem began.

Once I finished graduate school, I had no reason to stay at the library that extra hour to write poems. It was 1978. My daughter was five years old and in school during the day while I traveled the county, teaching freshman composition on three different campuses. Afternoons I spent taking her to her ballet, tap, and every other socializing lesson her little heart desired. I composed my lectures on Florida's I-95, and that was all the thinking time I had. Does this sound like the typical superwoman's lament? To me it meant being in a constant state of mild anxiety that I could not really discuss with others. What was I to say to them? I need an hour to start a poem? Will someone please stop the world from spinning so fast?

I did not have the privilege of attending a writer's workshop as a beginning writer. I came to writing instinctively, as a dowser finds an underground well. I did not know that I would eventually make a career out of writing books and giving readings of my work. The only models I knew were the unattainable ones: the first famous poet I met was Richard Eberhart, so exalted and venerable that he might as well have been the pope. All I knew at that time was that at twenty-six years of age I felt spiritually deprived, although I had all the things my women friends found sufficiently fulfilling in a "woman's life," plus more; I was also teaching, which is the only vocation I always knew I had. But I had found poetry, or it had found me, and it was demanding its place in my life.

After trying to stay up late at night for a couple of weeks and discovering that there was not enough of me left after a full day of giving to others, I relented and did this odious thing: I set my alarm for 5:00. The first day I shut it off because I could: I had placed it within arm's reach. The second day I set two clocks, one on my night table, as usual, and one out in the hallway. I had to jump out of bed and run to silence it before my family was awakened and the effort nullified. This is when my morning writing ritual that I follow to this day began. I get up at five and put on a pot of coffee. Then I sit in my rocking chair and read what I did the previous day until the coffee is ready. I take fifteen minutes to drink two cups of coffee while my computer warms up—not that it needs to—I just like to see it glowing in the room where I sit in semidarkness, its screen prompting "ready": ready whenever you are. When I'm ready, I write.

Since that first morning in 1978 when I rose in the dark to find myself in a room of my own—with two hours belonging only to me ahead of me, two prime hours when my mind was still filtering my dreams—I have not made or accepted too many excuses for not writing. This apparently ordinary choice, to get up early and to work every day, forced me to come to terms with the discipline of art. I wrote my poems in this manner for nearly ten years before my first book was published. When I decided to give my storytelling impulse full rein and write a novel, I divided my two hours: the first hour for poetry, the second for fiction;

two pages minimum per day. Well or badly, I wrote two pages a day for three and one-half years. This is how my novel, *The Line of the Sun*, was finished. If I had waited to have the time, I would still be waiting to write my novel.

My life has changed considerably since those early days when I was trying to be everything to everyone. My daughter is now twenty-five and in graduate school, not a ballerina, Rockette, or horsewoman but a disciplined student and a self-assured young person. Thus I do not regret the endless hours of sitting in tiny chairs at the Rock-Ette Academy of Dance or of breathing the saturated air at the stables as I waited for her. She got out of her activities something like what I got out of getting up in the dark to work: the feeling that you are in control, in the saddle, on your toes. Empowerment is what the emerging artist needs to win for herself. And the initial sense of urgency to create can easily be dissipated because it entails making the one choice many people, especially women, in our society with its emphasis on the "acceptable" priorities, feel selfish about making: taking the time to create, stealing it from yourself if that's the only way.

II

Writing in No-Time

Writing in No-Time

LUCY FERRISS

"I have no time!" It is the writer's—especially the woman writer's—most frequent complaint. More frequent for women because, as Virginia Woolf gently pointed out to us many decades ago, we are not well-versed in demanding time or space for our writing. I'm sure I am not the only writer who has been stopped, just on the brink of a precious hour alone at the computer, with the well-intended comment launched by husband/mother/partner: "I'm glad you're getting this time for yourself."

"It's not time for myself!" we want to scream. "It's time for my writing!" When we're done with the writing, we may want to add, we'll take advantage of that preferred time for ourselves, thank you.

But the husband/mother/partner would only look confused at such a response. Hadn't they meant that, about the writing, when they said "time for yourself"? Isn't it the same thing? Recognizing their innocent confusion, not wanting to put a damper on things, we bury the scream and say, "Yeah, I'm glad, too," and then we go to the computer, fuming.

Before we waste the writing hour with an hour of anger, let's take a couple of minutes to look at the history of this time problem. For me, this is personal history, which I'll wager to be not that far removed from the various personal stories that make up our collective history as women who write. Mine starts with my earliest days as a writer, when I could hardly distinguish between being a writer and being a reader. Those were the days when I was known as a dawdler; when my ability to read far outstripped my ability to tell time; when my mother made the serious mistake of allowing me to keep my bedside lamp on as long as I liked, provided I had a book propped on my knees. My time had no value placed on it, no priorities. I was aware that I often got into trouble for not finishing tasks or for being late, but I could no more locate the source of that trouble in the minutes or hours I spent absorbing or making up stories than I could locate the source of water in hydrogen and oxygen. Water was water, and I was habitually tardy.

Then life began to organize itself. There was clay-time and singing-time and gym, birthday parties and ballet lessons, setting the dinner table and cleaning out the cat litter box. At first these categories had some fluidity—there were long mornings, the year I attended afternoon kindergarten, when it seemed my mother kept no track of me. Whether I was building a cardboard city or dreaming up a story about that mean boy Darrell Scott up the street made no difference, so long as I wasn't whining or torturing my baby sister. Gradually, however, it became clear that certain things took precedence. At school, there was a half-hour of "free time" after lunch, in which we could play jacks or write stories or stare at the wall; if we misbehaved, that time was taken from us under the assumption that it was an indulgence, on a wholly different order from learning geography or doing jumping-jacks. At home, when asked what I was doing at a given moment, I found that answering "setting the table" or "practicing the piano" meant that I could continue the activity uninterrupted until it was complete. "Reading" or "writing a story," on the other hand, ranked about as high as "watching TV" or "nothing": these things belonged to no formal category and could be cut through, as in "Oh, well, then, listen to this . . ." or "Come help me here, then." Watching TV in fact ranked higher than writing, in that we were allotted ninety minutes of TV per day, and any interruption involved payback.

As I advanced to high school, I began to learn tricks to vault past the formal time blocks that were assigned to the recognized categories of life—school subjects, socializing, chores. I could do my homework fast and then be free to use the remaining "spare" time any way I chose. I didn't go out on dates—too skinny, too inept—and so I had Friday and Saturday nights to while away. As when I was small, no one cared what I did with those empty stretches of time; and yet, while I used some of the time to write—in my diary, in poems and stories—I complained, like any teenager, of being bored, of having nothing to do. Time weighed heavy, not because I was too young still to see myself as a writer, but because time defined as "spare" had begun to lose value. The people I knew, after all, were achieving identity through recognition, and recognition came from things achieved in publicly sanctioned time: beautiful, popular girls dated; smart girls studied hard and spoke up in class; upwardly mobile girls earned money after school; talented girls took extra classes or sports. Even those stoic girls who had to help their mothers at home or work in the family business knew what their duties were and what could be gained from the hours spent.

Paradoxically, it was during this same era that one *product* of my writing time—the well-turned phrase—actually acquired some value. If I agreed to write the lyrics for the school skit, I could get out of helping with the costumes. If I rang the right moral bells in an essay I called "The Value of Friendship," I could net five bucks and an identity in my school. Once, faced with an English class dulled by vocabulary drills and one-page essays, I approached the teacher and announced that I was writing a twenty-page short story about a girl stuck in a well; might I be excused from assignments for the remainder of the semester? To my astonishment, the teacher humbly agreed, only asking from week to week how the work was progressing. The last weekend before classes were out, I scribbled some drivel about how the girl had lost her memory and could only be aroused by a dripping faucet. But it dripped on for twenty pages, and I got my A. The hours had been well spent, you might say; they had garnered results and eliminated more tedious work.

None of this had anything to do with writing, real writing, where the process had no clear goal and the way was tangled by language and the demands of the self. Real writing copped no immediate rewards; it invariably involved a certain amount of tediousness; it had about as much value to the outside world as a nap, and it took longer. Slowly, inevitably, there came to be other ways in which I spent my time, and before I knew it, I was grown and the other ways became demands, and I found myself lamenting how life drained my time and how there was none left, none at all, for me to do my writing in.

At present, I support a family of four, including two attention-greedy children. I teach and I volunteer and I take care of my parents, and so on. Of course I also write, though not at the speed or output I'd like. When I am pressed on this point by close friends, I come up with what I have called the Almost-True Confession. What all this activity amounts to, I confess, is my greatest excuse ever. First there was school, then work, then more school, and now I have work *plus* family. I have discovered formal time structures so extensive and thick that there is simply no place left for truly great writing, so that the world will have to be thankful for whatever stories I manage to eke out of my frenetic existence. No criticism is allowed—how can you fault a working mother for not measuring up to Virginia Woolf, much less Shakespeare? I can show you the minutes I have available: a half-hour in the morning before the children are up; two hours in the evening after everyone else has gone to bed; the occasional Saturday afternoon. I don't shop anymore or go out with friends. I have arranged my life so that there is simply no spare time for my writing at all. And not only am I thus let off the hook of ambition, but the world also sanctions my kvetching.

I'm lying, of course. Not about the amount of "spare" time, which is slim indeed if you keep track of such things, but about its relationship to the writing. In the first place, the writing life had chosen me before I became a mother or the financial support for others. I knew how far excuses could be begged, and it wasn't far. Plus, somewhere along the line, I had come to realize the intrinsic value of the writing process, how for me it is like breathing or quaffing thirst, necessary to my existence. However I might argue time constraints to others, by the time those constraints became as great as they are now, I already knew that no amount of outside commitment would soften my devotion to words on paper. What the Almost-True Confession amounts to is this: a bending of the knee to the very notion of formal time structures, to the social idea that "spare" time begins and ends at given moments and can contain various possibilities including writing within its parameters. But my writing began, as I have said, before I understood clocks and commitments. To enter the realm of my imagination, my "writing head," I have to forget time. Forget spare time, writing time, cooking time, teaching time, sleeping time. I have to obliterate time altogether.

For a while, when I had to share a tiny apartment in San Francisco during the week, I took over ownership of a shack three hours up the coast, in Mendocino County. I went up there not so much for time as for space. The place had no electricity or plumbing. For cooking and light, there was propane; for heat, a woodstove; for water, the stream a mile away on the lumber company's land. The icebox ran on a block of ice. In keeping with the primitive nature of the place, I made myself a rule for my weekends alone: no mirrors and no clocks. I spent my days hacking paths through the woods with a machete, prowling the beach for miniature abalone shells, and writing. I ate when I was hungry and slept when exhausted. I never knew what face I wore, or what hour it was, or—most important—how much time I wasted walking or writing. I learned to operate in the land of no-time, and I did some of my best work—not as product but as process.

Not only do daily time pressures, or one's awareness of them, cripple writing; the larger fear of imagination giving way to "real" life can block the exercise of imagination from the start. I know a woman—call her Brenda—who wanted both to write a novel and to have a baby. But Brenda had seen mothers who tried to write novels, how hard it was for them. So she determined to finish the novel first, before she got pregnant. The years ticked by, each one a gradual narrowing of the time Brenda saw as allotted to novel-writing as opposed to baby-making. She could not finish the thing and, by the time she threw in the towel, she was on the outer cusp of the child-bearing years and had infertility problems. So Brenda ended up with neither book nor baby, only a cup of bitter regret.

Now Brenda might never have finished that book, baby or no baby. But the fact that she perceived an upper limit on the amount of time she had in which to write her novel clearly put a check on her ability to imagine, to work in the realm of imagination. It figured her unwritten novel not as process but as product—and as a product with a deadline that amounted to death for the process. I picture her always at her desk with one eye not necessarily on the clock but on the calendar.

This, then, is my True Confession: that some of us cannot—indeed, must not—structure writing time. The secret lies not in having an hour, or a day or a week or even a year, in which to accomplish something we call "writing" but in returning to a state in which the words "hour" and "week" have no meaning. It's very hard to conceive of such a state, in our clock-in, clock-out world. My days at the Mendocino shack, I'll admit, were unusual, and I can never return to them. Meditation, some say, exists outside time, but for me the closest parallels to writing are less transcendent and more workmanlike. I think, for instance, of domestic tasks, especially those with rhythm and beauty, like ironing. Back and forth goes the smooth heavy metal block, back and forth: collar, cuffs, sleeves, placket, front, back. I cannot iron well in a hurry, and when I am ironing, it is almost impossible for me to keep track of time. Hanging up clothes, too, seems to defy time structures, and I've had others tell me the same is true for gardening. You put your mind to these tasks, and you do them until you cannot do them any longer—until all the weeds are pulled, or there is a knock on the door. There's a hypnotic quality to these states of being, and yet they consist entirely of conscious work. Yet how do we, faced with the constant presence of the clock, pressured to bargain for minutes ("I will start supper precisely at 5:45 if you promise not to bother me until then"), drop our conscious selves out of time?

Again, my best parallel is domestic. In a guide for 1950s wives and mothers that a friend sent me for a laugh, I found the following advice: no matter what distracts you from a particular task you have set yourself for the day, whether it be cleaning the cupboards or sewing your daughter's ballet costume, be sure always to come back to that task; do not turn from the distraction to a different project, or you will end the day feeling you have accomplished nothing. All right, then. I am not a 1950s housewife; I am a writer. I am a writer all day, all night. No time-structures bind my writing. I begin it when I awaken, and whenever something distracts me from it, I turn back to the writing when the distraction is over.

Is making love a distraction, then? Well, yes. So are eating and work and playing with my kids. They are distractions I choose—freely, even gladly—but when I am finished with them, I don't glance around for what to do next; I simply turn back to the writing. Or I begin with the writing. Take, for instance, that mini-span between having dinner ready and actually corralling the herd toward table. I give my children a ten-minute warning, which is really fifteen minutes, and you know they're going to stay far from me for that brief span, lest they be roped into laying out place mats. If I'm keenly aware of the span, I might reread what I wrote yesterday, or organize files on the computer; *fifteen minutes isn't enough to get real writing done,* says my persnickety inner muse; *don't frustrate yourself.* On the other hand, hey, it's a gift—no value attached to these fifteen minutes or taken from them, nothing to lose. So I boot up a new file, I start the next chapter. In a quarter of an hour ("*Mo-om,* you said supper was *ready*"), I've got a paragraph. So save it and serve the lasagna, what the hell.

Or there's the morning alone with the sick child. He's supposedly coloring on the floor of the living room—which is, incidentally, where my "home office" is located. Five minutes, I ask him. Don't talk to Mommy for five minutes, and after that, I'll play ticktacktoe with you, I promise. This time I start at the midway point in a story left hanging from the week before. I manage not five minutes but maybe five words before he interrupts. He wants to know where a brown marker is. On the windowsill, I tell him, and go back to the screen. Those last two words suddenly look not quite right, so out they go, and a new phrase comes in. How is it, he wants to know then, that red and blue and yellow can make brown? We'll try to blend it with paint, I say, in five minutes. Don't talk to Mommy for five minutes, remember? And I set down the next sentence, with the word "brown" in it. This paper is see-through, he says; the markers go through, it's wrecked. Crayons, I tell him, that's what you're supposed to use in coloring books. It's wrecked! he snuffles. Mommy will make a Xerox of the page at her office, I respond, my face glued to the computer screen, and meantime you do the other pages with crayon. Both pages, he says; the other side's wrecked, too. Both pages, I say, if you promise not to talk to me for the next five minutes. Aha. There's the next sentence, forming in my head. Only the paragraph needs to begin differently—it needs to begin with what my character's lover says, there needs to be speech.

As this slice of life makes plain, I never get my five uninterrupted minutes. Maybe I was foolish to try to write with a convalescent five-year-old in the room. On the other hand, there's some advantage to cobbling a paragraph together word by word—to rereading and rethinking the sentence I've laid down before I rush on. Later, I can streamline the thing, maybe take out the bit about brown. Again, the trick is simply not to see the morning's effort as wasted, and particularly not to give up on the morning's chances just because I know my child will not grant time to my writing. The frustration that can be bred by such scenarios is nothing more than the frustration that comes from privileging formal time structures—*this* is domestic time, *that* is time for writing—which inevitably creates expectations about the results of that allotment of time. Those expectations themselves, I've argued, diminish the act of writing. Conversely, the morning scenario I've painted, with its throwaway time, holds no expectations other than making it through to lunch; and the writing process itself becomes a kind of challenge, a new way of plucking words and voice from the inner space where my imagination still holds forth despite my little rascal's insistent presence.

Finally, there's the potential for immediacy in writing snatched from the jaws of clock-time. If a faculty meeting ends an hour early, I can assign myself the task of finishing chapter 5 in my new novel—something I might be able to do, in rough draft, in an hour, since I'm less than a paragraph from the end. That assignment, for me, will result in an hour spent hating the computer screen, or deciding to grade student work instead, or even finishing the chapter by rote rather than inspiration, because the fact is I'm not ready to finish that damn chapter. A better choice—given the hour, my fatigue, the setting—is not even to flick on the computer but to set down longhand that conversation I overheard on the way back to my office. Enter, suddenly, a description of the wind whipping fall leaves across the bare ankles of the young, anxious woman who was talking. Enter the smell of the corridor when you step inside, a pungent mix of mold and that morning's donuts. Enter the light cutting across the dust on my window. Suddenly the phone rings and it's my husband, wondering where I am, didn't I promise to be home by six? Needless to say, I haven't finished chapter 5—I haven't finished any-thing—although I have got a dozen hot sensory impressions on paper, impressions that would have been lost otherwise but will now feed into the novel, or an essay, or something, sometime. And maybe I'm tardy, getting home, but I'll be forgiven this once, especially since the bit of scrawling I got done puts me in a fabulous mood all evening.

And does chapter 5 ever get finished? You bet. Only never on time, never as an assignment, never as an effort gauged by the clock. We for-give ourselves this lack of discipline. Why? Because we are writing.

On those few days when an ocean of time presents itself, of course, few of us can write nonstop. We stare, jot down notes, pull books off the shelves, delete awful phrases, fiddle with our hair, push lines of dialogue across the page, and sometimes—rarely!—zoom along in a story like a dolphin through the ocean, leaping and diving until that inevitable inter-ruption arrives. Some days I take a cue from a writer friend of mine who turns on her computer when she's making morning coffee and turns it off only when she goes to bed. With my mischievous munchkins, that scheme can backfire, but it certainly sends a message about priorities. All this to say—again, taking a page from the 1950s housewife manual—that writing does not occur in our spare time, it occurs in our lives. Spare time, "time for ourselves," is itself one of the distractions we may choose to allow. Who's in charge here, after all?

The next time, then, when that caring individual says, "I'm glad you're getting this time for yourself," try turning the tables. Tell him/her/them how glad you were to have spent time with them, or to have done the laundry or earned the day's paycheck. Let them think you're being snide or cuckoo. Who cares? Clocks and calendars are not writers' tools. They have their place in the other worlds we inhabit, but we need to banish them from that place in our minds where writing takes shape. While it is true that writing cannot happen when there is no time for it, in some crucial way it can *only* happen in "no-time."

Excerpts from a Talk by Tillie Olsen

The following are excerpts from a talk by Tillie Olsen with a group of women writers at the "Women's Voices" writing workshop held at the University of Southern California at Santa Cruz in July 1978. The entire tape of the talk (during morning and afternoon sessions) ran for nearly six and a half hours, including comments and questions from the workshop participants. To excerpt from such a lengthy body of material is a formidable task. I undertook it because I firmly believe that what Tillie was saying as she talked with the other women writers gathered in this workshop setting is not being said in just this way by any other writer I know.

Such necessary excerpting means that much is left out. I have foregone the customary procedure in this case of using ellipses every time a word or words are omitted because I felt so many would interfere with readability. I have used ellipses only where relatively long sections of the talk have been deleted. In cases where there were very lengthy breaks in the talk, when people left and came back together again at another time, I have used asterisks to indicate that a new thread of talk was taken up.

I regret that the tapes I had were not able to pick up the exact questions and comments of the workshop participants clearly enough to render them transcribable. In cases where it seemed necessary to know the specific remarks to which Tillie was responding, a suggestion of the question has been inserted parenthetically.

What is necessarily, unfortunately, lost in a transcript like this is the physical presence, the feeling of mutual support and understanding that was being nourished among the workshop participants during Tillie's talk. What such transcriptions retain, however, is a tone of conversation, the sense of being spoken to directly (and personally) as a woman and a writer. There is, I think, value in that directness, the intimacy. For this reason also these excerpts are printed here: for those who were not, as Tillie would say, "circumstanced" to attend this writing workshop, to hear this talk in person.

It should be noted that Tillie Olsen's exceptional book *Silences* (Delacorte Press, 1978) was not yet out at the time of this workshop, and she had been asked by the coordinator of the workshop to speak out of the concerns raised in that book. The reader is referred to *Silences*, vital reading for all women, all writers.

I would like to thank Marcy Alancraig, from Berkeley, California, coordinator of the now three years of "Women's Voices" workshops at USC, Santa Cruz, for her assistance in taping this talk for me in the midst of all her other duties during the workshop. Credit should also be given to the Women's Studies Program at USC, Santa Cruz, for their support for these important workshops. I would also like to thank Tillie Olsen for her cooperation with my editing and for giving her permission for these excerpts to be printed in *Trellis*, despite the necessary deletions and incompleteness.

MAGGIE ANDERSON

❧

[Reads from *Silences:*] "How much it takes to become a writer. Bent (far more common than we assume), circumstances, time, development of craft—but beyond that: how much conviction as to the importance of what one has to say, one's right to say it. And the will, the measureless store of belief in oneself to be able to come to, cleave to, find the form for one's own life comprehensions. Difficult for any male not born into a class that breeds such confidence. Almost impossible for a girl, a woman."

The fact remains that literature has been used and too often taught in a way to shut people up who aren't bred to that kind of a confidence. Yet one of the ways in which we can be enabled to get that sense of the importance of what one has to say is, if we are fortunate enough, to live in a time in which there is a movement for human freedom of which we are an essential part. The women's movement, in the last century, as in this century, has been responsible for a great deal of opening up and of voicing out of a sense of oneself, out of a sense that one has something to say that is not there, or enough there, in literature. . . . Our coming together here, in this way, as a workshop, is so important too, to the getting of that sense of oneself and the importance of what one has to say. Workshops like this were unknown even five years ago. This is only the second year of a women writers' workshop on the West Coast. . . . Writing does result out of our being together, out of what happens when we are not in the isolation that several of you mention, that terrible isolation that you need to break.

If you are a person of color, or—and this, like being a woman, crosses and involves both—of a class whose economic circumstances necessitate most of your life having to go into everyday work, then you simply don't have *circumstances* for writing. . . .

Part of my luck, my resources as writer have been my five colleges: the great college of motherhood; the great college of human struggle; the college of everyday work. Yes, and the college of literature, reading a very great college; and then, late in life, the college of contrast, where for the first time I had closeness to people who had "means," enabling circumstances in their lives, and saw the difference it makes. The college of motherhood: there is a certain source sense of human life that, so far, only mothers have been able to be close to, that yet is not even in literature, let alone inherent in other fields of human knowledge, including belief in the enormous innate capacity in children. This is partly what *Silences* is about: human creativity and the muting of it. It's about having to grow up in a world in which the color you're born into, the class you're born into, the sex you're born into, can be (and have been so far) determining as to what it is you can do with your inborn art capacities, the ways in which the world chooses to recognize creative achievement. We don't have enough writing yet about circumstances. Virginia Woolf's *A Room of One's Own* is our great predecessor, the first great study of the relationship between circumstances and what the world *recognizes* as creative accomplishment. . . . When we talk about creativity, we must not make those male separations, that creativity has only to do with achievement in certain forms. We must recognize that it exists in everyday life; has many other forms.

❧

. . . I love to repeat a more and more well-known story out of Elizabeth Cady Stanton's *Eighty Years and More*. It's about the time when her baby was ill and she called the doctor. The doctor was mystified. The next day when the doctor came again, the baby was fine. He asked her what she had done, and she told him. "Ah!" he said, "mother's instinct." "Instinct!" she said. "That was damned hard logical reasoning." We accept that we are "intuitive," that we do things by "instinct," but actually it's a secret process—even when it seems to be intuitive or instinctive—of lightning-fast reasoning, and putting together of understandings and experiences that we've had. . . . We must be very careful and remember to stand up for our intellect. And to notice how the intellect expresses itself in everyday life, because it *does*, I assure you, it does. That's one of the great things I learned from my college of work, how the intellect expresses itself in everyday ways. . . .

And, now, quilts do begin to hang in museums. Why are those quilts so moving? Because the pioneer women had only scraps, everyday scraps, and out of them, with the kind of mathematical genius that's able to make patterns, and with sense of color, vibrancy of color, that we endow with respect when a recognized artist uses it—out of that, they made these quilts. And furthermore, these works of art were useful; they kept people warm. A marvelous story is Alice Walker's "Everyday Use." And along with that should be read Dorothy Canfield Fisher's "The Bed Quilt." Susan Glaspell's "Jury of Her Peers" reveals to us how the sense of justice weighs itself out in everyday life.

. . . In "One Out of Twelve," I quote W. E. B. Du Bois from an article he wrote near the beginning of this century, called "The Damnation of Women." It was primarily about the situation of black women, but in it he said that "it is only at the sacrifice of the chance to do their best other work that women bear and rear children." You who are mothers need not gasp and feel doomed, because it is changing as circumstances have become more favorable—not the beginning of enough or fast enough yet—but we do have more writer-women-mothers. Yet basically, it still remains true: only at the sacrifice of the chance to do their *best* other work can women bear and rear children.

John Berryman, the poet, who must have had, I don't know how many wives, let alone women, how many children, wrote "Them lady poets must not marry, pal." Meaning if you're a woman who insists on being a poet, forget about personal life, personal fulfillment, let alone kids, all that *he* had. I call this "The Patriarchal Injunction": if you're going to enter a "man's domain" (because, you know, literature for centuries was a man's domain), then you must unsex yourself, divest yourself of what a man in literature could have, including the privilege of having children. I use this strange word, "privilege," although mostly it's the opposite of privilege in this world that's unfit for, indifferent to human life. And no one but you is responsible for their well-being, caring about them. And yet, even under these circumstances, the yields of motherhood, the yields to me, the yields to others of us are there.

I'm not talking about a situation of free choice, because such doesn't exist, yet it seemed, seems, like choice. But when you have to lop off a portion of your being, your fulfillment, without really weighing it out as you only could in a situation of freedom, then that is no longer free choice.

❧

Strong emotion. Emotion is something we all have to contribute to literature: emotion deep in us, seldom or never articulated. Scorned; put down. (We ourselves, as some of you have said here, have been scorned, have been put down, have felt that we're not "very good" and "our words are weak and small.") In deep moments, we know how much, already, we have lived. Even supposedly common experiences, how deeply we have lived them. I often quote Blake's "For a tear is an intellectual thing."

. . . Intensity of emotion: emotion has been put down because it's a "woman's quality." Somebody repeated here what we're told all the time: that men have had to suppress it. It's a writer's job to question anything that's told to us, *everything*. (It's every human being's job, really, to question everything.) We must never simply accept what is told to us. The fact is that men have been legitimized, have been permitted to express, emotion after emotion after emotion denied to women. And yet, we so accept that emotions are what women are about, and restraint and control are what men are about, that we do not look at the everyday actual reality: the emotion of anger. It's been legitimized for men—even to the extent of expressing it as violent rage, as the whole visibility given to battered women shows. Yet, men have had legitimized wife-beating, the expression of anger in the most violent kind of ways, as well as subtle ways. Virginia Woolf's *To the Lighthouse* shows some of the kinds of rages men are free to act out.

I'm generalizing again, talking about what is most characteristic, and it varies according to class too. That makes a difference as to what you are allowed to express, what you have to control, what is legitimized, fostered, what forbidden. . . . If a man feels desire or attraction, he can act on it directly; think of this powerful emotion permitted to men, almost completely denied to women.

In my long ago *Yonnondio*—a scene on an ice truck, on a hot summer day, and the nine-year-old Mazie, who loved to swing up on the ice truck, shove the ice over. Once, a chant goes up, "Go to London, go to France, everybody sees your pants." She almost slips, goes under the wheels; never again that lithe joy, that sense of power. That's a very powerful emotion girls are robbed of, boys keep, "that lithe joy, that sense of power."

There are other such examples. We must not go on repeating and seeing only what we are told. We women are allowed only a limited range of emotions against our lived reality, compared to men.

∾

. . . The book *Memoirs of a Working Women's Guild,* for which Virginia Woolf wrote the preface, was written by women who were not at home with the pen at all. Few of them had had even sixth-grade education, and how stiff they were with that written word! Virginia Woolf was a member of the Working Women's Guild, got them speakers every month for three years, attended meetings faithfully, was fascinated, moved, instructed by these women. But she had to conceal her respect, affection, esteem for them with her posh friends; cover over by being amusing, about them, about her participation. Even with closest friends, if it's a sex/class/color world, you have to dissemble sometimes, cover up.

. . . But Virginia Woolf was handed these life stories that these women had been asked by their Guilds to write. The women were selected by their own Guilds because it seemed that their lives spoke best for the rest of them. Virginia Woolf agonized in their notebooks: "Is this a book? How can this be a book?" These were not literature as literature is usually defined. The only "literary" quality about them was a writer's selection of significant detail. The problem of "standards" again. But Virginia Woolf decided to write the preface, which she ends by making one of the most important statements and guides for us: "Whether that is literature, or whether that is not literature, I will not presume to say, but that it explains much and tells much, that is certain." And this, too, is part of the greatness of literature.

❧

. . . But now we get taped. We don't write in our own words, our own stories. A century after, it's still someone else writing Sojourner Truth and Harriet Tubman for them. But unlike them who were illiterate we can write our own accounts! We don't have to have Robert Coles or Oscar Lewis or Studs Terkel or anybody else tape us. *Memoirs of a Working Women's Guild* has been brought back into print and is now taught in classes. It tells, *as human source,* what the lives of those women were like, and adds, in their own words, [reads from *Silences:*] " . . . to the authentic store of human life, human experience. The inestimable value of this, its emergence as a form of literature, is only beginning to be acknowledged. As yet, there is no place in literature analogous to the honored one accorded 'folk' and 'primitive' expression in art and in music." But even there, it's given only a secondary status.

❧

. . . We have to help keep even the writers who do get published alive, very, very often. This is very important if you have read something that means something to you, *send a postcard to that writer!* You have no idea how essential that is. And write thanking the publishers for the book.

Poets & Writers in New York is a wonderful organization helping to keep poets and writers alive. They have a directory you can get for addresses.[1] You can call them if you need help or information. They also have a down-to-earth, informative publication, *Coda.*[2] They are a valuable resource, and the first organization that has recognized the kind of writer who previously wasn't legitimized. Before, you were only in a directory of writers if you published books, and then with established presses. For Poets & Writers you need only to have published a few things, a few stories or poems to be listed. That's rightful. That's the way it should be. Several years ago a directory of *Women Writing,* by that name, also appeared. Use this directory to send the postcards to writers. There are fine writers who never hear from anybody. I think of Norma Rosen, who's written four books—one of them, *Touching Evil,* a favorite of mine—Sarah Wright, who wrote *This Child's Going to Live.*

Publishers don't even want to publish good established writers any-more because they haven't sold "x" number of copies. Few publishing companies are independently owned by publishers anymore. They're owned by conglomerates whose only interest is profits. Why should you publish a writer who's a good writer, but who only sells a few thousand or ten thousand copies, when you can get a "how-to-do-it" book, or a cookbook, or a sex and violence book that will sell tens of thousands? I can't even begin to describe the frightfulness of the situation. When I was in New York last time, good writers were feeling as if they don't exist anymore. Nobody asks you to come and read, to speak; you can't get your new books published. Your published books seem to have ceased to exist unless you go to the library to look at them, to reassure yourself. . . .

[Selecting from a stack of books she had brought along:] Ron Kovic's *Born on the Fourth of July*—he was the veteran who came to national fame or notoriety during the protests against the war in Vietnam. He was a paraplegic, in a wheelchair, and, nevertheless, was bodily removed and harmed when he tried to protest the war. This young man, who had never thought of himself as a writer, went off, patriotically believing, full of dreams of glory, and he writes about that: about the war and about becoming a paraplegic, coming back, himself changed, into the changed atmosphere of his own country. He realized suddenly that he had some-thing to say, that he *must* write. . . . And this is not one of those "as-told-to" books, or a taped-transcribed-edited one. It's his own work. It's one of the few accounts we have of growing up male working-class in this country, and illustrates again the great latent capacities we have with-out even knowing it unless circumstances suddenly permit. I brought this along, not only because it is an actual first generation of one's family to come to writing account, but also because it shows you that he could've gone through his whole life and never known he had it in him to write. Again the chanciness of circumstances. I hate that. Bertold Brecht said: "Unhappy is the land that needs a hero." Writing should come natur-ally out of natural joys and sorrows, out of human blossoming. But it strengthens us when we know about the origin of such books: the power of circumstances. And we do not poison ourselves by feeling that it's ourselves—why we aren't writing—that we aren't disciplined, or tal-ented, or serious. Instead, we are freed to do what we can, when we can.

Agnes Smedley's *Daughter of Earth:* a book all of you should read.

Autobiography, but she calls it "fiction." What distinguishes this book is what distinguishes *Memoirs of a Working Women's Guild* from most other fictionalized autobiography. These books write other human beings in the full dimension. They've broken through what Matthew Arnold called "the thick walls of self." Everyone else isn't a fool or an obstacle; caricatures. You find respectful understanding, passionate caring.

. . . Albert Camus came from an illiterate mother and a working-class family. He got a scholarship and "crossed the tracks." But he tells, in his *Journals*, about the first and only time he brought a schoolmate home. He read what was on that schoolmate's face, and he felt shame for himself, his home, his family. He says, in his *Journals*, "If I was almost thirty before I was able to expunge this shame, it was because it would have taken a heart of the most exceptional purity not to have felt this shame." . . . Going home, already a great, so respected writer, how much could Camus talk with his mother, whom he loved very, very dearly, of his life, his ideas, the people he knew? He lived in a different world. . . . But Camus wrote in his *Journals* that he could not look at his mother (that is, when she was not looking at him) without his eyes filling with tears. "I love my mother with despair, I have always loved my mother with despair."

Alice Walker, a later generation, different color, different sex, made of her "loving her mother with despair" literature in *Revolutionary Petunias* and "In Search of Our Mothers' Gardens." All of us who come from people, who are close to people who do not have the development, the fulfillment, the greater uses of themselves in many different ways, the knowledge of different kinds of worlds that we do, all of us know that we might have been them, or they might have been us, had they been born as we were, one or two generations later. Circumstances. And if you "love with despair," then you do not, in writing, put down or otherwise caricature, your people.

❧

I want to say some more about forms viable, feasible for us. Letters, the epistolary form, a form used in literature, used in fiction, too. In volumes of letters, why aren't the letters of the correspondents also published? Maybe their letters have as much to say as the letters of the famous person. How many of us receive or have been handed somebody's letters, and been fascinated by them? There's no reason why volumes of letters of intrinsic value and interest, written by non-famous people, couldn't be published for what they are: that form of literature that "tells us much and gives us much, that we would have in no other way."

Here are letters of the poet Louise Bogan, *What the Woman Lived*. When she died in her sixties, she had one slim volume of poetry. It's true, each poem is lasting, is perfect, but she lived a fairly long life, a literary life. As you read these letters, you discover that it was a life very different from the life of a literary man. These letters, to me, have the stature of the poetry. Not only because they are consummately expressed, but because *it's what the woman lived*. A life is in these letters.

We know about diaries as a form. Read *Revelations: Diaries of Women*, edited by Mary Jane Moffat and Charlotte Painter, revelations of the treasures by women in diary forms. . . . We have had few journals that tell of the lives most people are living. . . . Older women, now, going to classes, going back to school—their emotions, thoughts, experiences. . . . There's so much in our lives that needs to be in journal form, or in the form of what I sometimes call "utterances."

When I first found again and looked at *Yonnondio*, after the forty years, I became conscious of how what eventually silenced me had made me a better and better writer. This started to be 1930's time propaganda: "the evils of capitalism—what it did to human beings." Somebody asked: How do you write so that it is not propaganda, so that it is literature? Well, if you accord people their fully human dimension, as best you know how, it will not be propaganda; it cannot be. What's more, there's nothing wrong even in propaganda. Propaganda has its honorable place. And necessity, too. We have much to be grateful for that came from people who didn't have time or development to create art, but went ahead and made a certain necessary point over and over again until people understood it, acted on it.

Literature of certain content is often put down as "only of sociological or historical value," or as "black literature," or "regional literature." But remember, if it tells much and gives much, it, too, is part of the greatness of literature. . . .

. . . *Conditions*, a comparatively new and wonderful magazine: in it we see again a burgeoning literary form, the interview; one with Adrienne

Rich, who always has something more new and more incomparable to say. But I ask why not, also, interviews with each other, who are not necessarily poets or other persons of reputation? I'm trying to think of some of the practical, available ways to put into printed form some of what is in us that "tells much and gives much, that we would have in no other way. . . ."

In this same magazine, Irena Klepfisz, nearly forty, writes about what it has been like, what it is like, having long ago made the choice to be childless, to live with that decision and face the future. It is a pioneering article, unforgettable. To me, literature. Not essay, a kind of personal statement.

I tell you these things because you are the ones who've got to carry on literature and expand it, in ways besides the ways I and others have written: besides the established ways. We have to get away from the idea that these are the only ways in which we can write. Women have had to be ingenious in so many ways, making art out of little scraps of cloth. Most of us are going to have limitations in our lives; if we are going to put our time into achieving the perfect poem, story, it may be that we have taken a wrong direction. I know women who are limiting themselves by trying to do what, for them at least, in this time of their lives is impossible, and, meanwhile, they're passing by other ways in which they could write and record. *Do what you can at the time of your life that you can.* Make out of those limitations, out of those scraps, what art you can, never losing your ambition, never losing your aspiration, but at the cost of aspiration, don't blind yourself to what you *can* do. I really grieve about, am concerned about it, because most of us are working under limitations. And work that can get done mustn't be lost as it's been lost in the past.

◆

There is a tremendous vulnerability in us to criticism. Never, as is done in too many workshops and writing classes, criticize, treat a piece of writing as if it had come out of an established writer, as if it were a published work. You *cannot* gauge from a piece of work by somebody who has not published a lot of writing what that particular piece bespeaks of the development of that person. You have to know a person over a period of time, so that you understand what the achievement in it is, what the weaknesses, what it represents in their stage of growth. I have said for years that someone should make up an anthology of what jaded writers were writing in their beginning, fledgling years. It would be relieving, strengthening. You would understand writing as a *process*.

. . . A lot of harm has been done to published writers by unqualified, irresponsible reviewers. And a woman is more vulnerable, a person of color is more vulnerable, a man who is marginal because he's out of the working class is more vulnerable. We tend to be crushed easily. . . . The confusion between what we had wanted to say, meant to say, and what we were actually able to say is a very strong confusion indeed. It's hard to separate yourself and see what you have actually accomplished. That's where others can help us, but, instead, what usually happens is that we're hindered. I think, if you are a newer writer, that you should stay out of situations where you know the "criticism" is destructive. You need the sustenance of others, living others, who are also struggling with writing, and the inspiring others who are also our companions through their books.

. . . There is a validation of self as writer from seeing yourself in print. It can be Xerox, mimeograph; shared with your circle or writing class. And when you're ready, send manuscripts out—select carefully where; know what they print and if your works fits; never judge yourself by rejections. Keep on. If criticisms don't ring true to you, disregard them.

[In answer to a question about commercial publishers and small, especially women's, presses:] Of course, if you *can* get published by one of the larger publishers, then your chances for distribution, for reviews, are infinitely greater, but I don't think we should turn our backs on the other ways to be published there are. And I believe that those women who do get published by commercial publishers have a special responsibility to do everything they can for good writers who are not that lucky, do everything they can to get them known, get them read, see that they get around and are listened to. But get published how and where you can: the small magazines, and the broadsides, your local paper.

Organizations like Poets & Writers help to create a community. And writers' workshops and readings are proliferating in this country. But we have to recommend readings by writers who aren't asked; we don't need to see the same faces, hear the same voices all the time.

❧

[In answer to a question about times when getting to writing is impossible:] Charlotte Brontë, the already famous writer of *Jane Eyre*, was silenced for a whole year after that came out. And, in response to a letter from a friend rebuking her for her silence, she wrote: "Submission when necessary; courage always; exertion when practicable. These seem to be the weapons with which we must fight life's long battles. . . ."

Submission is not passivity. Submission is not "giving in." It is not defeat. It is the recognition of the circumstances of your life. It's what human beings are faced with and must do in a world in which class, economic circumstance, color, and sex are so determining. We have to know how we're going to handle it so that it doesn't destroy us; so that instead we accomplish everything we can in our lives that aren't perfect circumstances.

∼❧

[In answer to a question about feeling guilty for doing your own work, writing, instead of taking care of others' needs first, primarily, children's needs:] This is so important to understand, particularly for women with children (let alone women with a paid job) who are trying to make some time for themselves, who are told over and over—"it's guilt you feel." It's *not* guilt you feel! What you're feeling is the working of an intolerable, insoluble situation, in which needs and demands of neither can be taken care of, or at best, one at the cost of another. Schools are usually not good places. Playgrounds or the street are usually not good places. This is not a world that nourishes children and makes them flourish. No one else but you (and perhaps a few family members) are responsible for and care about those kids. If you're *not* there, nobody else is going to be. If you have to be somewhere else, actual needs, actual situations that should be handled are not going to be handled. There's damn little you can do for your kids anyway because so much of their lives is determined outside you, beyond you. But it's not guilt you're feeling. When you're told it's guilt, it puts it in a psychological area where, presumably, if you just had the right kind of therapy, you'd be helped with your guilt. It doesn't enable you to see that intolerable situation for what it is.

. . . Why should the life of *any* human being have to go so much into maintenance of life when, if we were organized differently, it is not socially necessary anymore? If you have to work on a job, an everyday job, how do you steal the time—if you are trying to write—for yourself? When I was thinking of myself as a writer and working on everyday jobs,

I was more fortunate than most because I had, years before, done some writing. I had developed certain writer's characteristics, the ear for characterizing speech; a noting, questioning, recording; and I was really crazy about people. I didn't put them down as "losers" doing, quote, "shit work," an expression I never use and hate.

W. E. B. Du Bois calls that "the manure theory of social organization"; the old, aristocratic, class idea that the people who do the everyday work, well, that's what they are. Yet the world could not go on one day without this everyday work. In a different kind of society than ours, it would be respected. As long as any work is necessary, essential for the human being, it should be highly respected and highly paid, and it should consume only a small part of a person's life. We have the technological capacity to make this true.

I saw how things were crushed in people. And I recorded some of that in *Yonnondio*, the maiming of the children, the stunting of capacities. It's a process, of course, that has happened with all of us—including all those little kids who are maybe born to be writers, because of the way they are with language, and they grow up and, maybe, they're good talkers.

❧

You've asked me about myself. Everything in my life, my background, my childhood, my "colleges," my life as a writer, verified the presence of great capacities in human beings, the kind seen only when they come out in recognized forms of achievement, "success"; but I was fascinated about how these show themselves in everyday life. I was overwhelmed by the courage that people bring to everyday life. My god, it really *is* a miracle that half of us haven't wiped ourselves out. I love a couple lines of Emily Dickinson: "A day! Help, help! Another day!"

. . . I didn't waste those work years, those non-writing years. At the time I had my children, I did some reading. I kept quotations or ponderings tacked up over the sink. I memorized poetry. I did some thinking; I did some jotting down. I have a lot of notes. I would take clippings from the paper that meant something to me. Many women do that. They clip things; they save things. It's a writer's sense, a historian's sense: that there's something significant in this, something important, and I want to have it, use it in some way. The time I really began to write, much of it was done on the ironing board.

If I had entered that work situation saying, "I'm a writer, I'm better than you, this is so degrading to me," there would have been contempt, despair, I would have isolated myself, shut myself off. . . .

    ❧

. . . I started to say that, later on, when I wasn't so tired—when I changed my work and became an office worker—I used to knock myself out to try to get to work at least ten minutes ahead of time because it was an office where I had a typewriter; and, anyway, work was such a simplified place and responsibility compared to home! I had only a few things I had to do. It was clean; it was organized. But I *made* some time. When things weren't too fascinating during breaks at work, I would secrete myself and sit and read, or muse, or scrawl. And, later on, I used to look for the kinds of jobs in which I would have time to copy things out of books I couldn't buy; I'd pretend it was part of work. And always a 3 x 5 card to write on; a small notebook; the very act of making a note, recording, writing down, fixes it in some deep way. Somebody told me once that she took one of those jobs where she didn't have to travel to and from working during rush hour and always got a seat on the bus. She learned how to print big, because it was shaky on the bus, and that's when she got certain things recorded and written down. . . . You'd be surprised how pages pile up. . . .

    . . . There is, unquestionably, when we're at a certain beginning stage of writing, a kind of resistance to it—unless you're a very habituated writer. Those writers who've written most of what we read, who had a routine, who were professionals—they put in less actual time, fewer hours, on their writing than any of us puts in on even a part-time job. You know, "the quiet, patient, generous mornings will bring it." But we don't lead those kinds of lives. If we keep thinking about how we're not going to make it unless we have full circumstances, then most of us are doomed. Be realistic. William James said, "The world can and has been changed by those to whom the ideal and the real are dynamically contiguous." To change your personal life, too. But don't poison yourself because you don't have circumstances that writers (who don't tell you their luck) have had. Don't poison yourself because you're there with maybe kids, or, and, a paid job, or other using, demanding situations, and maybe a year has passed by (or more) and you only *thought* about writing. Don't foreclude, therefore, that you're not a writer. Don't write yourself off as just having had idle dreams. You *must* keep alive as much as you can. . . . In actuality of work, however partial, occasional, or if necessary, only in intention, aspiration.

Notes

1. The address is Poets & Writers, Inc., 201 West 54 Street, New York, New York 10019; the telephone number is 212-226-3586; and the Internet address is [http://www.pw.org].

2. *Coda* has changed its name to *Poets & Writers*.

3. Maggie Anderson, who transcribed these excerpts, currently teaches at Kent State University.

Doing What You Will Do

An Interview with Lucille Clifton
by Marilyn Kallet

MK I like to think of you at five years old writing sonnets in Depew, New York, and I'm wondering who helped you to get started with that writing. Who opened your mind to poetry?

LC My mother wrote poetry. It isn't that she helped me to write it, but I saw poetry as a natural part of what one does. My mother, who did not graduate from elementary school, loved poems. She used to sit in her rocking chair and rock and recite poems—very traditional iambic pentameter verse—"Abbu Ben Adham" was one, "The House by the Side of the Road" was another—old poems. But I saw that doing as a very normal part of what one does.

MK Maybe that's why your work sounds so accessible. The reader doesn't have to fight to enter the work. Though your writing is crafted, certainly.

LC I take great care with craft. But this is an oral tradition, really. I think probably the oral tradition is the one which is most interesting to me and the voice in which I like to speak.

MK When did you first recognize that you were speaking in your own voice?

LC When I was younger I used to copy—people all want me to say Langston Hughes and Gwendolyn Brooks, but no—the poets I used to read were Edna St. Vincent Millay and Emily Dickinson and Thomas Wolfe. I love Thomas Wolfe. Though of course I don't use language like any of them. I've been compared to Dickinson, but I don't write like her—I just write short poems. I've often been compared to Langston Hughes—I don't write like him at all, but I'm black, so people compare us. I think when I won a prize and I was going to be published, I realized, "Maybe I'll do this again!" And I had won a grant from the National Endowment for the Arts—that was so shocking to me. I've had two grants from them. I was very excited, encouraged. I was a housewife with little children. I had four in diapers at the same time. There are six children, and they are only six and a half years apart in age. So when *Good Times* was first published, they must have been four, five, six, seven, eight, and ten.

I really think that one can do whatever she or he has to. I was going to write poems. Someone has asked my children about that, about how my writing changed our lives. But I have been writing ever since they've known me. I was writing with the same intent— major intent. What I mean by that is that I wanted to do well. I wanted to do well this thing that I felt I must do. They haven't read the books on mothering, so they think the way their mother is is the way mothers are. They were not neglected kids by any means. So they didn't think there was anything odd about the way I mothered. Somebody asked my daughter on a television interview, "What's it like, her being your mother?" My children always say, "Well, everybody's mother does something. This is what she does." They don't see it as odd. Nor did I see the fact of having children as keeping me from doing the thing I felt I had to do. I had to learn a process that would allow me to do it.

MK Can you talk about that? That's really interesting and it might be useful.

LC It's just that what I learned to do was to write in my head. Even now when I get down to compose—and I compose on a typewriter. I cannot compose longhand at all, never have been able to—by the time I sit down to type, I'm not starting at the very beginning, I'm starting somewhere in the middle. I can keep a few lines in my head at the same time—and I can revise in my head—so by the time I sit down, I'm already on my way. It's just a matter, then, of following the poem.

MK I'm trying to picture you at the moment when you actually got to sit down and write, with these little children. . . .

LC I can't write when it's very quiet. My baby's thirty-two now, so it's not an issue. But because I was so used to little children—to their playing and, of course, making noise—I'm very good at focusing myself in the middle of noise. So now I turn on television, or I like music when I'm writing, because when you're writing and you have little children and there's silence, there's something wrong! So I am not able to write as well in silence. Sharon [Olds] came into the room the other day and said, "You have the television set on!" I said, "I want to write, and I've got to have something on."

MK Did you have any help with your kids?

LC No. Nobody wants to. . . . I had four in diapers at once. I couldn't have afforded it even if I could have found someone. But most people are not going to watch that many children. Later, when I had to get a job outside the home I did have help with the kids. But during their youngest years, I did not.

MK What kind of music are you turning on?

LC I love all sorts of music.

MK Your poetry is saturated with it.

LC Well, it should be musical. I'm not too crazy about a lot of rap or a lot of country-western. But I like Willie Nelson. I like jazz; R & B, big time. I love Bach. I like all kinds of music. I like Coltrane.

MK "Get what you want, you from Dahomey women"—that was the saying of your great-great-great grandmother.

LC Yes, my father's great grandmother was a Dahomey woman. As was Audre Lorde.

MK I feel the kinship in your work. How has that tradition held power for you?

LC I think that from the time I was a little girl, I believed—not that I'm not insecure, because I am big time in lots of things, but not so much in my selfness—I believed that I could do what I wanted to. I believed that when other people wanted to limit me in some way, they were wrong, that they didn't know what they were talking about. I don't have to believe what people say, because they are wrong quite a lot, especially about me. So I need to check things out for myself. I have always been a learner, and there are lots of things I like to know about. At one time the culture limited what even seemed possible for me to know. But I never went for that. They were just wrong.

MK This sort of inner reference comes to you through family history and stories, and how else? Are there people in your family who were strong?

LC Yes, my father used to say we were a family of strong women and weak men. He was probably right, through the generations. I think that we are a family of very strong women. I have four daughters. The one daughter with children only has two sons. My sister has three daughters. I think my line has been strong. I was born with twelve fingers, as my mother was, and my oldest daughter. I somehow think they have a bit of magic in them. Something that helps you with an extra knowing. And I think I do have an extra knowing.

MK Did they take your extra fingers?

LC Yes, when I was born. My oldest daughter was the only one I did not see born. They gave me a drug. The rest I watched being born; I was present. Before I was able to stop them, they had removed my oldest daughter's extra fingers. I felt really bad about that. So for her I wrote a poem, "I Wish for Her Fantastic Hands," for when she was pregnant. But she has two sons, no daughters.

MK Whom do you thank in your life?

LC Everyone. Even those who have not necessarily been positive, because I have learned a heck of a lot in my life. I have had a challenging life, but I have learned much from it. My daughter gave me her kidney—I am rather thankful about that. Since 1994 I have had breast cancer, kidney failure, then almost a year of dialysis. I'm a year away from my kidney transplant, four years clear of cancer.

MK Thank God. And you have your daughter's kidney?

LC Yes, and she's my youngest child—that one which I really did not want to have.

MK But she insisted, didn't she?

LC I have a poem about it. [Included with this interview.] Yes. She said, "If I could have talked, I would have told you 'give me thirty years, you're going to need me!'"

MK I'm thinking that you have incorporated the many obstacles in your life—including the illnesses—into your writing.

LC This is what my life is. Sure. I have poems in the book about cancer, new poems about dialysis, which I hated tremendously, poems about the transplant.

The book is going to come out. I hope it will be *New and Selected Poems.* It's not done. When I wrote *The Terrible Stories* (1996), I was trying to write a *New and Selected* but I ended up with new poems.

MK What else would you still like to accomplish?

LC I'm sixty-two. I really feel that I have not yet done my best work, and I feel really good about feeling that! That's why I thought, "I can't possibly die from kidney failure, because I haven't done my best work yet."

I have told myself that I will accept the sacred which comes to me. I'm not a religious person, I assure you, but I do think I'm a spiritual person. I sometimes have hesitated to publish poems with the sacred voice because they are not validated that much. But I think I want to accept and use those poems as well as the ones I usually publish. There's plenty to see, to do. I'm a very alive person, for somebody who can hardly move!

MK Do you have advice for young writers?

LC If something can start you, then something can stop you. Keep writing. Trust the poet in yourself. Trust the language. No poet ever gets exactly where they want to.

Every poet I know feels they almost did it. On my gravestone it's going to say "She almost did it." And that will be a triumph because—getting it right, who knows what that is—but doing it anyway, not for the glory but for the thing itself. Poets serve poetry. It's better to want to write poems than to want to be a poet. It's better to be writing poems than to have written them. I know that there are no circumstances that can stop you because when my first book came out, I had four kids in diapers and I had no help and I didn't know about Pampers. My youngest daughter was the only one who had Pampers. I didn't care if she was toilet trained or not—I figured there's nobody twenty still walking around with diapers! What you will do, you will do.

MK What is the most important aspect of your craft?

LC For me, sound. A lot of people are triggered by what they see. I am triggered by what I hear. For me sound, the music of a poem, and the feeling are most important. I can feel what I can hear. Poetry wasn't made to sit on a page.

I think Stanley Kunitz talks about this—"the page is a cold bed."
The first poets didn't write anything. The first poets didn't use poly-
syllabic language. Every culture has its poetry.

I teach in a program, so I can say this: I think that poets now,
especially in programs, write for the page. So it's a poem that you
can see, but there's no music in it. Also, they tend to be written for
critics and to be evaluated. Poetry is a human art and needs to be
written for humans. It needs to matter. It is a history of what it
means to be alive in this time and this place. And that matters.

—Olympic Valley, California, July 22, 1998

❧

donor

    for lex

when they tell me that my body
might reject
I think of thirty years ago
and the hangers i shoved inside hard
not to have you.

i think of the pills
the everything
i gathered against your bulge
and you
my stubborn baby child
hunched there in the dark
refusing my refusal.

suppose this body does say no
to yours again
again i feel you
buckling despite me
fastened to life like the frown
on an angel's brow.

Hedging Bets on Motherhood

PAMELA WALKER

Most kids would rather have their mothers on the brink of suicide in the next room than happy anywhere else.
NORA EPHRON

I knew more about babies than your average new mother. Growing up on the plains in what William Gass calls "the heart of the heart of the country," I was indoctrinated early in age-old agrarian ways whereby older children, especially girls, care for younger. I was the second of my mother's four and her only girl; my youngest brother was born when I was ten. By the summer of my thirteenth year, when my mother went to work in the office of a box factory, I was put in charge at home. In all fairness, I believe the arrangement was my brainstorm. I wanted money; I earned twenty-five cents an hour and I worked a forty-hour week. Doubtless, it was this experience, stuck at home with baby brother on sultry days when I longed to be at the pool with girlfriends, that cured me of premature longings for a baby of my own.

I was thirty and single when like clockwork the notion of motherhood struck with private urgency, taking me by surprise, for in truth children, like all trappings of adulthood, terrified me. I had spent the first decade of adulthood avoiding pregnancy like disease through religious devotion to birth control along with sheer good luck. This is not to say I was one of those women who abandoned you after you gave birth. I was the friend who brought your family dinner when you came home hurting from the hospital, the one who took charge of your tiny baby so you could sleep. I had a way with children, always someone else's, and I made my living as a teacher. Adulthood eluded me, but I had my finger on the pulse of infancy and adolescence.

I attribute my fear of adulthood to one bitter night on the first of December in 1968, when my brother Jon was hurled through the windshield of a Volkswagen driven by some maniac kid who lost control and rolled his mother's fastback five times in a snow-covered field along U.S. 1 in Iowa City. The driver and the passenger riding shotgun, supposedly the death seat, walked away whole. I was twenty years old and one week married to my college sweetheart. I started writing stories about Jon and me as children, and even before one was published in the college literary magazine, I was hooked. The only times I felt remotely alive in the years following Jon's death were the hours during which I resurrected him on the page.

Banishing motherhood appeared a small price for saving my life. I had models. Willa Cather had no children, nor Flannery O'Connor, Carson McCullers, Katherine Anne Porter, not the Brontës or Jane Austen. Shirley Jackson had five, but she was the anomaly. The idea of dirty diapers and pabulum coming between me and my aspirations filled me with palpable horror long before I read Sylvia Plath. My best friend at Iowa State married my older brother and quit school before their son was born. Once during my own youthful marriage, my period was late and I remember telling my mother that I was worried I might be pregnant. Mom reassured me that unplanned pregnancies can be a blessing in disguise, this from a woman who bore her first three children in three years— her "stepping-stone kids," she called us—yet grew so wild with frustration that she was breaking hair brushes over our heads by the time we reached middle childhood. I got off the phone and informed my young husband that if I were pregnant, I had to get rid of "it." I was taken aback when he insisted he deserved a say in the outcome.

By the time I met the man I married in 1985, the jig was up, no doubt about that. I became a mother belatedly precisely because I had been unwilling to give up the writing life, no matter how unsuccessful it might have been, until it was almost too late. Were it not for the obsessional nature of writing, the control it has held over my every decision from choice of livelihood to marriage and motherhood, the be-all and end-all nature of motherhood might have appealed to me much sooner in the game.

When a year's investment in ovulation predictor tests failed, I made the rounds of fertility clinics, toting sperm to labs, popping Clomid and plotting my waking temperature. My first pregnancy went a full twelve weeks; the next was gone before I missed my period, not even an embryo, just a still vacuole on the ultrasound screen. "Bad egg," the attending physician mumbled to the nurse. I lay upon the gurney, awed by how precisely heart-shaped is the preembryonic human heart at the center of the ovum.

I refused to fall prey to genetic hubris, wasting precious time and money on experimental therapies with bad odds. I harbored no desire to languish in the stark halls of shiny hospitals, emerging empty-handed. I always knew that if I could not carry a child, I would adopt, and at the age of forty, with two miscarriages in five months, I was more than willing to forsake blood ties. When my husband, Rich, and I arrived in Santiago de Chile to meet our infant daughter, Juliet, I believed I was adequately prepared for the changes motherhood might work upon my life. Yet here's the truth: no matter how much you know, it's never enough.

It's not enough that you adore this most precious baby chosen for her beauty and her spirit—*ánima,* the Spanish call it. "She reached out to me with her arms and her eyes," our lawyer told us about finding Juliet at La Casa del Niño in Santiago. She was six weeks old and indomitable. It's not enough that you fall in love with your baby's button nose and bushy eyebrows, that her dark almond eyes enchant you. We'll split the duty fifty-fifty, you reason, even-Steven; we're a modern couple. Chalk it up to naïveté: the baby brings a will. When colic racked her being, I alone upon this earth could bring her solace. On Rich's chest, she writhed. Her shrieking ripped my heart apart. But put her in my arms, and she was silenced instantly. The power was haunting; the magic, overwhelming.

Nothing could have prepared me for what Marguerite Duras calls "the colossal swallowing up which is the essence of all motherhood, the mad love . . . and the madness that maternity represents." I'm talking about a mother's terror of abductions and cabs jumping curbs, horrifying scenarios from the late-night news that send a shudder through me as I'm speeding down the parkway to the city. I let up on the gas, shift to the middle lane, and drop my speed to fifty. I'm talking, too, about a loss of time and self profound and absolute, every bit as daunting as I imagined it to be.

I used to keep journals of dreams and thoughts and secrets. A journal a year was nothing. I do not recall a single entry serving as the basis for a story. Journal keeping was simply a way to know myself through the luxury of thinking my own thoughts. The journal I currently keep is made by Quillmark of Random House. It is covered in a paisley fabric; its lined pages are thick and ivory. I write with a Pilot Razor Point whenever I steal a moment.

I began this journal on June 19, 1989, two months before we met Juliet in Santiago. Day after day the birth mother's release failed to arrive. Without it, we could not file the final U.S. Immigration papers. On June 27, I wrote that the Chilean child welfare agency refused to accept the documentation of state licensing provided by our home study agency. These bureaucratic delays added six weeks to an excruciating wait, each day a new torture that I was stuck in New York half a world away from Juliet. My arms ached to know her weight. Yet more than all else, I lusted for my baby's smell as though I were a tigress separated from her kitten, as though the most primal of senses were essential to bind us.

In *Silences* Tillie Olsen writes it was no accident that the first story she considered publishable began, "I stand here ironing. . . ." During the twenty years Olsen bore and reared four children, working at paying jobs as well, "the simplest circumstances for creation did not exist." The hope of writing became the air she breathed until her youngest was in school and "beginnings struggled toward endings." Juliet is now nine, and I have yet to fill my journal's 160 pages. Late at night, when the house is quiet, too wired to sleep, too tired to write, I lose myself in *Unsolved Mysteries* or, better still, dramas of real cops taped in blue tones with hand-held video cameras as they arrest scrawny young men who speak in twangs. Even when I eke out a few hours now that Juliet attends full-day school, my thoughts run helter-skelter, wild like the winds of a cyclone, and I cannot harness them. I end up cleaning house with a heavy heart. When words fail, cleaning gives quick, if ephemeral, results. Motherhood requires a record leap of faith that the writing will wait, growing richer even as I iron.

One child makes you a mother. Much as I love my daughter, and truly I do—she is a miracle—another was out of the question. As Alice Walker said, ". . . with one you can move. With more than one you're a sitting duck." Realistically, hedging bets on motherhood as long as I did goes a long way toward assuring that your first will be your only. To look at me, you might think I'm well fit for the physicality of motherhood: I am blessed with a lean body and a surfeit of energy. Yet during Juliet's first year, my strengths were not equal to the rigor of arriving four days a week at the Bronx school where I tutored.

Money would have helped the physical punishment of motherhood if not the melancholia. More money, and I would have rented car space at the garage next door for twice the monthly. More money, and I would not have been slogging up Amsterdam Avenue through wind and rain and snow with an infant. I would have taxied her to the baby sitter, taxied home, and written all day. Of the two women I know who do not work outside the home, one keeps her house in the Chicago suburbs immaculate and the other plays tennis at a private Virginia club several times a week. Now that their children are in school, they do volunteer work. They both have plenty of time to write—they don't, of course, because they're not writers—but I see that if I were playing their hands, I'd be writing. I might even take up tennis if I were so privileged as to escape the hustle in the infernal dollar-an-hour racket.

Like Tillie Olsen, I am sustained by the mere hope of writing. On countless dreary weekends filled with a never-ending succession of tasks undone as soon as they are done—feeding, changing, straightening—I used to dream of Cummington Community for the Arts in Massachusetts, a colony that provided a children's summer camp for parents who worked in private studios. The winter before Juliet turned four, I applied for a residency. In the spring I received a devastating call from the director: Juliet was not eligible for the program until her fifth year. As a consolation prize, I was offered a one-week residency in June. It wasn't much, but it was something quite miraculous all the same.

I borrowed a laptop and set off for Cummington, where I was afforded a huge studio with brilliant natural light on the top floor of an old farmhouse, looking to bright forests as far as the eye could see. I took long walks on mountain roads with other residents. I breathed the green, the trees, the sky; I heard the songs and frantic calls of birds. For five glorious days I lived an idyll, luxuriating in reading and writing, sleeping and dreaming. From erratic notes jotted over the previous year, I started this essay, right away getting caught in a wrong tack from which I could not extricate myself and drafting one worthless beginning after another. I was not working well but I was working, I told myself. Hours passed unnoticed, and suddenly it would be dinnertime.

The deal I had extracted from Rich over dinner at his favorite Mexican restaurant was that he would take vacation to work at home on his computer projects while Juliet spent each day with the baby sitter. Within two days of my departure, plans for the home front, tenuous hopes as they turned out, began to fray. Juliet was overcome by asthma—which had never troubled her before my absence, nor has it since. She could not go to the sitter, so Rich could not do his work. My lark became his nightmare. On the fifth day, he called: "We're coming tomorrow." By this time, I could type no more. My wrists were in spasm. Sharp pains shot up my arms if I so much as tried to press the shift key. I was ready to throw in the towel on soul-searching and to meet my family.

As cruel irony had it, Cummington lost its battle for life the year Juliet turned five. I possessed neither a backup plan nor the financial means to create one, so she and I spent the summer at home, quite literally. Though we made three long voyages to Amagansett, Long Island, to visit a friend at her beach house, we did not frequent the playground or the movies. We never even paid a visit to the zoo though it's free on Wednesdays and fifteen minutes from our house.

Juliet is an independent child with her own rich and secret world of fantasy. "Mama, go to the kitchen," she tells me, and I dare not spy on her. Even so, we're talking at best a half-hour, during which I might read some notes or write a phrase, one lone phrase, before she sought me out at my computer. I couldn't get a thought in edgewise.

I wrote by hand at a local diner, slogging away without direction or inspiration. I wrote late at night as hot summer days slipped inextricably into weeks, and suddenly the season was two-thirds gone while I had nothing to show for my dogged efforts to write something, anything, preferably a thing of beauty or at least of truth. Defeated at the beginning of August, I turned my attention to a small piece of research I had completed the previous spring in graduate school. I had returned to school after a twenty-year hiatus for state certification in special education, a decision forced upon me by the realities of motherhood: I needed that which I had always shunned, a day job with a pension.

Granted, writing about education felt second-rate, yet I was impressed by the ease with which my words flowed onto the page. If the blank page of fiction is like negotiating a foggy sea alone in a canoe without paddles, composing an academic article was more akin to finding oneself on a cruise ship with a Caribbean sun radiating from the azure sky. By the time you sit to write, you have marshaled a whole army of authors to back you up, and with that kind of moral support, I was actually able to think and write in the midst of my child's brilliant hurly-burly. Within two weeks I rewrote the article and submitted it to a journal. A month later it was accepted for publication.

When the article was published just before Christmas, I felt like a writer again to see my name in print. I passed out copies like Hanukkah gelt at graduate school. One of my professors to whom I had complained about being unable to write said, "See, you are writing." A piece which implores educators to develop genuine sensitivity for youngsters with learning disabilities is no shame. It's not as though made-up characters are chomping at the bit in the furthest reaches of my mind. My new degree landed me a day job at the cutting edge of public education, which I augmented with night work, teaching adults to read. My husband, a union man, toils six days a week in network news to garner the same salary a five-day schedule brought him ten years ago. Terror, which has burrowed its way into every fiber of our lives as parents, is the driving force, the source of energy reserves we never knew we possessed.

I do not miss the journal writing per se. In motherhood I have found I can live with less—four to eight entries a year. Yet I do miss the fullness of time from which the voices emerge, and of course I miss the voices themselves. Above and beyond the loss of friends through death and leave-taking for sunnier locales, much of my loneliness as a late-life mother results from this chasm rent between me and characters I have yet to meet. I sense them still. I hold onto hope that the words will come back—if not in a flood, then deeper with humanity, a gift of motherhood.

Since Juliet's birth, the speed of passing time grows merciless. Years zoom by at breakneck speed, and suddenly I am the mother of a third-grader who plays piano and eagerly awaits her budding breasts. She makes books and dictates stories. On a black background, she paints a turquoise tree, filling the whole canvas; her sense of color, form, and space is brilliant. She places several feathers in its branches. "Now, it's done," she declares, throwing the paintbrush in the slop sink. "I'm going to watch some TV, and you can clean my brushes."

A child is a creation unto herself, making up the world as she rolls along. The sky's the limit to this fairy child. I am the assistant, at best a guide who makes her discoveries more possible. Tending to my daughter's needs keeps me whole. Before meeting my husband, I had come to fear I would never marry again, nor bear children and place my mark of immortality upon this world. So I wash the brushes, thinking thoughts I have no time to write, dreaming dreams I don't remember. I have to believe that I am ready for the voices when they come.

The Artist as Single Mother

KATHERINE SMITH

Creation is often thought to be a product of a mind carelessly meander-
ing over long periods of time. In my own life as the single mother of a
very young daughter, this concept is an obstacle to writing. Given the
realities of my life—I do not often have more than half an hour or an
hour at a time to write, and even these hours are too often purchased
with a self-destructive guilt (I could be picking my daughter up early
from daycare instead of writing this essay)—I have made for myself the
following credo: it is perhaps true that a mind freed of care creates the
"best" art. But I do not strive to create "good" art; I simply strive to
continue creating. With or without a child, for me, as I suspect for most
artists, creation is necessary for self-creation—a space, however limited,
where the self can expand and breathe independently of the world where
one "functions," whether for self or others.

Writing is vital to my life, even if the limited time I can give to my
writing tends to dictate the form (mostly poems and short pieces) that
writing takes. For while someone who writes full-time is more able to
dictate the form of her writing, single parenthood is not conducive to
certain genres of art: the long, plot-driven novel, the epic in painting,
perhaps sculpture. These art forms require not only a quantity of time
and solitude but a purposefulness that is difficult to associate with single
motherhood. The artist/single mother must be deft at spinning her life
from a web of impossibilities and learn to enjoy a diet of winged crea-
tures flown her way by chance.

The single mother needs to know that any solitude, however brief,
contains the seeds of freedom; a quarter of an hour alone in the river

of self on a raft of words can give one's life that sense of infinitude so sought-after by all artists. On the other hand, purposefulness is constraint. It is not difficult to create when creation is freedom, if only momentarily, from the demands of everyday functionality. But if one is to turn one's creations into works of "art," one must make that art visible to the world, and visibility requires purposefulness in a sense the single mother knows only too well: the chores of sending out manuscripts, arranging readings, applying for grants and fellowships are analogous to the changing of diapers, dressing and feeding, and other tasks associated with the child, not to mention the innumerable duties associated with the workplace. All of these tasks of the artist/agent/mother, in themselves trivial, take a sort of administrative watchfulness that can seem impossible given the constant stewardship of life itself with which the artist/mother is already faced. When does one find time to fill out the forms, send out the curriculum vitae, stuff the envelopes for contest guidelines, do the networking, when one is at the same time concentrating one's energies on the diverse tasks of a full day at work and evenings and weekends spent with a four-year-old? It is all too easy to put off the nurturing of one's poetry, ferrying it forth from the dream world of one's own desk drawer to the social world of the printed page; to put off this ferrying forth which requires so much ambition and purposefulness that seem fruitless in relation to one's everyday life. And how are the hours of solitude, the time snatched from the jaws of functionality, to seem worthwhile if they simply lead to one further duty: that of being secretary to one's own passion?

For the mother/artist, ambition can cause terrible pressure, but the work itself can also be a source of energy. Personally, I have chosen to raise my child and to carry the burden of my own ambition. I do this because I have a deep need to have the products of my creative life validated, if only in a limited way, by the world, almost as if the world were the oasis to which I bring my thirst.

❧

The single mother, like others who have found themselves by necessity surcharged with responsibility for life, is too often praised uniquely for her ability to function, to survive. Need all a woman's self, all her usable energy, be invested in functioning? A world where the mother is never free from responsibility for her children or from her vital income-producing work, will be a world in which few single mothers will be artists. Only a privileged few, only a heartbreakingly select group of strong single mothers, will survive as artists in a world where functioning on a primitive basis is the only priority of women. (Of course, in America, the land of Self-Reliance, functioning is often considered the primary moral goal. For while this country is a paradise for that part of our lives in which we are the healthy—the rich, the strong, the normative—it is a hell for that part of our lives in which we are the ill: the poor, the disenfranchised, the different.) In some respects, single mothers can find themselves in the same predicament as did all women a hundred years ago, tied to an endless stream of domestic responsibilities, with, at present, the added burden of making a living. There are no easy solutions, private or social, to this problem. Least acceptable is to decide that the vision of single mothers can be excluded from the total perspective supposedly given by the arts. For the woman to remain dependent on the father of the children, the answer of the "family-oriented" 1990s, is the worst of all possible solutions in a world in which creativity counts.

❧

A private solution is simply for the artist to do what she can, to turn her back on a world that values above all the grandiose (America is the only country in the world to continue to value art above all for its length, its bigness) and the controlled (the obsession with craft at the expense of delight). There is still room for play in this serious world, still room for the improvised in the life of the mother. There is perhaps less and less room for the masterpiece in the lives of women, those masterpieces which have been suffocating humankind since the last of the great patrons, the Medicis, was buried in the tomb. Yet the urgent question remains to those of us for whom art matters: in a world in which artists provide their own livelihood through an hourly wage and are sole providers for children as well, what is the place of the imagination?

❧

Creation is not about duty to others; nor does it concern duty to self, that wearisome specter that haunts the pages of women's magazines, advising mothers to neglect neither their personal appearance—their hair, their makeup, their clothes—nor their inner lives, their spiritual and sexual resources (for women the imaginative and the sexual are often considered undifferentiated, as if they had no imaginative life apart from or beyond the sexual). Self-help books for single mothers abound in practical advice on caring for self, children, boyfriends, often even advising women to draw or write poetry in lieu of practicing their sexuality. But this belittles our selves, our sexuality, and the works of our hearts and hands. Our expression is something at the same time more primitive and more transcendent than a simple wish to "refuel." We are not machines. The works of our hands are made of our nothingness, our doubts, our fears; we too hang onto the material world with all our might, unravel fibers from that slender cord in which are also tangled our hopes.

❧

The sun's glare sinks into green water, whose current effortlessly carries it off downriver so that only the diffused glow of an early spring sunset spreads over the trees on the bank. An hour ago I watched a woman weep as she struggled to pick a three-year-old child up from the floor of a daycare center. Two older children, brothers of the little girl, stood near the exit, wanting to leave. I watched the woman and the child struggling, oddly aware of myself as being as distant from the pair. I spoke to the woman and she turned away, muttering something about getting dinner ready. What kind of life is it that reduces single mothers to a machine-like existence, where only functioning matters, where only the conflict is meaningful, whether it be with children, society, or self? What kind of world is it where the only beauty to be found must be bought at a shopping mall with money better spent on new winter clothes for the children?

❧

Driving past the local utilities payment center frequented by the poorest of my city's southern district, I see, waiting patiently beneath the arcade of the seedy run-down mall, a woman with a little boy. The little boy has a crew cut his mother runs her free hand through. Even from the road I can see the color of the envelope she is holding. It is blue, the color of the local electric bill. The young woman is teasing her little boy, playing with him. Both of them are laughing as she waits for the payment center to open, probably paying as most do here—in cash, at the last minute, to divert a cut-off.

Standing in the early morning fog that hovers over the arcade, the two look very alone, their rusty black Mustang parked beside them for company. In their laughter is the courage of art.

The sun sinks over a hill as I write these words, leaning over the scrap of paper crushed onto the steering wheel of my humming car, my daughter cradled in the arms of someone who is not her mother. I write these words as I watch the sunlight glint off a scrap of bark covered with red ants, lying in the parking lot next to the roadside where I have pulled over to write imperfect words whose fragmentary nature is due not to any lack of wholeness but to a life lived with full arms, with fingers that must too occasionally loosen their grasp of the work that brings in the money or their grip on the child, to pick up a pen.

This is the mercurial moment of solitude that centuries have tried to deny me. This is the instant of irresponsibility by which the future may judge me. This is the instant that could cost me my job. This is the instant that could deny me custody of my child.

In the brave new world of the end of this century, neither loss of child nor loss of employment is held to be of much consequence in the imaginations of those who have never irreparably lost either. Every loss, every risk taken in the interest of creative growth is seen to lead to consequences retrievable by subsequent action. The single mother knows better. Like all artists who produce under adverse conditions, the single mother who takes the time to paint, to write, to sculpt, to write music knows the real cost of creation in human terms. And knows the untenability of a life in which there is no risk.

Solitude is the risk she takes. The writing is a relief from drudgery and routine. Sometimes the riches garnered from stolen time repay doubt. "Simmering" offered such a payoff of much-needed nourishment, with the promise of more.

Simmering

Though the invisible vowels
are rich as ice cream licked by a tongue
of black ink,
though my brain crackles
in little explosions,
like breakfast cereal
that my pen scoops up like a spoon, though ideas
are strung through me

like strands of paper-thin spaghetti
lifted from a casserole of red wine sauce, thoughts
like the crusty crust of brown bread spread with a creamy
pungent cheese,

I can't eat,
can't pay my rent, feed my child, heat
my apartment against February cold
with this poem, shouldn't
be wasting my time here

with this hallucination, this imaginary supermarket, this oasis
from the real world. I should not be
writing this poem,
or listening to the slow rain,

or staying home to cook something that takes as long
as bean soup, writing this poem while beans soak
with carrots, celery, leeks,
taking up hours
of leisurely simmering,
earning their richness from nothing.

Writing Between Dreams

to Ernest Boyer

ELAINE ZIMMERMAN

It is after midnight. The kids are asleep. David has not come home yet from his job in the city. I begin to write an obituary for my friend Ernie Boyer. Ernie just visited Connecticut, and I am stunned that he passed away so soon, though his illness was known.

I fall asleep, wake up, write more in my head. Worry if I can hold on to this till morning. A cloud surrounds the writing. There is something comforting about it—like a quilt, an empty field, or summer haze. Death and sleep hover near each other.

He stands in front of the crowd, comprised mostly of school principals and policy leaders. He looks frail, thin and removed. Ernie speaks slowly, builds up, and then he's flying. Words spin out of him. All on the failures of the education system and the sharp curiosity of children. He drinks educational change the way others take in soup or tea. Whatever was fragile is gone; the room is hushed and in his eyes. You can see yourself and all you have hoped for the next generation in his presence. This is a gift.

After the talk, he lingers. He signs every person's book, talks with each one, almost misses his plane. On his way to yet another city, Ernie Boyer offers hope, challenge, and intimacy. Each conversation is his last, but no one knows this. He leaves his letters and legacy calmly in each person's hand.

His wife, Kathryn, puts a blanket around him as soon as we are alone in the car. She is a midwife, knows about the beginning and end of life, wraps babies in their swaddling clothes and is wrapping Ernie as lovingly and simply.

It is Kathryn who convinced Ernie that working only on formal education was too limiting, that learning begins before birth. She was seeing babies who needed serious attention. Kay worked with pregnant teens. She understood again and again that health and learning begins well before children open the kindergarten door.

Ernie Boyer began to watch the babies with her. He became a key leader on school readiness, the poet of sorts on the importance of early learning experience. This famous codger talking about infants and child care to school superintendents shook the industry, all because he was smart enough to marry Kay and wise enough to listen. Ernie spoke on neighborhood, family, the impact of television, values. Near his dying, he released yet another book expanding the framework of quality education.

In the car, wrapped in a wool blanket, he says, "Tell me everything, everything." He pulls out a notepad. Reads the articles I hand him. Frail and gray, he is still devouring information on children's learning and strategy to help them.

He says, "You are ahead of the curve. This is the next step." We hug. He walks with Kay straight from the car and our conversation to a small helicopter waiting for him. He is too frail for airport bustle and climbs slowly up the staircase, on his way to the sky.

I wake to Benji next to me. There was a shrill cry, like a peacock in darkness. He had had a bad dream, full of witches. Was his howl a witches' howl, or was he shrieking back at them?

I hug him as the trembling subsides. Then put him back in bed. David is home now, next to me.

Benji screams again, this time from his bed. Now he has earnest questions. "How many minutes till we get up?"

"Three hours."

He says, "No, how many minutes?" And we are off multiplying three hours times sixty minutes at four in the morning. Numbers bounce from room to room. Witches have been replaced by mathematics, contemporary pillow talk.

I whisper to David, "Ernie Boyer died."

He says, "I know. There was an article in the paper."

"Why didn't you tell me?"

"I thought you would have read the paper."

"He was my friend. I was just with him."

He says, half asleep, "I guess I should have said something."

We doze. Then, a loud bang in the living room. Sounds like a window opening. I hand David the portable phone and say, "Use this if I don't come back." There is nothing downstairs. I come back up.

He laughs and says, "Next time hand me the television changer." I don't understand, and then it's clear he thought the phone was for hitting the burglar on the head. He wasn't thinking to call the police, to get us help.

I'm pondering this, hitting burglars on the head with a portable phone and how David watches too much television anyway, and I trip on marbles that the kids had in a pile on our floor. Then I can't stop laughing, how writing about death brings up the living. How every bit of day comes alive in the darkness—trying to write between dreams, the witches' howls, marital twitches, Benji demanding math—and how life is just as simple and humbling as these tiny glass balls that can throw me off balance in the dark. Ernie Boyer would have laughed.

He left us gracefully. In some drive that took hold of his heart, he said good-bye with passion and elegance, offering vision, not endings. All these slips, human foils of learning and relationship, were his fodder for learning. And if there are any classrooms in heaven, he's already pulling teachers into neighborhoods and playing with the very young.

Writing Fellini

COLLEEN J. MCELROY

Over the years I have learned that my ideas percolate in the twilight and dawn of sleep, when I am awake and not awake, when I take notes on life. That is the time when I am less concerned with rules and social decorum, with restrictions and limitations of the imagination—when I am neither here nor there.

Usually it is just a comfortable time when I can lie in bed and let myself go into or out of sleep. It's that time when, as callous as it may seem, I don't attend to my partner, or to anything else pressing me to do anything but write. More often than not, I am thinking about nothing in particular. Perhaps my best sleep sedative, the bedside television, is turned on. It's the one my father sent me twenty years ago when I was recovering from pneumonia, the black and white set with a three-hour sleep timer that resembles not so much today's programming as it does those grainy shows of yesterday, a time out of time. It's perfect for my entrance into sleep, the sound turned down until it is barely audible and I hear voices out of context, washing away the day's distraction. A jumble of words from characters to whom I have no commitment, voices that erase the linearity of conversations and allow my thoughts to wander.

That's when I begin to make associations. I take those images as they come: absurd, vengeful, comical, sad, or so utterly philosophical, they surprise me with unrealized wisdom. Some are vaguely connected to incidents I've recently experienced; some from the past; some from a draft of writing I have yet to complete. My bedside notepad becomes the receptacle. Perhaps that is why I don't have any single journal—my notes divided between the small notebook I carry in my purse, the bedside notepad, and all those infernal bits of paper torn from the edges of newspapers, magazines, the backs of sales receipts or shopping lists, anything I can find at the moment. I scribble down a line intact before it is lost in the quagmire of my imagination. I write in the margins, scrawling and scratching out the words as fast as they come to me. Punctuation is of no importance; grammar is momentarily forgotten. "Get it down! Get it down!" I say to myself. And I rush into the idea before the demands of the day's schedule return to plague me. Not all of these fragments are usable, but their appearance signals an urgency to write. Once, en route to someplace distant, I was compelled to pull to the shoulder of the highway and add to my journal several lines that had floated into my head. A highway patrolman, seeing my blinking hazard lights, stopped to offer help. He rapped on the window, and I rolled down the glass and snarled, "Go away! Don't you see I'm writing?" (When the Muse hits, she sometimes hits hard. But you'd best answer; she hates being ignored.)

Although my most productive writing period is from midday to early evening (I revise during late evenings), not all of my ruminations come in the night before sleep, or when I am otherwise distracted. I need time for contemplation in the mornings when I first awaken. This "mind wandering" time is often triggered by my dreams. I am a lucid dreamer, and can remember dreams sometimes for days. My dreams come in many forms: a series (usually heroic and guess who is the hero), prophetic (predicting something, however enigmatic), and bless Hera, sometimes they offer rough drafts for writing, though I hate it when I wake up and know I've finished, in my dreams, a novel of such import the world will shudder and redefine literature. The only seriousness I pull out of dreams of that nature is that they send me back for more revisions of my writing.

I write songs in my dreams. I prime myself before going to sleep by listening to instrumental music from a certain period, depending on the project at hand. Instrumental music plays an important role in my writing. It can provide mood without words. I don't want lyrics, unless it's opera when words have been collapsed into rhythm and movement. But opera works well to help my ear for poetry, which I define as the music of language. I listen for the melody inherent in sounds and words, the syllables that are no more than the woofs and tweets of the body's musical instrument: language. Like musicians, poets play with two-beat and three-beat measures, changing rhythm by attending to the sounds of words, the vocal music of poetry.

I have been involved in projects that required me to write lyrics, not just poems set to music, but words that were fully intended to be part of a musical score. When I worked with Ishmael Reed on the choreopoem play *The Wild Gardens of the Loup Garou*, I was asked to add a love song to the first act. Love song? Love poems are the most difficult—they tend to drool, if you're not careful—and love songs are spider webs: beautiful, entrancing, and sticky. I tackled it with mood music—lots of violins—a glass of wine and candlelight before bed. My dreams did not fail me. The next morning, I reached for the note pad and wrote the chorus:

Lost in love, wanting love.
We are weary travelers lost in love.

Pithy but effective. (Of course, traveling, my obsession, naturally plagues my dreams.) Then came the hard work: shaping, embellishing, and revising, using the machinery or craft of poetry. The dream had simply led me into the possibilities of image. I can capture them if I'm lucky. It's like trying to photograph fish when you're scuba diving: you're out of your element and the fish won't stop and pose for you. But you keep working at it until finally, you get one or two in focus and full view.

Dreams are full of trickster images. You have to know when to trust them or even how much of them you can trust. There are dreams that disguise themselves as part of your imagination, and are really traps set to ridicule you. (I'm sure the Muse has a sense of humor; why else would she go vacation and leave you stuck mid-page? Or send out your subconscious to cause havoc?) I remember a peculiar dream that left me with what I guess I could call a song, that is, if I intended to try my hand at vaudeville, complete with top hat, tailcoat, and a cane. One advantage I have in dreaming is that I'm offered full sensory images: sight, sound, smell, and sometimes, texture. So there I was, center stage with the footlights high and the smell of backstage sweat and leather drifting in the air. It was my big number. Get the picture? I belted out the lyrics, Ethel Merman style:

Here we are, sitting around thinking
But a chicken doesn't ask you when it's born
Oh no, I say, a chicken doesn't ask you
A chicken doesn't ask you
A chicken doesn't ask you when it's born

You just gotta love the Muse for that one. Still, the fear of something resembling the chicken lyrics made me concentrate very carefully on revision and reshaping for the several weeks afterwards. Fortunately, the warp and weft of my dreams usually leave me with more workable images. I have produced, in fact, poems that started in a dream that sort of drop-kicked me into subjects I hadn't yet tackled. One poem, "Shelley at Sequim Inlet," came out of a series of dreams. Although I am as taken with the topography and unpredictability of northwestern landscapes as the next poet, I've spent many years avoiding the usual northwest poets' subjects—the weather, seagulls, geese, Dungeness Spit. Then one spring, when I had been thinking about going to the ocean, to La Push on the most northern tip of Washington State, I started having a series of northwest dreams.

The first dream didn't strike me as particularly significant; after all, I had moved to the Northwest partly because the ocean was so near. The sea, the presence of water, is comforting. Walking along the beach clears my head, and gives me room to think. Perhaps the atmosphere is much like those twilight hours when I'm half asleep, or perhaps it is that I was born under the water sign of Scorpio. Whatever the reason, I feel an affinity with water. In Bellingham, I lived within sight of water, fish, gulls, and a string of island glimmering in lilac mist on the horizon pervaded my life. And for a while, after I moved to the Seattle area, I lived on Bainbridge Island in closer proximity to Dungeness Spit and Sequim—true "northwest subjects." Now I live above the Ship Canal, where I have a clear view of gulls, ravens, and hawks: their comings and goings, the infamy of their greed and constant wars in their search for food. But I had not consciously pursued birds and such in my writing until these dreams began. One night, a line emerged: Gull, thou never were—no doubt taken from my subconscious misquote of a line from Shelley—leaving me with partial images but offering the heart of the poem, which became:

Shelley at Sequim Inlet

Gull you never were a bird to float
on balmy breeze   high on a manure pile
you were king   your feet planted firm
on a farmer's boots   the smell suits

your dirty white coat   bird that is gull
you are no romantic speck hovering
in search of scraps   warm rot or rust
dirty bird you bully this northwest coast
and any other that offers loot   heavy-winged
you circle spews of foam as it some great
gossip nailed you to the spot   hawking
for gang wars   keeping the neighborhood
awake just to break your brother's back
        What gall you have gull
        What open lust and luck
        What single eye and hip-broke walk
no petal soft bearing whips you toward garbage
fighting's your only relief from the constant
call for food   and heaven is the air
alive with the smell of dead things
come on gull   voodoo caller of the sea   riffraff
faker   We know you   despite your shrill delight
your cracked-beak squawks say you're grey with fear

The beauty of notetaking when I first awaken is that I've let down my guards, all those governances of logic and association. For that poem, I didn't have to consider all the other poems about gulls and Sequim and northwest weather. The world was fresh and new, and everything was possible. This is the part and parcel of creativity.

Of course, I don't always fall asleep to create, but what happens in the twilight time of half-sleep never ceases to surprise me. It releases me, like a parachutist on free-fall, into a space where I can see more clearly. If I ever have any doubts about the effectiveness of creating in "twilight sleep" (which is the birthing process my mother opted for when I was delivered—but I don't really want to think about those ramifications), I need only recall the poem that truly came from sleeping with one eye open.

For years, I tried to write what I call a "genesis" poem. I envied Nikki Giovanni's Nikki Rosa, Carolyn Kizer's "Pro Femina," and Ishmael Reed's "I am a cowboy on the boat of Ra." I hadn't taken any easy routes. For nearly five years, I had tried to write a poem that used the Egyptian deities of the underworld: Dis and Dat. Problem was, I am a black poet, and everyone thought I was using dialect. Then in 1975, I went to a Fellini film festival. Eight and a half hours of Fellini. Clever, right? You brought your lunch; you slept; you stayed there for eight and a half hours. It was sort of "Fellini on the rocks." I stayed awake for *La Dolce Vita* and *La Strada*, but by the third film, no amount of coffee could sustain me. I don't remember much until I awoke in the middle of *Satyricon*. On the screen, Rome was burning and two men, escaping the smoldering city, had stumbled upon a slave girl, lost in the melee. The three of them struggled with speech—the men patient in their Italian, and the girl lyrical with the clicks and glides of what was meant to be some African dialect. But speech didn't matter as they took comfort from one another in those few minutes before the fire reached out for them, and they all fled, each to their own sense of survival. The whole encounter was probably no more than a ten-minute section of the film, but I had awakened to it, and the poem that had been brewing in my head began to take shape. I left the theater with that image in my head. On the way out, church bells began to toll the hour, the bell tower bathed in a ghostly spotlight against a midnight sky.

I think I began writing in the car. I know that by the time I reached home, the poem was struggling to get out. I wrote the draft in long hand, my thoughts racing with images while my body slumped into fatigue. I couldn't write fast enough: one page, two, and finally, three. Some words were no more than loops and squiggles, a kind of subconscious shorthand that was reducing itself to heartlines as my energy dissipated. When I reached the end, I simply dropped the pencil and fell asleep almost before my head hit the pillow. But this poem had begun, pulled from the detritus of prewriting and triggered by Fellini's fleeting image of a slave girl with her language of birds, wind, and water, with her finely honed sense of survival. "Song of the Woman Who Knew Too Much" began with:

> The land is cold and its men gather earth for no reason. Their eyes fail to give them pictures of the inner world. They are angered by small changes in clouds.
>
> I am Diamonane, daughter of seven voices, my language as old as soft hands across a man's bared chest. Bones mean nothing. It is the flesh, hot and

sweet, it is there that you flower and die. You have seen me walking slowly at the edge of foreign seas, you have seen me choking on diesel fumes of cities, eating muskmelons under the striped tents of incense-filled bazaars, quarreling with the fish-hawkers in the French Quarter, or standing, head bowed, at edge of a clearing among Dutch settlers in those first New England snows. But always, always, my cape, full and black, billows and flows even on windless nights.

I had planned to turn the poem into stanzas the next day, but what I'd written took on its own form, its own sense of existence. As I recall, my revisions were minor: strengthening repetition to increase rhythm, reducing adjectives, discarding the last line, strengthening the vocal play of sound echoes. It was my first prose poem, those three pages of images pulled from the brink of sleep. Or was it sleep? After all, I had been working on that poem for over four years. I had spent those years working various drafts, dreaming the poem, if you will, in bits and pieces. And then it emerged—perhaps from the "triggering town" that Richard Hugo describes in a book by the same name. It had percolated, matured, wandered down the corridors of my imagination before being brought to fruition in that moment when all things were possible, that "twilight sleep": where artists have incubated a magical blend of experience and imagination.

But most of us have become too Western. We have forgotten how to trust the dream, embrace its tangents, and at the same time, distrust its arrogance, and use our inner ears for distinction, to know that, day or night, the dream is how we imagine the world, how we create.

Walking into Poetry

PATRICIA CLARK

Even on my busiest days, I find time to take a walk. I blame it on my dog: "She really needs to get out. I can see the difference when we do—she's so much happier." Sometimes I invite the man I live with to come along, but it's a routine of ours: I invite, he declines, and we both end up relieved. Yes, it's true that I want to be alone for an hour. But finally none of these explanations is exactly right. I really go walking in search of a block of blank time. It is vital to my mental health, to my mental fitness. And the walking time, silent time, is the seedbed for poetry and writing of all kinds.

In Grand Rapids, it's June, and the green and golden light has been calling to me since 6:00 A.M. I've been at my desk long enough to have worked my way through discouragement and into something interesting. Now I know where I am in a poem I'm writing and what the next step might be. Looking up, I notice that my dog, Rosie, has been staring at me, perhaps for as long as an hour. I've put her off, but now the time's perfect. I gather the leash and the training collar, and we're ready to go. Heading out the back door, leaving it unlocked, out through the gate and to the sidewalk of Johnston Street, we'll head east to Philadelphia Street, turn left and walk half a block to Griggs, then one more block till we reach the big oaks of Mulick Park.

Two houses down from mine is the house where the Skavlems live— a large, Catholic family with nine children now grown up and gone. Michelline and Tom are friendly, but they keep their distance; beyond expressing concern about my unmowed lawn when I'm out of town, they don't ask for details about my life. Tom shares lawn-care advice with me and snow-blows my front walk on wintry days. One day I noticed the blue and white statue in their backyard. It immediately carried me back to my childhood street in Tacoma and to the Christoffersons' house, which boasted an identical statue of the Virgin Mary. I thought they were the holiest people I knew. I remember going there after school, or on a Saturday perhaps during Holy Week, to kneel and pray the rosary. Other family members went with me, I think. Was this during my introspective phase when I considered being a nun? I had been told in Catholic school the powerful, transformative stories of those who "received a calling"—but my classmates and I were also a little cynical and could tell a recruiting speech when we heard it. Nuns were "brides" of Jesus. But doubts remained, as I recall, about how much fun such wives might have. Those Catholic school years come back, suddenly, with a rush of fearful recognition.

Once I'm out the door, down the street, my bare legs feeling the breeze and the dog nipping my heel to herd me along, the sensory delights of early summer bring me inevitably to those other streets. Memories bring with them a thousand scents, sounds, and images for poems. I'd forgotten the Christoffersons, their statue, my failed vocation, all that early life of mine that I simply filed away for years under the false heading "the large happy family." Much remains to be confronted. Why do I have a shiver of fear remembering the nuns? What were my first-grade nightmares all about? Why didn't my parents take action about my teacher that year (a nun who had a "nervous breakdown" after the school year ended)? Why was I sick in church so many mornings, often enough that I was a regular outside on the steps, with head between my knees?

We go left on Philadelphia, then right on Griggs, as Rosie strains the leash for the shade of Mulick Park. In cities, of course, one is drawn to green places, to the oasis in a desert of asphalt and cars, and yet I wonder sometimes if another need doesn't bring me to the park—the desire to hear and see the children at play.

❧

Perhaps now it's early winter, late December (still a time in Michigan when parks are gathering places for people), and the inches of new powdery snow glint gold, blue, and pink in the waning sunlight. If walking in summer is pleasant, winter seems even better sometimes: I kick along in the stuff, scattering diamonds. The dog wants to turn the corner before I do, the corner of Rosewood and Griggs. Left we go, then, toward where the sounds of children playing carry to us from the slope a block away. The bright-coated children are sliding, calling out, screaming, lobbing snowballs at each other, while their parents are parked streetside, engines running in minivans, waiting and steaming the windows up. I'm slow to make the connection, or perhaps it takes some time to admit it. But one day it hits me—how I deeply desire to have a baby, how there is something in the park that I can't bear to see some days. I know I must write about this particular ache of mine. Would it occur to me so easily without this walk, without the landscape right in front of me? I credit these walks, these well-worn paths and places for my growing understanding. Walking helps me face my obsessions, helps locate pangs and longings that I will write about, and it's something that comes out of the silence of walking. We see what is right in front of us, finally. When the children run to us—and some of them always do—they ask the dog's name; she rivets their attention, not the woman holding the leash. My eyes linger, memorizing their eyelashes and the red bows of their mouths.

One day the sight of a tuft of grass sprouting, like a clown's hairdo, out of the sidewalk reminds me of a long-ago fishing trip when we reeled in, after hours it seemed, a miraculous catch: not a salmon or a trout, not a steelhead, but a spiky purple sea urchin caught in the saltwater off Neah Bay. I still remember the mixture of dread and awe with which we confronted our catch. Shadows of male shapes in a small boat: my father, grandfather, younger brother. Something about walking brings back people from other times in my life. One day a voice comes back—the laugh of Nelson Bentley, a teacher of mine in a beginning class. I walked in Seattle for years and wrote poems that Nelson encouraged. He's gone, but I have his presence, guardian angel-like, along with me.

If the silence has filled me up, sometimes I want words, so I recite poems I know by heart (Wallace Stevens's "Sunday Morning" or "A Postcard from the Volcano" or some Emily Dickinson, Robert Frost, Robert Hayden, Elizabeth Bishop) or a few lines of my own I'm working on. The poet Mary Oliver writes about walking and writing, contrasting walks with a writer's use of naps: "For myself, walking works in a similar way. I walk slowly and not to get anywhere in particular, but because the motion somehow helps the poem to begin. I end up, usually, standing still, writing something down in the small notebook I always have with me." [1] Unlike Oliver, I walk without a notebook. I prefer leaving my hands free. There's always the leash anyway, which Rosie's now pulling for home.

One reason I have continued to enjoy my walks is Rosie's presence and the memory of many experiences we have had together on various "regular" walks of ours. One was in Knoxville, Tennessee, when we used to walk near Middlebrook Pike. There was always mood-blue chicory waving along the roadside, and I would release Rosie from her leash for a bit to race through the tall grasses, her head popping up from time to time as though she were coming up through waves. The rhythms of our walk propelled me into an ecstatic experience that I tried to capture in a poem. Here's the last half of it, in which I try to put my finger on what has occurred to cause such a flight:

That's when it happens
to me—in sunlight, or in rain, heading
down a road somewhere, heedlessly,
breathing in whatever flowers in early spring—
redbuds, dogwoods, the anomalous

crab-apples. I don't leave my body
behind, and don't desire to. Instead,
it's as though every pore opens to drink in
sensation, the body like a sponge,
and it's almost painful—one could get
singed or blinded by the sudden light.
It doesn't last, of course. I know someday
I'm going to die. Somehow that doesn't

matter much when I'm on the move,
and the fields wave their grasses freshened
by rain. To live deliberately and lightly,
denying nothing, is what I'd like, the way
horses feeding in the pasture across the pike
step carefully in their huge, slow bodies.

Flies harass them, landing on their ruddy
flanks. Again, again, they flick them off.

I think that movements of bodies, movements in walking, can release
something in us—if we can only get away from the noise and if only
we can stay in the "now" of our experiences. The result is synergy in
such remarkable times; we may arrive at an unanticipated place. And it's
worth the trip. I remember not to rush. I remember to stay in the moment of this moment of life.

～

Where is it I go when I walk? I go out in a regular path and return.
Now I walk not just around Mulick Park but all the way to Breton Road,
through a neighborhood where I hope to live some day. I've even picked
out a house for us there—a Tudor house made of stone, a big two-story
place where we'll have some elbowroom. On my walks, I step away for a
short time from my life and have a chance to see it from the curb. I walk
out in stress and hurry to find freedom; the trick is then to return and
make the freedom possible. I'm finding my way—I don't have a role
model for this life of not being a mother, not being a caretaker for a
houseful of people. But I am figuring it out, step by step, as I move
through the streets of my neighborhood, as I clear my head in a busy
day of teaching, living, writing. I walk to locate myself better in all these
things. And sometimes it seems to be working.

I'm home in my study now. I've been reading *Writing Toward Home,*
Georgia Heard's book about engaging the writing process. She describes
a concept she learned about in Spain called *querencia*—an instinct that
animals have and that humans possess as well. Heard writes: "In Spanish, *querencia* describes a place where one feels safe, a place from which
one's strength of character is drawn, a place where one feels at home. It
comes from the verb *querer,* which means to desire, to want."[2] Heard
believes that writers need to describe this place for themselves as clearly
as possible and to find it if they can.

Walking has brought me back here, through afternoon shadows and
smells of bread—from the Butternut Baking Company down on Edna
Street. I'm returning to the poem I was working on, though shortly I
must turn my attention to student papers and student poems. Some days
I find the poem I've begun is not as good as I thought it was in the morn-

ing before our walk, but other times I am pleased at what I have wrestled out of silence. I feel a kind of internal humming, the whole grand machinery of the body and mind working as one, that says, "Set to work, begin again in earnest. Indeed, you can balance all of this. It will balance." I begin again, remembering Heard's chapter and her discussion of *querencia*, and I think *But that is the place I get to by walking.*

Notes

1. Mary Oliver, *A Poetry Handbook* (San Diego: Harcourt, Brace, 1994), 119.
2. Georgia Heard, *Writing Toward Home: Tales and Lessons to Find Your Way* (Portsmouth, NH: Heinemann, 1995), 4.

The Prime Necessity

DENISE LEVERTOV

The most important factor (along with native ability, of course) in any poet's survival and development is that he or she recognize the necessity of apparently doing nothing and of giving each potential poem time to incubate. Daydreaming is not a luxury to the poet. Guile and a certain degree of ruthlessness (preferably disguised) may be called for in order to find time for it. The poet may look, and at times even feel, as if he or she is doing nothing in particular, is self-indulgently reading novels or window-shopping or wandering about the streets or fields—but if these or any other seemingly irrelevant occupations act as an incubator for poetry, the poet is in fact working, and must cast out guilt and scorn criticism of his or her behavior.

Sometimes it is guilt, sometimes ambition and impatience or the ingrained Protestant work-ethic which makes a writer who registers an "idea," a "feeling," promptly set to work to "find words for it." Whatever the cause of that brisk, painstaking, or frustrating search, it is a mistaken enterprise. Innumerable possible poems have been distorted into, at best, dull approximations of what they might have been by such hasty and laborious action. A poem has to come to its full term just like a baby, and early induction of labor may prove fatal to it. When it is ready to emerge from darkness, its words do not have to be sought, for they *are* it.

Once it is born, the poet (its parent) will have it in her or his care— and if it is not one of those short poems that comes into the world as a prodigy, with teeth, hair, and the immediate ability to walk and talk (or rather, to fly and sing) the poet will have to attend to its growth and education, in other words to revise. But even in that process, if the words that must be added or substituted don't come of themselves, summoned by some further creative daydreaming, not by strenuous pursuit, they will never properly graft themselves to the poem. When competing synonyms present themselves, only the poet's ear (silver or gold, and never tin) must be the deciding judge.

All of this is what literary criticism, with its agendas and theories, does not recognize. And the "teaching" of poetry, too, unfortunately often fails to convey that poems are living things, not inert. Thus too many would-be poets expend their energies in an effort which results in banalities, who should be letting the unknown poem work within them, at its own mysterious pace.

III

Sounds of
    Hazard
    and
    Survival

Writing the Impossible

HILDA RAZ

I'm a writer—of poems, essays, reviews—a list maker, a doodler. And I'm a teacher, as well as the editor of the literary quarterly *Prairie Schooner*. All the dilemmas endemic to women writers are mine. But once, not long ago, I was not a maker of particular texts or a professor or the editor of a venerable magazine but only another woman with breast cancer. Maybe you already know what I learned: a million women, some of whom write and edit, have had breast cancer too, and many have used their writing as a strategy for survival.

How I learned to survive cancer as a writer/editor: each day in the course of my work, I'd tell a *Prairie Schooner* contributor the reason her work had been caught in the paper jam at the magazine. Shameless, I figured pity might help her forgive an unforgivable delay. But each writer had a story to tell in exchange. She or her (mother, sister, daughter, friend) had also had breast cancer. Pretty soon, within the month, my telephone began to connect me to absolute strangers, writers whose work I knew. Stories, advice, jokes, book lists, messages of cheer and despair were their unsolicited gifts. Before the year was over, I had the start of a collection of manuscripts by these writers and their friends about their experience with breast cancer. And I started to write one. My new book of poems, *Divine Honors*, was published recently in the Wesleyan Poetry Series. The book of essays I collected and edited, *Writing in the Margins: Women Writers on Breast Cancer*, will be published soon by Persea Books.

Meantime, I was ensconced at home with my assistant and a collaborator, editing a special issue of *Prairie Schooner* in my bedroom—one editor on the bed, coeditor and assistant on the floor or at the kitchen table. This group was reassuring. The work would go on. Of course I was scared. But my terror was tolerable during the day, working in company.

Back in the office the crush of messages continued. And the news. Several contributors to *Prairie Schooner* or their friends were diagnosed with breast cancer. Now I was the experienced patient, so I began to telephone these writers as others had called me.

What news did I have to pass on? I'd ask, "Remember our preadolescent bodies, our flat chests over gorgeous rib cages? Remember pulling on itchy sweaters over an undershirt? Remember T-shirts and our delicious collar bones? How strong we were, how confident!" As if mastectomy could connect us to those bodies. But this is the way I was feeling:

Terror

Like air you seep into my body cavities
and take up residence, open charge accounts,
root, stalk, and flower a perfume of rush
and drum, violet as sunset, a bruise
over stitches. I walk, you walk.
Then I run—if I'm lucky.
Unlucky I lie in the bed or worse,
too weak to rub the ice itch. God!

Want nothing, says her voice, so I do.
Then you go away. You're through.

For now, the activity, the voices, advice, the sound bites on the telephone, or the pixels of e-mail messages kept me feeling pretty safe. I realized the magnitude of terror only in silence.

For years, silence had been necessary for work: we'd learned our lesson from Virginia Woolf when she said a woman writer needs a room of her own. A quiet place for making texts. A room so small perhaps it's only a pad of paper in the hip pocket of her jeans. This kind of privacy and silence were dearly earned, a site of making. Now, sick, I learned silence was the place where terror lived. What to do?

I moved my computer into the living room and never turned it off. In the middle of a conversation, I learned to hobble away from the table to sit down and clack onto the always-receptive keys whatever came next in the piece at hand. For four years I worked this way. People who came to visit grew restive. So I learned to invite people in groups, to talk to each other. Soon they didn't mind when I phased out, or disappeared on line. And then they didn't notice. Now, the holiday turkey in the oven, the family of friends at the sauces, here I am in *this* text.

All day I have been searching for a good way in. At last, at 12:42 A.M. precisely, after dinner and talk, browsing through an issue of Robert Coles's magazine *Doubletake,* I fall upon, on page 114, a passage by Francine Prose: "I can't imagine what miracle I expected . . . so that these isolated words—pianos, hands, light, water, women, furniture, hair—would organize themselves into stories and reveal their complex meanings." She is talking about stories by Felisberto Hernández published in Spanish, a language she can't read. I am talking about a compulsion to make of her list—any list—this essay, whatever the surrounding circumstances. This compulsion belongs to the writer. It won't be argued with. Any list is a skeleton. I can no more help starting to build than I can not flinch from fire. Every verb choice—or whether to make it negative or positive—presents the chance for the text, makes me a present of a text. And nouns! No matter that another's list of nouns—Rilke's house, bridge, fountain, gate, for example—has been used before. The task becomes mine, like breathing or turning on the light, braiding my unruly hair or drinking a glass of water, pushing from my body the head of my child.

At dinner a busy friend, now retired, told about her comb collection. What? I said. Yes, she said, if you watch the ground as you travel from your office to the bus, from your house to the store, from the park to the lake, you'll find combs. Never, I said, I never did. Did you look for combs, she asked. Well, no. Next day I looked for combs. The first day I found six. No use to tell me people don't much use combs any more. The comb here, rhymes with poem, is a list title. The writer collects them. It's the editor who culls them.

I meant to make of this essay another kind of list: the things that *keep* us from writing. How do I, or you, or the Uruguayan Hernández, who died in 1964—or Francine Prose, for that matter—resist being diverted from the job of making order from chaos in a meld of languages and experiences we don't understand? Why did Prose fix on the Spanish stories of Felisberto Hernández? What shuts me up?

I think in the brain of the writer and in her hands lives the electrical compulsion to decipher. Never mind that she barely understands Spanish. The writer also needs to cipher, to encode, to make mysteries. Translations come later.

So here's a list of what keeps me from writing: fear, cancer, his suicide, their departure. I'd rather be swimming in the ocean, waving not drowning, than writing when I'm afraid, sick, or grieving. But what else can you do?

Maybe, if you play the piano, you won't need to transform lists into lines. Maybe you can sit for an hour and play a language the tongue never enters.

❧

A variation on the text: once, not long ago, I was not a writer of particular texts or an editor of a particular magazine but only another woman with breast cancer. I was afraid to be alone. Desperate, I moved my computer into the living room. Maybe I could write—too weak to hold a pen—while other people watched TV or ate dinner. Everything I'd held about conditions for work broke. A room of our own, maybe only a tiny room with furniture the size of a pad of paper in a hip pocket? I had a room. Cancer turned me out. Slammed the door. Alone = terror: numero uno on the list of silencers.

Ever since George Sand's disgusted lover left her for writing in her nightshirt in the middle of the night, we've known consequences come with the calling. To sit in a chair in front of a computer for five hours, especially if the room is occupied by other people, isn't familiar behavior. Yet if we are writers, we are scanning the room for material. Most of the time we have the good sense to write down and amplify our notes when we're alone.

Now I had to write during the holidays when the family was home— kids, friends, constant phone ringing, turkey in the oven, bread rising, fights brewing and settling. Recovering from cancer, I moved from a room where I'd worked in blessed solitude while the kids were growing up, nothing save blood or intruder to interrupt me—moved out because I was afraid to be alone. The interruptions that had disturbed me for decades now proved evidence of continuing life: boiling water, murmurs. And so, between conversations with my sons, stuffing and basting the turkey, talking on the telephone, I'd go to my chair, still talking or listening, to write a few lines, a stanza. The form of the poems seemed made from the complicated materials around us, lists, repeated directions, endearments, a notion of service behind everything here: house, kids, yeast, braids of dough Aaron shaped for the cardamom bread, my fingers on the keys, the pillow at my back, the timer bell John clicks off.

Without much time left, or even a place to write, we must write in the time and place we have. Look down. Combs everywhere.

Or better still, a familiar list: piano, hands, light, water, women, furniture, hair. Every word in its place in this text.

To write is necessary. The rest varies.

The Elephant in My Living Room

Depression and the Writing Life

LYNNA WILLIAMS

I'm smiling a little as I write that title, because it will be light out in three hours, and by then, surely I will have thought better of this, made myself understand why I can't write this particular essay, at least not this way. For now, though, before prudence and circumspection and my personal chart-topper—good, old-fashioned fear—overtake me, I can write myself into morning; I can write the truth. I am forty-five, and depending on how these things are calculated, I have been depressed, sometimes clinically, more often not, for about forty of those years. I have been a writer since I was eighteen: a reporter, and then a political speechwriter, and now a fiction writer. I have written every kind of newspaper story, from political campaigns, to serial poodle murders, to Mikhail Baryshnikov shopping for Tony Lama cowboy boots. I've written speeches about children and poverty, and speeches about sewage flowing into the Mississippi River. Now I write fiction, and I've published well enough that I have a teaching job and the expectation of a second book to go with the first. What I have never written, not once, is this particular truth: I have this illness. Season to season, year to year, it gets better, or it gets worse, but it does not go away. So I live every day with the elephant in my living room, the immovable object, the thousand-pound secret I decorate with a fringed lampshade and try to pass off as a lamp. An ugly lamp, inherited, passed among the women in my family like a gag gift at a shower—nothing I would have bought for myself, but something that I can't just give away.

Were I braver, less ashamed, more given to either joy or irony, I might say *screw it* and "own" my illness: tell the world and come home to put the lampshade on my own head. Ours is a culture of revelation, after all, and we could dance then, the elephant and I; we could out ourselves on *Oprah*, on a sweeps-week show called "Writers and Sadness: Hey, There's a Reason Dogs Die in My Stories." But that's not going to happen. I do not celebrate my depression; that isn't in me. I can't accept it; shame is too much a part of the illness, too central to who I am. So *Oprah*'s out, but neither am I committed anymore to "fixing" my depression, finding a cure, putting myself out of my misery. The list of what I've tried, whom I've seen, what I've taken, is a long one, and itself, fairly depressing. It's like the tag line to a bad joke: things go better with Prozac, but not for me. Things go better with insight, but not for me. After a while the fact that, despite enormous effort, I can't be, or haven't been, cured has become part of the sadness. It's a tricky equation, determining, with any exactness, what is pathology and what is pride. All I know is that I don't need another failure.

I am left, then, to tend the elephant, every day. I walk around it, when I can. I accommodate, I adjust, I improvise. Some days the depression makes basic things hard; other days it makes them impossible: sleeping, eating, talking, loving, moving from here to there. But I do those things, with varying degrees of success, every day. I do them not because they support life—I am not that sentimental about capital-L Life—but because they support my writing. And writing saves me, and that's not sentiment, either. Writing saves me because—listen to me—it is not my illness. Writing is not therapy; it is the sole thing in my life that the elephant, no matter the pressure exerted, cannot have. Not that it doesn't try. Writing is, after all, about possibility, and possibility is the opposite of depression. Honoring the possibilities requires taking risks, and taking risks requires belief in oneself; given that, it is amazing to me, not that I have to write but that I can. After all, there are plenty of other things I've accepted not doing, things I can't make room for in the house where the elephant lives. There are no children here, except in the photographs on the refrigerator.

What makes writing different? Perhaps it's only different because I've decided to grant it an exemption, decided to hold it apart from the sickness. Perhaps it could just as easily have been fabric art, or even brain surgery. But I don't think so. Writing, to me, means serving the story. In the act of creation, it's the story that matters, and that means I have to get out of the way. It is, absolutely, the hardest thing I will ever have to do. I have a friend who wants to tell jokes but can't, and every time she gets to the punch line, she says, "This is the funny part." This is the funny part: getting out of our own way is the hardest thing any writer does. When I write, I am—wait for it—just like everybody else.

Years ago I wrote a newspaper story about a rainmaker who showed up in a West Texas drought; apparently he'd never seen the Burt Lancaster movie, because he arrived in Abilene with the exact same cloud machine, just as shiny as Bert's, just as fake. He said making rain was simple: mix so many clouds with so much secret formula, and the next thing you know, there's an umbrella sale at Woolworth's. I can close my eyes and see that machine: the silver knobs, the red lightning bolt painted on the side. I think that if you fed that machine pellets of shame and fear, the clouds would rain sadness. The truth is I am afraid of fear; I worship control and normalcy and order, and never so much as when I am incapable of sustaining them. But, to write fiction, I have learned to be afraid, to honor chaos as a beginning, to view both fear and disorder as a necessary part of generation, of finding the story. Now I know the fear for what it is: not deadly, not this time, but a necessary part of staying with the work until it's done. Another friend says that if you're not afraid when you're writing fiction, you're not paying attention. I pay attention when I write—not to my own heartbeat, not to the rhythms of my own unhappiness, but to the interior and the event of the story, to its needs, its obsessions. I'm the writer, yes; I construct the story, yes; but I work for the moment when magic and analysis combine, and the story is more than I imagined. In those rare and longed-for moments of grace, there are only possibilities, and sadness is a universe away.

It comes back, though. When I'm not writing fiction, I live in the world you live in, the world where I cover the elephant up, make it pass for something else, for anything but what it is. So I'll finish this little piece—depressives are dogged, above all—but then I'll put it away, and no, I won't acknowledge the metaphor. Then I'll write another essay, funny maybe, about surviving as a Southern writer, when what you really are is a New Southern writer. New Southern writers are rootless, unable to tell one tree from another, possessors of no childhood memories, writers for whom a sense of place comes down to remembering where their car is parked at the mall. New Southern writers are, in fact, depressed, but I won't say that. When I'm done with it, the essay won't be a lie; it will just be firmly, resolutely, beside the point. It will be a piece about an elephant, in which the elephant is never named. It will be, in fact, Exhibit A in the case for my writing fiction. With fiction I have nothing to deny, and everything to declare, so a character in a story of mine will never have to say, "An elephant? What do you mean, an elephant? That's a lamp. Don't you see the lampshade? Jesus, I hope you never go to the zoo."

Note

Since she wrote this essay, Lynna Williams's depression has abated, with the help of "one more try" at seeking medical care.

Selective Listening and Resistance

A Writer's Capacity to Thrive

MARY C. LEWIS

Writing demands selective listening. The world beyond my desk has a daily habit of distraction—drattedly necessary electro-connection devices called telephone, answering machine, voice mail, *ad nauseam*. Then there are printed messages from family members, friends, bill collectors, and assorted other strangers who have obtained my address somehow. A writer has to select what to listen to, decide what can be ignored and what, if anything, must be dismissed because if it isn't, the message's implied or overt meaning could erode the possibility of her experiencing any benefits from writing.

I've gotten good at tuning out. It's amazing what a predetermined period of solitude, complete with the phone shut off, can bring to my writing. Tuning in to what I want or need to hear has been an unexpected byproduct of tuning out. Humorist Nicole Hollander calls this "a positive hearing problem." I don't entirely agree. When it comes to distractions from my writing, I hear what I want to hear, and I see this as an advantage, not a problem. An example of what I mean arrived in the mail recently, a greeting card from my mother with two statements: "Please don't work so hard" and "Try to find some joy in your life." I threw her first statement into the closet of my mind, where I keep presently unworthy yet potentially useful items, knowing I might extract her words someday and put a version of them in the mouth of a character. I mounted her second message on the bulletin board of my mind and displayed it like a certificate of merit. *I find great joy when I write*, I tell detractors.

A fifth-grader taught me the value of selective listening. In 1986, I began a stint teaching writing at an elementary school in Chicago. The premiere session began with my explaining a journal: its development as a literary form, making a journal personal, what might go in a journal, the advantages of keeping one. Blah, blah, blah. The sound of my voice drowned out my awareness of fifteen students, ages nine to thirteen, whose squirms and wandering eyes I discounted as neophytes' reactions. Finally, I noticed the hand of a fifth-grade girl waving at me.

I interrupted myself and allowed her to speak. "Miss Lewis," she asked, "when do we get to write?" The rest of the students chimed in, pencils poised in their hands, notebooks open. They were ready to write; they'd heard all they needed and were eager to do what they came to accomplish. That day I, supposedly the expert, learned an important lesson. Those young people showed me that when a writer tunes out damaging or distracting messages and tunes in constructive or encouraging words, including those from within, boundless growth occurs. Ideas sprout, mental pictures unfold, a writer can hear herself think.

When I am writing, I need intense focus to listen selectively. An internal meeting is underway, and those in attendance—my composite parts—confer while I stare at nothing in particular and await their decision. Why would a character say such-and-such? Might the character's words be misunderstood by another character, and if so, why? Within me and within the evolving world of a scene within a novel are the answers. I find them with concentration.

For fifteen years, as a full-time freelance writer and editor, I slaved an average of seventy-five hours per week on behalf of my clients. A life-threatening illness that began in earnest in 1993 and that will in all likelihood remain with me compelled me to pursue my present course as though my life depended on it. Since then, I bust my butt on behalf of my own writing—self-generated, self-rewarding historical fiction. I work so many hours at a scene or sentence that the afternoon passes into sundown and then night without much notice from me. And still I concentrate, every piece of me congregated around sensing and expressing.

In return, the pieces of me—images, voices, memories, and dreams—consult with each other and merge with my concentration, inching along finely graduated steps. An image gathers itself, or a gesture, sound, or texture, dancing among the grouped pieces, bits forming into shaped words. I strain from the weight of holding back distractions and the effort of paying minute attention, playing the role of recorder of this evolution and practicing my craft of composition.

Occasionally, an intruder slips into the internal meeting, uninvited and lobbying. I funnel my will through the piece of me called Focus. I am rude toward the sneaky intruder; at forty-something, I figure it's about time and give myself permission. If it takes the passage of afternoon into night, I will not waver. The meeting continues. When some words are on the table, I string them with loving care into phrases, sentences, paragraphs, chapters. A scene or character's dialogue emerges; with it comes an exhilaration I get from doing nothing else.

This cycle of energy feeds resistance, the other critical element for me to thrive as a writer. Often I forgo a "normal" routine. My clock runs differently; conversations and outings with friends and family are unpredictable and infrequent; and while I enjoy a couple of television series, I'm an unfaithful viewer.

More important, wearing the insignia of *Writer* requires me to repel doubt and fear. Whenever inner pangs nag me, questioning my qualifications—whether I have enough credentials to apply for grants, residencies, and fellowships; whether, indeed, I have the nerve to write about an era for which I have no academic background—I realize counteraction is necessary. It took me several years to develop sufficient courage to subdue the uncertainty. Much of that time, I heeded society's definitions of "success" and allowed those conditions to interfere with my capacity to thrive. I worried about the nerve-wracking experience of thrusting myself out onto an unprotected limb and exposing myself. How would I survive the harsh blows from bill collectors, grantors' rebuffs, editors' rejection slips? At some point, my doubts and fears became less important than the need to write. The internal gang kept meeting without my approval, and eventually they pushed me to collaborate. To my surprise and delight, I have yet to fall off the delicate branch on which I live.

A hint of resistance occurred one day in 1996 when, while writing a scene for a novel, I came upon a character's words. Auntie Netta, the guardian of her often combative and demanding niece Sanchelle, needed to reassure Sanchelle, who'd gone to New York City in search of fortune and fame and was having trouble obtaining them.

Auntie Netta wrote Sanchelle a concise note of advice: "Dream big, so big you feel like you are going to bust if you do not take care of it. Do your dream." Sometimes it is possible to generate the means to defend oneself as a writer.

The writing choices I make involve resistance, too. I have to suppress the urge to pick the easy way out of a scene or a character's dilemma. This became clear to me once I began writing the way I really wanted to write. Instead of taking on clients' assignments or submitting proposals for work, I began using ideas that sprouted from within me. Most often my ideas feature women who drive the plot, act as protagonists, and reveal or hide their motives while doing so. My experience with writing women's fiction has been immensely rewarding, but sometimes I've gotten entangled—caught in a web of stereotypes whose threads weren't always apparent.

The final chapters of a novel I wrote provide an example. When I developed a "map" for the book about Sanchelle, I constructed an ending that seemed appropriate. After several attempts and failures, Sanchelle envisions a way to make a life for herself in New York: she wants to start a women's apparel shop, with her best friend Danielle as clothing designer and herself as milliner. I thought Sanchelle would get there by borrowing the money from a man she would meet and come to love. I went merrily along writing the book until I reached the final chapters. Suddenly I became blocked (and panicked, since I was almost done).

I awakened one morning, troubled and frustrated, the blank screen of my computer monitor staring at me like an accuser. A thought rang in my mind: stop the presses!

In whose universe was it required that my precious character Sanchelle obtain a crucial resource for her success from a man? Several hours of pacing and germinating ideas led me to another ending. Sanchelle and Danielle got the money they needed from Josephine Maximillian, an elder with whom they had lived, whose financial legacy turned out to be as valuable as her emotional ties to them. I'd disengaged myself from a worthless, damaging trap. I'd dreamed big and done my dream, the way my character Auntie Netta urged me, as a writer, to do.

With that in mind, I became curious about the nature of thriving and consulted a well-worn source, the fourth edition of *Roget's International Thesaurus*. The synonyms for *thrive* included "increase, mature, sprout, germinate, be full of ginger, blossom, fatten." A few of the items surprised me. I'd never considered "thriving" as synonymous with "maturing" or "being full of ginger." To thrive as a writer, I realized, meant it was OK to mull an idea—allow my internal group to meet for as long as was needed for the words to evolve. It was equally fine to use spicy language and sassy, mature women as lead characters. In fact, this was being demanded of me. The scrawny limb on which my life dangled was fat enough to hold me. I could live with my choice.

My writing requires selective listening and resistance. Without those elements, I'd probably still be curled fetally around assignments from clients, safe and stagnant. Instead, I'm glad I can lend the women I write about an open ear and fierce focus, and earn my greatest joy.

The Glass Cage

ALEIDA RODRÍGUEZ

For many years, when my writing was solicited for anthologies or special issues of magazines, I always sent out a wide variety of work, but after the initial thrill of publication had worn off, I started to notice that, invariably, the pieces that addressed my exile, my mother, and my childhood in Cuba were the ones selected and reprinted again and again, making it seem as though that's all I have to say—a three-note piano. Since this happens continually (yes, it *still* happens), it feels as though I'm being told there's something *aberrant* (and unseemly) about my stepping out of the ghetto of ideas assigned to me, and a hushed embarrassment seems to accompany the return of my poems about psychological and spiritual states, the delights of visual art, or even my relationship with my backyard. My creative territory had been predetermined for me, silently, invisibly, and I began to experience such limitations as a glass cage. It also became apparent to me that this glass cage, though confining, would allow me a certain visibility—as long as I said and did the "right" things within it.

It is interesting to note that I have experienced this form of censorship at the hands of people who would otherwise be considered liberal, sometimes even radical—those who purport to oppose censorship in all its forms. Yet isn't it much more radical, much more *inclusive* in the fullest sense of the multicultural agenda, to desegregate subject matter and understand that minority writers must occupy a wider territory—even occasional excursions into the nonpolitical? Why is it so hard to believe that some of us can actually *enjoy* being alive and want to render *that* delight instead of obsessing about how oppressed we are? The dictator

I'm most interested in toppling is the internal one, the one who can do most harm. I hold with the Indian poet Kabir, an ecstatic Sufi, who says: "If you don't break your ropes while you're alive, do you think ghosts will do it after?"

Here's an emblematic experience with the glass cage (of subject matter, style, language) that minority (including gay and lesbian) writers get cornered into. In the late 1970s I was asked to send poems for an anthology of work by *Latinas*—a term that is much more inclusive than *Chicanas*—so I had hope for the book's potential. I sent in some things, and a long bilingual piece about my childhood in Cuba was accepted. In the early 1980s I was told the anthology would be published soon by Capra Press, and all that sounded quite good. When I received my contributor's copy, however, I was taken aback: it was titled *Fiesta in Aztlan*—a place I never would have known about except that I had taken a pre-Columbian art course in college—and the book's subtitle was *An Anthology of Chicano Poetry*. I was, I soon discovered by checking the biographical notes, the only non-Chicano/a included in the volume (it had since evolved into a coed collection, which was at least a good move). And to add insult to injury, a translation of the Spanish lines in my poem had been done without consulting me, and there were several things that were completely inaccurate or just plain tone-deaf. Why did no one think to ask me to do the translating, considering they were dealing with Cuban idiom? And couldn't they—these well-meaning people who wanted only visibility themselves—see how *invisible* it made me feel to be grouped under such a title? I felt as though I were crashing a party. I had no business being in such a book, except that my poem met the two requirements for Latino writing: it was bilingual and its theme was childhood and family.

The organization of the book also makes it clear that it is a *culture* that is being showcased, not the creative work of individuals. The volume is divided into chapters titled "La Familia," "The Streets of the Barrio," and "El Mundo"—the latter promising a wider territory but consisting instead of poems about prison, drug addiction, political anger, the humiliation of speaking with an accent, the suffering experienced in crossing borders, and the killing effect of menial jobs. This is "The World"? What an unhappy, circumscribed place it is! Not a single experience rendered in that section is a positive one. It could be argued that the book reflects the reality of 1982, but I'm afraid the "allowable" list of topics for Latinos hasn't been enlarged much during the intervening years.

Quite recently I had a piece published in a special Latino issue of a respected literary magazine, and though the cast now includes Cuban and Puerto Rican writers as well, the themes are still the same, and much of the writing is disappointingly simplistic or undercrafted. Carlos Fuentes, in his essay "How I Started to Write," says of his friend and mentor, the writer Alfonso Reyes: "He taught me . . . that Mexican literature was important because it was literature, not because it was Mexican." I'm still waiting for Latinos living in the United States (but also women, gays, lesbians) to realize that it isn't our identity, or even our suffering at the hands of oppressors, that makes us writers.

For myself, I find that overtly "political poetry" feels just like that— in quotes—in some sense posturing, laying claim to a ready-made (I am *this!*) or, to borrow a phrase from Annie Dillard, "robbing power from the cataracts of the given" and therefore not revolutionary at all but flatly reactionary. Instead, I find the subtleties of politics personally conveyed to be much more radical in their specificity, their ability to get under the skin—*infinitely* more delicate than the broad brush of polemics. It has been my experience that an unlikely emotion such as joy is much more subversive than anger. This may be because moments of joy have been much more radicalizing in my own life, responsible for *real* insight, than moments of anger, during which everyone involved is exiled—in other words, removed from connection, which is something I know a thing or two about.

Maybe it's my being a Cuban writer that makes me so sensitive to fascism—regardless of its source. My own "you can't go home again" is not abstract but tangible, a relationship with an absence that becomes nearly something, a phantom limb. I can't exist *there,* but *here* there are the mistaken assumptions about who I am, what my politics are, and what my subject matter "should be," just because I'm able to check off the boxes labeled Cuban, Exile, Lesbian. From writers and editors of magazines and presses to taxi drivers, every American is looking to reeducate me about what's *really* going on in my native country. But, while that's annoying, what disturbs me is being penned in (pun intended), relegated to a ghetto of experience and ideas by people who would keep me exiled and wounded in my work because that position seems more authentic to them, never mind what it does to me as a human being, or as a writer.

This pen of "acceptable" themes is that pernicious glass cage, which, though limiting, provides the *illusion* of freedom. Within it, we're permitted certain topics—our oppression, of course, being first and foremost, and we're allowed a "healthy" anger that won't really threaten anyone, but we can also write about home (how we live), food/sex (what we eat), and family (what eats us). This makes our work serve more of a sociological or anthropological function than an artistic one, and it is paraded in special issues or anthologies as glimpses into our exotic lives or customs, like a captured native being toured through Europe in a cage. In a bizarre modern twist, the glass cage is now sometimes chosen *willingly*, as it has served to make certain writers more "visible"—elevated like go-go dancers in their cages, they shimmy in their colorful costumes above the crowd, sometimes for a pretty sum. But is this a position of respect—a prominent Latina writer and her collection of antique Mexican blouses, riding the tattered skirt train of poor Frida Kahlo—or just another minstrel show, another hat dance, another cha-cha? Clearly, those willing to "do the multi-culti" to the expected, even the expected rebellion—*especially* the "rebellion"—are rewarded, a fact blinding them to the limitations of the cage. The little metal label affixed to the base of the cage identifies each one as Angry Latina or Powerful Lesbian or Exotic Exiled Writer or Indignant AIDS Activist, each person trapped into acting out the tiny handful of characteristics allotted to that "identity." The jury is still out on whether they're victims or opportunists. Either way, the harm they do—these writers whose aim is not primarily literary, who serve up what the liberal white culture expects (the colorful, angry, wounded, quaint, or earthy *outsider*)—is that they contaminate the well for those of us whose concerns are more formal and spiritual, for whom it's a dedication to a craft we love as deeply as we can, with a devotion to its needs and nuances, like something alive we have been entrusted with, and not a blunt instrument.

Thus it seems silly to me that when no one sniffs a pot of beans or spies my grandmother's braid in my work, I'm dismissed as not being Latina enough. But there's no way I can write from the Grandmother's Braid School of Thought (first of all, neither of mine had one), even if that has been deemed by *others* to be my appropriate source. So what are my options—invent a persona so that I can be perceived as "authentic"? How truly bizarre. It feels as though I'm being told to stop having such fancy thoughts and get back into the kitchen (of the mind), Little Lady— but by people I never would've expected. And can anyone determine what's authentic for another?

A couple of years ago, a well-known Latino writer, serving as guest editor of a major literary magazine, informed me that, while my work clearly showed seriousness (something he frowned upon, apparently), it just wasn't "earthy" enough—as though I should be creating the literary equivalent of pot holders, as befitting my last name. The irony of that adjective, as applied *against* me, is that I write a great deal about nature, and even when I'm not addressing it directly, my metaphors are often—well, for lack of a better word—"earthy" ones. Not surprisingly, I have found that my work fares better—that is, a wider range is better received—when it's a blind submission and there are no expectations to fulfill.

Because of my "identity," I go through the world having to challenge expectations about me, shattering the glass cage in order to create more elbowroom for my work to exist—I almost wrote "world" there, which is closer to my meaning. When I write, I am attempting to render the world that I experience through all the lenses of who I am. Fortunately or unfortunately, due to my particular set of personal and historical influences, I straddle, or bridge, many boundaries. In me, a lot of borders meet, and I am grateful for the opportunities my exile has provided me to cross-pollinate. Fuentes says, again in the same essay, "My upbringing taught me that cultures are not isolated, and perish when deprived of contact with what is different and challenging. Reading, writing, learning, are all activities aimed at introducing civilizations to each other. No culture . . . retains its identity in isolation; identity is attained in contact, in contrast, in breakthrough."

For me, it's not always necessary to tell you *what* I am—or, rather, who I am *externally* isn't always important to the specific poem I'm writing. What's become important is who I am *essentially*, my loves and quirks that are the result of a multitude of influences and that exist below any sociopolitical label adhered to the surface. What's important—for me—is to connect, to move beyond my experience of exile, though my life is forever underlined by that fact. Czeslaw Milosz has said, in a 1993 interview in *Poets & Writers*, "No, we don't want to be fixed in the throes of historical circumstances. . . . We consider a rich historical experience a curse. We want to liberate ourselves and move forward to experiences that are shared by other human beings." And yet, is Milosz any less political?

My choice to adjoin in the widest possible sense has radicalized me. I want to know: Why is a prison considered more political than a neighborhood? I want to know: in the *largest* sense, can I consider myself in exile if I am "at home" in nature? Why is it considered aberrant that I am more drawn to finding metaphoric bridges in my backyard—that tiny piece of the backyard we all share—than I am in burning them? Who says that whining or raging is more legitimate than delighting or loving?

And why is my interest in visual art considered a betrayal of my race? Does anyone tell a writer living in Latin America, for instance, that she can't write about the way sunlight falls on a bowl of pears because it's not Latina enough? I personally know a writer in Cuba who's writing a book about her fascination with Egypt. The rule seems to be: Stay in your native country and you can contemplate aesthetic or esoteric concerns, but move to a foreign country and you're no longer yourself, you're now an "identity." Your fascination with painting becomes a sign of your political abstention. Never mind your intellectual curiosity, your path is no longer your own, you become a representative for people who don't represent you in the least, your books must have a handle, an angle, no longer can you fill a book with uncategorizable fragments like Eduardo Galeano's wonderful *Book of Embraces*, which embraces everything. He's one of those rare people who can render political ideas in exceptional language, but he succeeds because he subverts through delight and humor, not polemics. It is the smallness, the human scale, of his concerns that makes his work universal, and he *assumes* that you, his reader, are his brother or sister, not "the enemy."

From my interest in painting, and its accompanying issue of perspective, I've learned that sometimes you have to look at something at a distance in order to make it small enough to fit into your brain. Though it's a great distance away, both geographically and temporally, I have an abiding fascination with ancient Spain—but neither because of anything overtly political nor because of my trying to clean up my gene pool (anyone with even a passing knowledge of that place and time knows how complex it was culturally and ethnically). I like thinking about something as big as Andalusia—the oldest Western civilization, the southern half of Spain—absorbing the invaders, their races, customs, languages, architecture, music, without ever acknowledging that it was being invaded. The result was a place in which, for awhile, everything and everyone coexisted peaceably and a rich complexity flourished. Much in the same manner as the Religious Right today (but, I must caution, *also* the Left), the "Catholic Kings" launched the Inquisition in an attempt to annihilate that complexity—homogeneity was their war cry. But I like knowing that, despite their efforts, flamenco has Oriental roots, and there are Arab words embedded in Spanish like Moorish tiles, a zigzag design of *A*-words: *almohada, almuerzo, alabao.* And, possibly, even my own name.

So what happens when a land doesn't acknowledge that it's been invaded or colonized? Paradoxically, it possesses a kind of integrity. Cuba used to be something like that (interestingly, Fuentes calls Cuba "the Andalusia of the New World"). Though it was the first stopping place for Columbus, and our native peoples were completely wiped out by the Spaniards, no Cuban I have ever met thinks of himself or herself as an oppressed and colonized person. Even the most uneducated, working-class Cuban (my parents being prime examples) is a little uppity, making no apologies for taking up space. We are not cowed by authority—that is, psychically speaking (explaining our national endurance under fascism and the flourishing of our culture even in exile). We have the self-possession (in the deepest sense, possessing only *ourselves*) of the people of a diaspora. It's as though we've always been roaming and Cuba's just the most recent place we've been kicked out of, but, really, we've *always* been moving—since Eden. And the further back we go in this thinking, the more territory we'll discover that we share (northern Spain, for instance, used to be called Celtiberia), the more interconnected we all are.

Thus, as I've lived and loved and lost but also *found,* I've begun to see myself not as an exile but as a nomad, a role that has less to do with politics than with the human condition—though I realize this is a very simple way of saying something that cannot be simplified. The advantages being that, though you're cast out, you determine your own territory, and, despite the hardships, it's a lot wider than the reservation or concentration camp—or glass cage—others would herd you into. But I'm talking intellectually here, since I have stayed put geographically for thirty years in Los Angeles, my hometown for now. It's my *mental* territory that I'm protecting here, my right to follow my whims, even if they lead me into the classics, or writing in metered verse, or exploring spiritual ideas that have nothing whatsoever to do with the Virgin of Guadalupe or La Caridad del Cobre. I was thrilled, for instance, to discover in my research into ancient Spain that Sufis were present in Andalusia—Rumi, my brother! Now *that's* something I'd love to spend some time investigating.

To be fair, though, I have to admit that for many years my identity as an exile was of great importance to me. It was a deep trauma that I bore with as much pain and ambivalent pride as the enemy's blue numbers at my wrist. I had been violently ripped from all that I loved, and because no salve, no surgery, seemed to exist for such a wound, I staggered around grasping the arrow in my heart, mad with pain. My pain, I felt, was evidence of my fidelity to what I had lost. So if I now rail at others for circumscribing my world, it is because the release from my internal glass cage has been hard won. When I was willing to let go of my special status as a tragic exile, I awoke to the fact that we are all exiles—from various physical places, from families, from the past, from childhood. Suddenly, what had previously alienated me from others and made the world taste so bitter—no joy to be found anywhere!—was what allowed me to be linked to all beings. But I would've floundered less if I'd had the following quote from Julio Cortázar's insightful essay "The Fellowship of Exile":

> Simply stated, I believe it is feasible to invert the stereotyped notion of exile which retains many connotations that we should be rid of by now. The unavoidable fact is that we have been expelled from our countries. Why play into the enemy's hands by treating the expulsion as a misfortune—a response that can only direct our reactions in a negative manner? Why should we harp day after day, in the press and public forums, about our condition as exiles, focusing always on the most painful details when this is precisely what those who close the doors to our countries want us to do? Exiles, yes. Period. Now there are other things to write and do—as exiled writers, of course, but with emphasis on "writers." Because our true effectiveness lies in our ability to profit

from exile, to take advantage of these sinister fellowships, to extend and enrich our mental horizons so that when at last we can focus on our own realities, we can do so with greater lucidity and effect.

Amen. It's true that if I hadn't experienced exile, I may never have become fascinated with certain ideas, like the idea of home. For instance: if not Cuba, which is forever lost to me, then where? And not only where, but how far back? When, not just where, was home? I'm trying to figure that one out through a process of elimination: for complex reasons, never with my family; not in Springfield, Illinois, where I was placed in a foster home when I arrived without my parents at the age of nine; not even, I've discovered, in the world of multicultural writing as it exists. All of those habitations were just too small for me. So I've arrived at the idea that I carry home with me (you should see the way I pack for camping) and that the doorway to my house is anywhere I experience delight— *there* is my true homeland. Not a headline event, this view lacks the sexiness of rebellion and coins no slogans. But it's basic and true—*for me:* What I write is by definition political, since I define politics as any action against annihilation—even when I'm addressing a hummingbird in my backyard or the sunlight coming through my front window. The fingerprints I leave on the things I lavish my attention on are my own, not indications of my race or my sexual identity or my country of birth. I consider a writer to be political when that person—regardless of sex, sexual orientation, class, nationality, race, religious beliefs, *or even subject matter*—alters me on a molecular level with the fire of his or her vision expressed in precise language. There is a quote by the late American painter Fairfield Porter, whom I admire beyond words, that has become a kind of mantra for me: "The most important thing is the quality of love. Love means paying very close attention to something, and you can only pay close attention to something because you can't help doing so."

It is my *nature* to pay attention to whatever happens to volunteer in my garden—tinged with the complexity of my particular set of historical and personal baggage. My love happens to reside there. We can conjecture that because of my abrupt uprooting I seek connection in nature, but, like a lover, I don't much care why—*I just want to be let in all the deeper.* Whatever the reason, when I step out into my yard, I am—as Scott Russell Sanders says so beautifully about the drowned land of his

Ohio childhood—"letting down a line to plumb the bottom. . . . To touch the ground even through a length of rope would be some consolation." My writing is the line I drop down, and when my voice emerges, it is sometimes the voice of the scrappy, invasive morning glory vine that says, *Move over and let me have more room.*

Sounds of Hazard and Survival

COLETTE INEZ

Last spring at a writers' colony in New Hampshire, idly tuned to a thrush solo of bubbling notes from the woods, my face pressed into a purple shrub of flowering lilac, all at once, I heard myself humming and groaning.

I was astonished to recognize the sound as a sort of sexual breathing, a primal voice harking back to the incantatory moans and grunts of my ancestors, first in the trees and savannas of Africa and later in the caves of Lascaux or along rivers deeply rooted in the Dordogne of southwest France, where my family claims its blood lines. These unintentional murmurings underscored for me the richness of my life as a woman intent on making herself visible.

My first remembered sounds were bells and birdsong. Deep fullbosomed bells called me to Matins, our morning prayers and jangling bells announced High Mass. Birds served as my alarm at dawn, calling me awake, piercing the dusk of Vespers at evening.

To this music I may add the clatter of spoons with which we scooped up our lumpy gruel, the slurping of cabbage soup, burps, snuffles, hacks, giggles, phlegmy whines, harrumphs, the nether sounds that issued from rumps or were mimicked in halls, and the drub-a-drub of sticks being run along the iron fence when nuns were preoccupied with the demands of the day.

Even as I slid into a well of sleep, birdsong from the top branches of the honey locust or basswood tree might seek me out before I entered the dream tunnel only to climb out again, yawn, sigh, smack water on my face, slip on my uniform when I lived with the children abandoned to the care of Catholic Sisters in Brussels, Belgium, before the German occupation in the spring of 1940.

The hushed shuffle and scuff of shoes seemed omnipresent. Shoes clicking or dragging Sunday visitors down hallways where I looked for my mother, who came two or three times, arriving in the guise of an aunt, pious and stern, a woman with whom I got down on my knees to babble a prayer learned by rote.

Footfalls echoed on stone for almost every enterprise of my childhood. Three times a day we formed queues for prayer and at the lavatory's rank of white porcelain sinks to wash our hands before eating. The WCs were few in relation to our numbers; pee pee and ca ca were swiftly executed to gurgling flush and pounding fists at the toilet door. We stepped lively to our Saturday bath, transacted in a wooden tub of hot water; filed to meals in the refectory and to music class, where we piped Gregorian chant in harmony, voices trilling and swelling in rooms adorned with crucifixes, emblems of Christ's sacrifice for our sins.

Hurry up, nuns barked. Stand up straight. Walk a straight line. Line up for class to study the catechism. Who made us? God made us. Who is God? God is the Supreme Being, infinitely perfect, who made all things and keeps them in existence. Sometimes my heart pounded at the heavy thump of Sister's brogues, the hiss of her voice as she pinched my ear. Sometimes a switch whistled in air and stung my flesh.

We learned the lives of the saints, penmanship, arithmetic, and world geography, countries pointed out to us on a pastel-colored map that snapped as it rolled up and down. Marching orders called out by a nun master sergeant demanding her snot-nosed troops account for themselves as they were ushered to Easter services at Saint Julian's or to winter outings on a frozen lake. I still recall the squeak of ice skates rushing to a stop, the clack of those strapped-on blades, a sad percussive note closing the doors of that icy heaven which had spun us like dancers on a frozen pond.

I suppose my sharp ears were whetted early when I contracted typhus—the only child in my ward to do so, I was later informed by Sisters. My quarantine took place in a large, pale room daily brightened by a glass of orange juice on a tray carried by a young novitiate. Her hurried steps outside my door, her soft, small voice still cling to memory, as do the resonant words of monsieur le docteur saying that the fever had broken and I would be well. Did he place his gold-rimmed watch next to my ear so I might listen to its heart?

Perhaps it was at that time of enforced silence I began to create conversations with my body parts. I would start with my feet, each toe given a name and allowed feelings to express. How you abused me when you jumped rope, big toes complained, as did my knees, banged and scraped in a fall. I found a warm nest between my legs, the "down there" I was not to touch, and together we sighed and whispered I forget what.

I spoke anxiously to the bag that contained my pee, begged it not to spill when I sank into fevered sleep. Sometimes my heart was a chatterbox; other times it droned on, bored with my affliction. I saw my fingernails with distinctive faces, somber, crooked, smiling. I gave them professions: bookseller, music teacher, ticket taker on the trolley car. They helped me while away the long sequestered hours, day in and day out, over a stretch of weeks from winter to spring, as I watched the red flowers of my rash wither and disappear.

When my illness flew out the window forever, I listened to birds in the shrubs and children in the yard sing "Cadet Rouselle" and "Il Etait Un Navire." In that rising music I sensed both the sadness of having been singled out by a fearful disease and the joy of being cured. My narrow world as a child among children lost to their parents through desertion and death would soon open its door to America.

Sometimes I asked if I were real and pinched myself when sailing to America, faintly moaning in my bunk bed as the ship rocked like a great whale I imagined had devoured me and would spit me out in the huge port city of New York. I had been told to look for skyscrapers, but they were swallowed in mist, muffled for me in the honk of fog horns, lost in the same way I felt I was when I came to live with an American family in their stucco house on Bayview Avenue—a home on Long Island with maple trees planted on either side of a street whose neat borders gave way to patches of open fields.

I am ten and hiding under a neighbor's lilac bush, eyes closed to better inhale the rich perfume of clustered flowers in full bloom. My cheek is red from a slap and my lips crinkle in a small *o* out of which sails a hum and then a pure whistle that imitates the local birds. Maybe the two-note slur of the phoebe, the "tchew-tchew" of the gray tufted titmouse, the thin, soft warble of bluebirds perched on high-tension lines and on branches of pine.

I pretend that I am a bird spirit, that I can talk in bird. When, after a long hush, a bird decides to answer back, I shiver with pleasure at my newfound powers of speech practiced in that lilac sanctuary or along the dirt roads and sandy beaches that looped the bay waters of the island.

What I dread are the sounds of tires squealing in the driveway, the slammed front door, the key jiggled in the lock, loud insistent voices blurred on the stairs, a banging against furniture, footsteps stumbling past my room, a scrape at the door, and the doorknob twisting.

At times, a pants zipper's "zreep" bares a pink bone that pushes against my dress. My foster father gives me dance lessons in the basement. We lurch to the tunes of "Siboney" and "South of the Border, Down Mexico Way." The click of swizzle sticks. One more "drinkee." Slurred words. Noises of danger. My foster family's sonic structure, its arrangement of destructive elements, the orchestration of its boozy world. Sounds articulated for me the menace and pleasures of life. And I was drawn to the instrumental play and music of words.

In French, the wistful word for dusk, *crépuscule*, charmed me as did the light-hearted syllables of *bicyclette*. We did not ride bicycles as children, but I saw them on the road, our Rue Chant d'Oiseau, transporting books, groceries, and flowers peeping out of waxed paper and tied with twine.

I bent my ear into vowels, the a-e-i-o-u repeated in my first and second languages, identical on paper but differently pronounced. I honored consonants, the hard and soft noises that curved my lips, and adored the humming of words like *marmalade, aurora borealis*, and *chandeliers* in English, which I did not speak when I arrived, except for a smattering: "hello," "mama," "good-bye." I appreciated the librarian's "shush," said with an index finger pressed to her lips. Ugly words fascinated me with their dark energy: *gawk, gaggle, khaki, putrid, pus*, and *tungsten*.

During years of practicing my whistle, I sang alto in church and school choirs, pleased to weave my voice into a melodic line of memorized music—mostly folk songs, hymns, show tunes, and ditties. Walking arm and arm with girlfriends, at parties when group singing was still common, or caroling at Christmas, I would comb my notes into a song without a score, not knowing how I did it and marveling at the progression of chords.

Gifted with an ear for music, I plucked out notes of "Hit Parade" tunes and themes from radio shows on the parish house piano, and I reveled in singing aloud when I pedaled my blue bicycle, a possession I treated lovingly as if it were my steed, riding it to the library, choir practice, school and along shore roads that lulled me with wind and water.

I know well that silence possesses noise and subtle communication—how much is said in the lift of an eyebrow, the line of a rigid mouth. But as a child I was in awe of sounds that seemed to give weight to events, anchoring the swirl of sensations, classifying them into good and bad islands of experience. The valiant cheer of neighbors tooting pipes and banging pots, the whiny throb of radio bands on New Year's Eve told me I belonged for that moment to a community I trusted.

That trust was dispelled in the middle of the night, the clug-clug of my foster mother's wedges on the stairs, the clink of ice cubes in a glass told me *look out, trouble ahead, escape.*

And I discovered that whereas my existence might slip-slide and stumble, I could exercise control over some of these sounds, later order them, put them on parade in secret poems I kept hidden in a speckled notebook. Verses about sunsets on Fly Beach, milk bottles delivered at dawn, dew drops on crabgrass were penned in tidy rhymes with dashes, unconsciously imitating that wizard poet Emily Dickinson. It never occurred to me I might write about my life.

Reassured by my own low voice, on sad or desperate occasions, I played a secret game in which I separated myself into two people—both me, one wounded, the other the consoler. "There, pretty darling, there, it'll all come right," I smoothed my forehead and ran my hand over my hair. "You'll be just fine." I purred and hummed, pitched my voice deeper, concocting a fantasy mother to quiet my crying. Even in adulthood that hurt-child-become-a-woman permitted her other self to commiserate and soothe with cooing sounds like a mourning dove.

Living near bay water, I taught myself how to listen to the wind, the varying tones—consoling or high-pitched like the tearing of silk or low and moaning, signaling a storm. Vigilant, I meditated on sounds repeated on the shore, the monotonous plick-plick of waves lapping the docks or the roiling white foam slapped against the coast.

Machines I barely understood sometimes reassured me with the glitter and shine of their metal snouts, sides, and backs catching the light as they sped by. I respected their noises crisscrossing paths of earth and sky. On back roads the roar of distant cars—few and far between in the 1940s—joined the whiz and drone of buses, the chug-chug and wail of commuter trains.

A passenger plane dreamily cruising over the grid pattern of our houses and yards would easily set off flights of fancy. Even bombers growling out of Mitchell Field oddly mollified me; I knew they were powerful and mysterious devices sent to defeat Hitler's and Tojo's enemy fleets. Weren't we told by elders that dropping bombs guaranteed victory and the coming of peace?

In the years that followed, the natural world became a haven I clung to when escaping my foster home and its hazards. Eventually, my haphazard caretakers would throw me out of the house on Bayview Avenue. I would find work as a telephone operator in a neighboring town with lodgings in a furnished room near the railroad track. Friends would help me move in.

My companions were books of poems and novels, often five a week, borrowed or bought, and I turned pages to the cadence of speeding trains that rattled my windows at night. At seventeen, my ear had begun to incline toward the rhythms of a safer place: classical music on WQXR, poetry committed to heart, tapping keys of my first Underwood, a pen scratching words on a blue-lined yellow pad.

At that writers' colony last spring I kept my usual journal of jotted-down sights and sounds:

Nectar on the lips of purple Lady Slippers. Dragonflies drone on rain-soaked paths. Meadows glitter and buzz. Blake T. tells me deer come to the red pine forest the MacDowells planted sixty years ago. I was a toddler then on the Rue Chant d'Oiseau taking my place in line to implore the Holy Mother. "Marie Vierge, Ecoutes Mes Prieres. Virgin Mary, Hear My Prayers." If only I could have tapped that child on the shoulder, and said to her: "You will be a poet."

Lilac edges turn rust-brown, cones of flowers whiten to moonsilver. Rugosa roses are next in line ready to kick into summer. From its hiding place of leaves, a solitary whippoorwill repeats its exuberant notes in the dark.

Finding the Groove

JOY HARJO

Once I was so small I could barely peer over the top of the backseat of the black Cadillac my father polished and tuned daily; I wanted to see everything. It was around the time I acquired language, or even before that time, when something happened that changed my relationship to the spin of the world. My concept of language, of what was possible with music, was charged by this revelatory moment. It changed even the way I looked at the sun. This suspended integer of time probably escaped ordinary notice in my parents' universe, which informed most of my vision in the ordinary world. They were still omnipresent gods.

We were driving somewhere in Tulsa, the northern border of the Creek Nation. I don't know where we were going or where we had been, but I do know the sun was boiling the asphalt, the car windows open for any breeze as I stood on tiptoes on the floorboard behind my father, a handsome god who smelled of Old Spice, whose slick black hair was always impeccably groomed, his clothes perfectly creased and ironed. The radio was on. I loved the radio, jukeboxes, or any magic thing containing music, even then.

I wonder now what signaled this moment of revelation, a loop of time that at first glance could be any place in time. I became acutely aware of the line the jazz saxophonist was playing, a sound that could only have been John Coltrane. I didn't know the words *jazz* and *saxophone*—or the concepts. At that age I was in a world that did not depend on humans for naming. I was slowly fitting myself to this configuration, as do all children in this constellation.

I don't know how to say it, with what sounds or words, but in that confluence of hot southern afternoon, in the breeze of aftershave and humidity, I followed the improvised horn line of Coltrane to the beginning, to the place of the birth of sound. I was suspended in whirling stars, a moon to which I'd traveled often by then. I grieved my parents' failing, my own life, which I saw stretched the length of that rhapsody. We were a small but crucial point in the construction, every thought, every flick of an eyelash, every dragonfly wing, every word mattered. We were nothing, yet we were everything. We were present at each angle of existence, poised at the center of the world as we drove together in my father's prized black Cadillac, through that humid summer day.

My rite of passage into the world of humanity occurred then, via jazz. Coltrane's horn had made a startling bridge between familiar and strange lands, between mystery and the need to breathe. Molecular structure is shifted according to tone and grace, reshapes the DNA spiral. Coltrane was not the first explorer, but he was one of the most gifted, could find new configurations of tones where there had been none discovered or known and bring them back to earth.

As that child I sensed this music had to do with me, the journey of my family as the soul made its way through lungs and blood, from Alabama to Indian Territory. We were there when jazz was born, for though the music is predominately West African in concept with European harmonic structures, jazz could not have happened without the influence of the Muskogee people, without the shape of the particular lands marking the southeast corner of this continent, without the energy thrown off from the struggle there.

On that humid afternoon as I began my own particular journey, I found a way toward the realization of knowledge in this world, a way to hear beyond the ordinary waves of language. A love supreme. A love supreme.

I am still on that journey. The stuff I need for singing by whatever means is garnered from every thought, every heart that ever pounded the earth, the intelligence that directs the stars. The shapes of mountains, cities, a whistle leaf of grass, or a human bent with loss will revise the pattern of the story, the song. I take it from there, write or play through the heartbreak of the tenderness of being until I am the sky, the earth, the song and the singer.

IV

❦

The Crucible
of
Family

The Writer in the Family

JULIE CHECKOWAY

I once heard Toni Morrison say that the greatest problem we face in America today is the absence of ancestors. Our wise ancestors are gone, she said, and there is no one to turn to for genuine smartness on matters of the heart. We have Geraldo and Oprah and Ricki Lake, Ted Koppel and his parade of flashy experts, we have Headline News every hour on the half hour, but no one in America today has a mainline into soul smartness.

Morrison said roughly this in an auditorium in Atlanta, where she and other writers who had won the Nobel Prize in literature had gathered for a symposium.

That's right, all of the Nobel Laureates said. *We are orphaned, left without family,* they all seemed to say, shaking their heads.

In the plush Jimmy Carter Presidential Library auditorium, which was filled to capacity, attention was being paid to what Morrison and the other writers said. The audience was breathless, amazed, listening, ears cocked. In the room, camcorders and tape recorders whirred and buzzed. Flashbulbs flashed, freezing the great writers in the act of all that head-shaking.

The irony was unbearable.

Hey, you! I wanted to shout out from my seat.

You writers, I wanted to say.

Don't you realize that you're *our ancestors?*

I believe that a writer's duty *as a writer* is first to him- or herself. That point is inarguable. A writer has to make a hard-nosed commitment to writing, or the writing won't happen at all. A writer has to seek out time to write and then guard that time like a pit bull. I got married a few years ago, and committing to writing feels like getting married. Saying yes to the whole enterprise day after day takes a willing and stubborn soul.

But a writer's first duty as a writer *and a human being,* I have also come to believe, is to nurture other writers. A writer must be midwife at the births of other writers' voices. A writer must share the wisdom she or he has learned in her writer's solitude and give that wisdom away, with kindness and generosity and gentleness.

It is, I am certain, the giving of an heirloom, an absolutely necessary behest.

I wouldn't be on this planet and writing if a whole lot of kind and patient writers hadn't taken time away from their own writing to read mine and to offer words of encouragement and advice, to line-edit, coach, cajole, hold my hand when my writing stank, listen to me cry over the telephone when my writing seemed to take forever.

For four years while I worked on my first book, my friends Lavinia and Brucie and I met once every two weeks—through pregnancies and miscarriages, through love affairs and sleet and rain and shine and thunder—to talk about our writing. For four years, we ate gingersnaps and drank herbal tea in each other's living rooms and commiserated and caballed.

Brucie and I helped Lavinia keep writing a book after she gave birth to her second baby and thought she'd have to stop altogether, forever. Lavinia and I helped Brucie keep writing short stories while she divorced her husband and sued for the custody of her two little boys and lost that battle and then while she began to publish and win prizes all over the place and didn't quite know what to think of herself anymore.

And Lavinia and Brucie spoon-fed me hope through four pretty miserable drafts of my book.

They never abandoned me.

We never abandoned each other.

Writers, especially beginners, are a ravenous and needful lot.

I was a cannibal when I started out. Early on, when I was an undergraduate in the creative writing program at Harvard, I would have eaten my writing teacher's right arm off if I had thought it would have made me a better writer. Once, when I was nineteen, I visited one of my writing teachers in her office, climbing a set of steep, creaky stairs to ask her whether she thought I had what it took to be a writer.

My teacher was in her late thirties. She had written three novels already and was at work on a long book of nonfiction.

"Do you think I can do it?" I asked her. "Do you think I have it in me?" I asked.

"I don't know," she answered quietly, and then with the sort of *koan* one might expect of a Buddhist priest, she asked, "Do *you* think so?"

Beginning writers ask the sort of question I asked. Rilke's young poet asked if the verses that he had sent the master were good or not, and Rilke answered him with great kindness—in a small volume of letters— that as soon as the writer would cease to ask such questions, he would know his writing was good.

Beginning writers are wanters. During the time of their apprenticeship, they want face-time, they want talk-time, teeny-weeny line-edits, phone conferences, e-mail exchanges, a dinner at your home (on the *good* china, not the everyday). They want to be welcomed as guests at your table.

And something more intangible.

They want the reassurance of an accomplished writer's nearness and the certainty of that writer's devotion, the way that infants want the breast.

⤺

Most beginning writers will settle, however, for a little nudge of honest hope.

About twelve years ago, when I lived in the Midwest and was studying at the Iowa Writers' Workshop, my friend Carole and I traveled together to hear Maxine Hong Kingston speak at a small Jesuit college on the banks of the upper Mississippi. It was February and gray. The auditorium that day was peopled largely by nuns in habits and women with blue hair and hard-shelled pocketbooks. Had they read *Woman Warrior* and *China Men?* I wondered as I took my seat. Did they know what they were in for?

Hong Kingston had a new book coming out—*Tripmaster Monkey*— and she read passages from it. The book was wise and funny, and she was funny and sweet and puckish, her long gray-black hair parted in the middle and tucked behind her ears. Hong Kingston had just returned from China—her first trip there, to visit the village of her ancestors, and she spoke some about that, too, that day, about how, in China, she had felt both at home and not at home and how those two feelings seemed just right.

It was my second and last year in graduate school at Iowa, and I wasn't having a terribly easy time. I had found the workshops brutal, sometimes arctically cold. In Iowa, I shivered with the want of writerly warmth. In Iowa, I hadn't really felt like much of a writer and hadn't found too many other people who seemed to believe I would ever be one. I was so miserable, in fact, that I had decided to leave the entire United States behind and go to China myself for a couple of years. If you spun the globe around, China was about as far as a person could get from Iowa City.

On that day that I heard Maxine Hong Kingston read from *Tripmaster Monkey*, I was twenty-four, a rather desperate soul.

After the others in the room had finished having their copies of *Woman Warrior* signed, I snuck up to the front, to the dim corner of the stage where Maxine Hong Kingston stood.

I looked at her and I breathed deeply. I looked her straight in the eye.

She looked back at me with anticipation.

"I'm a writer," I blurted out. "I'm leaving for China soon. Do you have any advice that you could give?"

Maxine Hong Kingston took her hands out of her pockets and put them on her hips. She cocked her head to one side and thought for a moment; then she smiled. She put her hands back in her pockets and said with absolute seriousness: *Keep your eyes open.*

And I got it.

I went away happy.

I took Maxine Hong Kingston's simple advice to heart.

In China I kept my writer's eyes wide open.

And my first book came from that.

An entire book probably arose from that one moment of straightforward, writerly kindness.

❧

"You're a *writer*?" a woman asks me at a cocktail party or a dinner party or in the checkout lane at the supermarket, and before I can answer yea or nay, the woman has begun to tell me about a novel she's been writing for years. She speaks of the novel ardently. Sometimes as she speaks her eyes close, and it's as if she has traveled elsewhere. Her hands gesture as gracefully as swans in front of her.

By the next week maybe her novel arrives on my doorstep in a package.

Three hundred and sixty-seven pages.

Single spaced.

Perhaps I have asked the woman to send me her novel. Perhaps I have not.

The point is: now that I hold in my hands the package marked *Priority Mail*, what in the world do I do with it?

Most writers kvetch about this kind of thing, the way that lawyers and doctors kvetch about how they're always being asked for free advice. True, being asked to read an enormous manuscript by a person you barely or hardly or don't even know can feel like being asked to take a pro bono gander at somebody's 1967 tax return or a suspicious-looking mole. But from time to time, I have found it helpful to my own soul just to go ahead and take the hulking, honking three-hundred-and-sixty-seven-page, single-spaced manuscript (that I did or didn't ask for) and read it. Sometimes (I'm not saying I'm a sucker or a martyr or that I do this all the time, and I don't exactly mean this as an invitation to the general public), I take the hulking, honking, three-hundred-and-sixty-seven-page, single-spaced manuscript inside my house and I read it as lovingly as I can.

Then I send it back to its writer with the most encouraging letter I can compose without lying.

Simply said: it's good karma.

❦

My best friend is a prize-winning poet named Jane. She comes from a family that's even more shattered and crazy than my own. My parents are long-dead, and that is terribly sad, but Jane's parents are alive and downright dangerous. Her mother is a drunk who says things to Jane like, "You'll never find a man to marry you if you keep those rotten animals," referring to Jane's dachshund and her munsterlander, the two dogs who have kept her happy company for years.

When Jane was a girl and her stepfather and mother used to fight, her mother used to bring out a .45 and shoot it at Jane's stepfather, always just missing, bullets always whizzing by. Then, even with the gun pointed at him, Jane's stepfather would advance at Jane's mother with a fist or a broken bottle, knowing, Jane says, that her mother hadn't the courage to shoot to kill.

Embedded in the floors and the walls and ceilings of the houses Jane and her mother used to live in are bullets that missed their mark.

Jane's real father was a brilliant scientist who, along with Timothy Leary, had blown his brains out on drugs and who also did Jane the tremendous favor of encouraging her to tune out and turn on. Jane and her father used to bond by freebasing, snorting a couple of lines. Very familial. It wasn't until Jane was in grad school at Syracuse and she had the understanding of Raymond Carver and Tess Gallagher that she began to get clean and sober.

When that happened, the drugs went first, but Jane was still drinking heavily. The drinking felt like the hardest thing to give up, perhaps because it was simply the last.

Tess Gallagher was a tough and demanding workshop teacher. She rarely allowed a student to miss handing in a poem. But like a good writing teacher—her eye not just on poems—she saw that Jane was struggling.

"If you need to skip a week of writing, that's OK," Tess used to tell her, and there was something in Tess's level of understanding of Jane, something about Tess's caring enough to say *you don't have to write right now*, that made it possible for Jane not to stop writing but to *keep writing* instead.

In all of her time with Tess, Jane never missed a poem or a class.

Once, Raymond Carver took Jane to lunch in those first days after she gave up drinking. He himself had been sober for a number of years. He took Jane to lunch and just talked to her. Then they had a little walk. After lunch, when they were standing at a windy street corner in Syracuse waiting for the light to change, Raymond Carver looked over at Jane and said softly, the way a good father might have spoken to a child whose mind he had quietly and correctly read, "Sometimes," Raymond Carver said, "when you're about to cross the street, you think, don't you, of how easy it would be to just, on an impulse. . . ."

He gestured to the passing cars, at how they whizzed by, at how simple it could be for a person to step in front of one of those cars, how easy and split-second it could be to end things.

"You think that. Right?" he asked Jane gently.

Jane nodded.

The light changed. Cars stopped.

"That's all right," Raymond Carver said. "I know that feeling."

The walk sign began to blink.

"It gets better," Raymond Carver said to Jane, and then, to get to the other side, Jane and Raymond Carver crossed the road.

❧

Here's a story I have told many times but have never written down.

Once, years ago, when I was a student, I had a professor who was, I am certain, a terribly lonely and unhappy man. He wrote brilliant books, and for one semester he came from far away to teach a group of twelve of us about writing.

On the first day of class, the unhappy professor arrived in the classroom with a pile of manuscripts in his arms. They were our manuscripts.

"I've read these," he said, throwing the heap down upon the seminar table. "And I simply don't know what to do with them. They're terrible," he said, motioning to the scattered pages.

The unhappy professor sighed. He looked down at the table and shook his head. "I don't even know why I've bothered to come here," he said.

There were twelve students in the room, and we exchanged glances. We didn't know why he had come either, but we knew without speaking that it was going to be a long and painful semester.

In fact, the unhappy professor was disgusted with all of our work, not just the first manuscripts but every manuscript that followed. He was relentless in his pursuit of our flaws and unfamiliar with the language of praise. He bore down upon us in class and told us that we were nothing, that we were useless, that even our attempt to write was useless.

We were, in his mind, irredeemable.

Once, he wrote in the margins of a story of mine, which I later went on to publish and for which I later earned prizes: *You have utterly failed. Do you realize that?*

Sometimes during that long semester with the unhappy professor, when I knew he was holding office hours, I would slip by the unhappy professor's door in an attempt to catch a glimpse of him at his desk. I do not know exactly why I did this. I think I wanted to reach him in some way, to have from him a kind word or to offer him the same. I do not think he ever saw me pass by because he sat with his back to the door, the slope of his back the opposite of an invitation to enter. He sat typing the new, unhappy novel he was writing and he appeared completely un-interruptable, as if it would be impossible ever to reach him, as if no one or nothing had ever reached him before, or ever would reach him, in his entire lifetime.

I hated and I pitied him.

Then one day the unhappy professor failed to appear in class. In his stead came another professor, the happy professor, who explained, wringing his hands (an uncharacteristic thing for the happy professor to do), that the unhappy professor had had to leave. Something terrible had happened, the happy professor said.

My first thought: a nervous breakdown.

But when we pressed the happy professor, when we asked him what it was that had happened, he told us that the unhappy professor's only son had died, that the son had fallen, or had been pushed, or had jumped— no one knew for certain—from a high window in a city far, far away.

Shamefully, I had thought more than once, and uncharitably, that the unhappy professor seemed himself the sort of person who might one day jump from a window.

Now I regretted that thought.

We never saw the unhappy professor again. He went home to see to his son's affairs, to tend to his son's funeral.

The twelve of us in the class sent the unhappy professor a dippy sympathy card, which we all signed with tense and earnest signatures. We wanted to send the unhappy professor something more than a card, but we couldn't think of anything that would have pleased him or anything that would have pleased anyone, not just the unhappy professor, in such a bitter time of grief.

One day, the unhappy professor wrote to us. Not *to* us, exactly, but *about* us, in a letter he penned to the happy professor.

"Tell them, please, that they are all fine, fine people," he wrote.

And when the happy professor told us what the unhappy professor had written, the twelve of us didn't know if we should feel relief or redemption. But we knew that something important had happened. Something to do with forgiveness, his forgiving us our flaws and our forgiving him his unhappiness, perhaps, and something to do with how the unhappy professor had been, in a strange but certain way, our father and how his dead son was our brother, although that it is not how any of us would have explained it then and that is not how some of us might explain it, even now.

But that is what it was.

∾

At thirty-nine, my best friend—Jane, the poet—still struggles with feeling safe. Sometimes in the mornings, when she is lonely or afraid, she sits in the benign darkness of a clothes closet in her house.

"In that closet, I take myself apart, then put myself together. To be sure that I can," she says. "To know that I can start from nothing and I can make myself into something. And then I can feel safe enough to go out of my house."

It all sounds a little melodramatic, but I've come mostly to accept Jane's rituals as necessary to her sense of narrative order in what has been a disorderly life.

For example, instead of keeping a street address, Jane always uses a post office box—so no one in her family will ever know exactly where she lives. Recently, though, she's gotten herself to a point where she can stand in a room full of people and actively ignore her own belief that someone nearby is about to kill her.

Not all that long ago, this woman who sits in closets sometimes and has to rebuild herself in darkness, stood up for me in the light of my own wedding, as my maid of honor, as important to me as any blood sister. She paced down the aisle of the sanctuary, a little shy but pretty behind her glasses. She wore a periwinkle-colored silk dress, and she carried in her arms a spray of roses. And whenever I got wigged out by all that was happening before, during, or after the wedding, she just kept reminding me about my soul—about how far it had traveled in order to come to a place where I felt I deserved to be married to someone good and kind and generous.

Over the years that we've known each other, we've maintained a steady correspondence about writing and the writing life, Jane and I. Jane always has wise things to say, things that make me grow as a writer and as a person.

When it comes to writing, I cannot start a poem unless I've got the voice down, she once wrote. *You experiment and experiment, hash the material through, try different paces, etc. . . . then suddenly something clicks, and it all comes into place. It all comes into place because you've got the voice—and the voice dictates all the other elements of the poem—pace (line breaks), diction, image, everything. The arrival of the voice is a touch of the Muse . . . feels like magic when that happens.*

Another time, she wrote, *I think in shapes—sort of shadows of shapes which change and surface and submerge into dark, and something to do with shapes overlapping is the area when articulation begins to be possible. And I feel all of this physically, just as phrases are physical, rhythmical, before they are embodied in words.*

How do you *think?* she once asked me.

No one, to my knowledge, had ever asked me that before.

❧

Here's a true story from my own life about writerly karma.

A couple of years ago, a woman in her sixties, the mother of a good friend of mine, a very nice woman indeed, asked me to take a look at the manuscript of a book she had just written. It was a novel, and it had been written on a dare. A group of old and faithful college roommates from Radcliffe had challenged each other to write romance novels for post-menopausal women, and my friend's mother had been the only woman in that group actually to take the dare seriously and complete the task.

Now the manuscript was in my hands. I took the book home. The woman had told me to take my time. The woman and I had planned a lunch date for some months later. In the meantime, I read the book—every page of it—and prepared myself to make a response.

The novel was a tough read because it hadn't decided what it wanted to be yet. The manuscript was a cross between a mystery and a romance. The villain of the book was a rather harmless Peeping Tom, and from time to time the heroine became "moist" between her legs when thinking about the book's handsome protagonist, a middle-aged doctor. The problem was, there was no incremental change in the main character, no big bang.

I began to worry.

The writer had taken herself seriously. I knew she would expect from me a serious response.

I would need to tell this woman the truth: that the book was structurally flawed, that its main character had to deepen, that the manuscript required a good two or three more drafts, that the writer needed to decide more clearly the genre in which she was writing.

But to balance the negatives, I had also to tell the woman that I had found the writing more than competent and in many ways brave.

To backtrack, this woman was not exactly a stranger. I knew her, and I liked her. In the city in which I lived at that time, she was a civic and community leader of seemingly boundless energy and great cheer, a mother and a school administrator. I remember thinking once that she was the kind of woman I had wished I had had as a mother. Mine had died of cancer when I was five.

This woman, too, had had cancer. Many years ago, when her three boys were young, she had overcome cancer of the eye, though the cancerous eye had had to be removed and was replaced with one fashioned of glass, a glass eye so real every time I saw it—with its certain pupil and its auburn iris—that I frequently forgot which eye, the right or the left, the woman had lost.

I felt I must address this woman without pity and with kindness and by looking into her real eye, the eye from which she looked at the world. I don't know why I felt that. I just knew it was what I must do.

The lunch lasted about an hour. We met in a restaurant and ate salad and talked about the novel. Upon hearing my comments, the woman seemed not crestfallen but quietly thoughtful and then at last grateful. She said as she left the lunch that she now had renewed energy to rewrite. She even left the lunch and called one of her sons and told him that I was a fine person.

I left the lunch feeling as though I had done a fine woman a good turn.

I hadn't shot her down. I hadn't needed to. I had been straight with her but still encouraging. I had done my best to treat her with the truth and respect that anyone who writes deserves.

And here's the karma part: Through a set of events I couldn't have written as fiction, this same woman became, not long after, my mother-in-law.

Which is all by way of saying that, although I long ago grew bone-tired of hearing people bandy about and misuse the phrase "family values," I have to re-invoke that phrase here and re-invent it in order to say a few things that I have learned about the writing life.

Everyone who is a writer is a writer in *two* families, the family into which she was born and the family of writers on the planet that spins beneath her.

And the writer in the family of writers can choose, or not, to pass familial goodness on — the wisdom of work, the wisdom of books — with as much goodwill as she can muster.

This I have come to believe: you must look into the seeing eye of the world with kindness.

And sometimes — though you *must* not count on it — all of this *may* come back to you in the strangest, most remarkable and beautiful of ways.

The Pure Place

TESS GALLAGHER

Getting lost in the flowers I
don't come home.
RYOKAN

She was doing one thing as if it were hers alone to do—each day going to the place and doing only that thing in that place. I saw my mother leave the house. She never asked permission, and she didn't say where she was going. She simply went.

She would be gone. And she would be gone. The house, her surrogate domain, did without her. I was the eldest of five and a girl, the only girl until my sister was born, when I was thirteen. In my mother's absences I took charge of the house from chaos. I self-assigned the making of an order there, kept it habitable, swept, mopped, put things away. At the same time and perhaps as consequence, my own room became a retreat, a hibernatory alcove. It was lined with rough pungent cedar boards shellacked to a ruddy glow. The wood was alive with knotholes, a host of mysterious eyes and Munch-like silent cries. These mostly benevolent witnesses, imbedded in the walls, stared out at me. Through a set of paned French doors curtained with tulle, the gauzy colors and shapes of my brothers and parents, as in a chrysalis, passed from kitchen to living room. Their voices rose and fell. Clamor and silence, swell and surcease. Inside this room I took myself further away by reading books, drawing and painting, and by writing weekly letters to my maternal grandmother in Missouri, my first correspondent—letters that would later burn in the attic where she had put them for safekeeping, along with her handmade quilts.

But even if letters burn—so important to write them. And important to receive those penciled tablet pages, sometimes accompanied by the flour-sack print dresses Mary Minerva Morris sewed for me by hand.[1] A letter to a child is like a star falling onto the front porch, magical with faraway life, yet dulled out, half-understood, and needing to be reimagined for brilliance. I can see my grandmother's beautifully penned handwriting yet. My mother's mother—whose letters crossed America from Missouri to me in the far Northwest, where she would never go, but where her only daughter had made her place which included, most prominently, a garden. Our letters with news of gardens, what was ripe or coming on—I must have written and received such letters.

Always we knew we could find Mother in the garden. Often we joined her there, helped with planting and weeding the vegetables, picking the beans and strawberries. How intent she was! How present and absent at the same time, not talking except to utter instructions, to show my brothers and me what to do.

I had discovered passion in the classical piano lessons my logger father paid for. But my mother's passion for the garden, her unapologetic seizing upon that engagement, season after season, year after year, has gradually impressed itself as deeply upon me, connected as it was to that mysterious time before she was my mother, a time that did not belong to me except as she loved the garden.

The house, the sure domain of my classmates' mothers, was her reluctant, intermittent sojourn during spring, summer, and autumn. Only in winter did she surrender to being "inside," as she called it, with all the distaste of animal for cage. Otherwise she could be found bending, or down on her knees, digging, or tending to the garden with watering hose, or behind the electric mower, or stock still, eyes squinted against sun, gauging how some plant was doing.

Passion and freedom and the example of industry—I gleaned these at my mother's side. But also I loved how boldly she absented herself, the fact of her being away, *outside*. As she was outside, so was I *inside*— inside in my passion and industry, my yearning for language and story. I went, as she went, without permission. I began a habit of going to my room, doing what my mother called "piling up with a book." I was piling up. At some point my mother noticed this stealing away. Mildly at first, then more vehemently, she took exception to my absence: my piling up. *What* was I piling up? What unaccountable accumulation? What secret store? These were her implicit but unasked questions.

Perhaps it was more than the small wood-framed house could bear—a woman and a young girl unlearning its demands. Neglecting it for periods. Thinking back, it seems I was always being called away from my alcove, my nestled bed-tending of books, read so ardently they wrung tears from me. I recall often that to be in company meant exile. I was brought back to the necessities of the household. My mother called me back. The book would have to be put aside, my place carefully marked with a pressed pansy from the garden. I drew the bedcovers up over its suspended promise like an imagined, ever-waiting glade such as the deer like to enter at dusk.

Only since my mother and I have become widows, living near each other for the past several years, have I begun to realize that she also had been called back into the house against her will during those times. She had wanted not to be alone in the work of the house, which was *away* from her passion of the garden. I was with her and without her in the housework. I left the beginnings of my own inner garden and helped her lift and carry the daily burden of the house. I see from this distance that we were reciprocal conspirators those days, hear her saying silently: *You can have your freedom if you help me have mine.* I let her have the garden. Day by day she let me have, more often than not, those delicious islands of time alone, sunken to a depth with books and painting and music.

Astonishingly, in all this time, it has never occurred to me to ask *why* my mother was going to tend the flowers. It was self-evident that we ate from the vegetable garden. But the flowers that bordered the yard—these were her real treasures.

There is a terrible velocity to family life in any period. So many actions. So little time and inclination to account for them. For so long I have had no idea what questions to ask my mother about her gardening, so my consciousness of it assumed, over the years, a mute regard. The longer I have been watching her go there, the more I have been aware of how much her gardening companions my own yearning, since childhood, to sustain a worthy engagement with language on right ground.

Perhaps I did not ask why my mother loved gardening because I sensed I might disturb her own natural immersion in what one might self-consciously call "the mystery of it"—that which she entered without seeming elevation. I might have feared making her too conscious of her unquestioning impulse to be where she had to be, past reasoning. Maybe I felt I would be turned aside, not admitted, had I asked.

In some unspoken way the garden took precedence over all else for my mother. I sensed, but did not know then, that it was the site of her rendezvous with herself. Yet, beyond that, it was also an intuitive and sustaining way of absenting herself from *self* altogether. It was the one place she spent herself unstintingly. To come upon her there, contentedly alone, was to enter the kind of solitude sometimes glimpsed from a passing car, that single horse grazing in a field, its four hooves following along behind the immensely absorbed head reaching down and out to the grass with lips and teeth.

Where did her mind go?—another unasked question that has incubated in me from childhood. In the garden she was *away*, and all yearning seemed quenched. She moved in a peaceful cocoon of coincidence with herself and the world. It was deep, this space. In it I could feel the richness of the soil, the jutting of an implement into it, preparing it, across time, for seed. She was connected to all those on the planet who had ever raised gardens in times before. So many of them women. And she was connected naturally and importantly to her own mother and the gardens she had helped make with her as a young girl and later as a young woman before her marriage.

I think now that I was drawn as far inward by reading and musing as my mother was drawn outward by her garden and that, finally, there is a place where, some thirty-five years hence, we have at last joined. Her example to me of achieving a freedom of spirit, whatever one's circumstances, was offered so boldly in my youth that it became an inner template: she marshaled herself. I saw her do her own bidding. Gradually I, too, would form this habit with my writing, reading, and musing—to do my own bidding, which is one of the primary mandates of any writer or artist, or indeed, as with my mother's example, of serving one's passionate engagement.

Accompanying this sending of oneself into the solitude of place and spirit, of taking oneself aside and *toward* an endeavor, was another example she gave me. Fruitfulness was not elsewhere; the worthy place of cultivation was near at hand. This was a considerable gift for a working-class child who could easily have assumed that those subjects a writer should honor were lofty and far from the actions of the life evolving around her.

Because the garden sprang with such abundance so near at hand, it became an abiding inner metaphor and visual certification that the place and ground of my own literary garden could credibly spring from those people and lives that mattered to me. It also ratified the dignity and wholeness and veracity of my language—strongly rooted in the language of those around me, their values and ways of seeing.

The word *daring* comes to mind—that I was nourished by my mother's daring to eschew, for periods, motherhood's intense and relentless servitudes. In a time before the mandates of women's liberation, the primary female figure of my life dared to take herself away, to claim another world at the center of our demanding household. I did not know then that the garden would be her stalwart, most abiding companion, outlasting even husband and children.

So it has been with my writing. It has continued to be a vocation that has companioned, consoled, and enlivened me, a place of enduring fruitfulness. This has been especially so since the death of my husband, Raymond Carver, with whom, for ten years, I shared a writer's life. Many people and activities, including my beloved secondary vocation of teaching, have sustained me for periods. But my writing has been and is the "pure place"—a phrase my mother and I came to consider in the following conversation. Although what we each mean by this phrase has different doors, we enter the same room, or in this case, the same expansive garden in which our ultimate freedoms find important and resilient forms for expression.

I don't want to supersede the reader's apprehension of what is transpiring between us in our dialogue—mother and daughter, gardener and writer—except to note that my own attitudes and searchings are, I hope, evident in the questions. I admire my mother's steps to the side, her renegotiations of the questions. Something rare emerges gradually from our exchange—her peculiar, exemplary fidelity to her view of what the garden is and her own part in it. These elements of her thinking, imparted as actions, became infused into my life as a writer and are present by inference in our exchange, even when I don't comment directly.

One of the things I love in retrospect about my mother's responses is that the more I try to lift the plane of discussion to some mental or spiritual consideration, the more she slams me back to earth, to *doing* and *being* as inseparable. There is great energy in her mental physicality, and this is continually accessible to me as blessing and resource.

I am finally more than thankful that both of us have lived long enough to accomplish this dialogue and to understand crucially, once more, that the garden, *the pure place*, has always been near at hand and is now firmly ours. It could have been otherwise. Our chance to connect might never have arrived. But a certain grace has attended us. The mutual solitude of living alone near each other occurred and mercifully left us at each other's disposal. How many children gulp down the mysteries of their parents' and grandparents' sustaining forces without either having had the occasion or the audacity to ask the revealing questions that might draw them to each other freshly, vitally, as these questions have drawn my mother and me?

❧

[The following is an interview Tess Gallagher conducted with her mother, Georgia Bond, about her gardening, in Port Angeles, Washington, October 17 and 19, 1995, at her Bay Street home.]

TG Where did you get the habit of going to the garden?

GB Well, I thought a house is just a prison. You could stay in a house forever and nothing changes, unless you change it yourself. But if you go out in the garden, every day you see a change. Something has changed it. It's changed itself. Without me. And that's the thing I like about it. It changes without me. You go out every morning and look at your plants, see how they've grown. But you come back in the house, and it's still the same old house. Nothing has moved. Nothing done. A house just makes a slave out of you for nothing.

TG You felt more free outside.

GB Yes. If you don't go outside every day, in a week or two you won't know your plants, they've grown so much.

TG So when you go out to the garden in the morning, do you walk around and take note of everything?

GB I do. I like to see if anything I've started is taking off.

TG I read about an eighteenth-century garden associated with St. Francis that was laid out in the shape of a naked woman. What's the shape of your garden?

GB Well, I don't think it has much of a shape. It's just a rectangular lot, a piece of ground, bordered with flowers, with a house sitting in the middle. There's an orchard, a woodshed, and a vegetable garden.

TG And a patch of iris under the cherry trees. And then of course there's the circle up on what we call "the point"—a big jut of land that overlooks the Strait of Juan de Fuca.[2] And there are borders of rhododendron all along the property, with trees around the house and also along your neighbor's property to the west.

In early Japanese gardens, there were rocky islands and these were actually considered the garden itself, so that for centuries the word *shima*, or *jima*, meaning "island," also meant "garden." Do you have any islands in your garden?

GB Not really. I have beds, you know, like the one up on the hill.

TG Where you have spring plantings and gypsophila. A border of rocks that contain plants in a circle.

GB Yes, you could call it an island.

TG What about the vegetable plot itself as a kind of island?

GB No, that's just more of a necessity place.

TG Necessity Island!

GB Yes, "Necessity Island." A place to grow things to eat.

TG In eighteenth-century England, public gardens and some private gardens were considered serious works of art in themselves. I also read that in Japan the creators of one garden even signed the backs of two rocks as one might sign a painting. Where would you put your signature on your garden, if you were going to sign it?

GB I think my signature is already on it, from the trees and things I've planted. It's a growing signature. I don't think it needs to be written out.

TG What is the thing you enjoy most about the garden?

GB Well, whatever needs to be done, I'm going to enjoy doing it. That's where your enjoyment comes in, doing what has to be done.

TG If the garden is instructing you, what does it say?

GB It's saying cultivate me, take care of me, and I'll reward you. That's what the plants say. If you don't take care of them and keep the weeds out, they won't do much for you.

TG You've been working in the Bay Street garden for over thirty years, with another twenty years of gardening on Caroline Street, where I grew up.

GB Let's see. We moved out here the day President Kennedy was shot [November 22, 1963]. OK, it would be thirty-two years at Bay Street. Yes, I've put a good fifty years into these gardens.

TG Does the garden now have a different meaning for you than when you started it?

GB Well it does, because now it sort of takes the place of people. Everybody's gone now, but the garden has stayed. And it's grown. It's taken the place of my husband and even some of my friends who've passed on.[3] Nothing about my garden left with those people who left.

TG So there's the sense that you're participating in the garden's bounty, no matter who comes or stays in your life.

GB Yes, that's it. You get to see if things you're trying to grow will take off, maybe surprise you, I suppose, like people do. For instance, I wanted a butterfly bush. Stevie had one and she told me, "Well, some woman said you can just break a limb off and bury it and it will take root."[4] So I said, I'll get a limb before I go home. The morning I left, I went out to get me a limb, and one had already been broken off. The kids or something had brushed it. It was about six inches long. I brought that home, stuck it in a pot of dirt, and you should see how it has grown! Just a limb. She's going to die when she sees I've got a butterfly bush off hers.

TG So there's a sense of magic. Of taking a scrap or part of one plant and bringing it to life on its own.

GB It's always a challenge with nature, to make things grow. You can take a piece off of geraniums and make them root. The same with fuchsias. They're easy to start.

TG So you feel rewarded when that happens?

GB Yes. A lot more reward than you get out of a house. Even if you had everything just perfect in there. Your dad's mother, she never went outside that house. She went around with her apron tail, dusting off the furniture every day. I thought if I had to do that all my life, I'd go crazy.

TG When you read the garden books you have about English and Japanese gardens, what ideas affect how you think of your own garden?

GB Japanese plants don't interest me much—bonsai and rocks. I like English gardens, with lots of roses and shrubs. They're more like the gardens I enjoy on the West Coast. With bonsai they cut the roots off. I think that's kind of cruel. I don't care for that. They cut a plant down until it will just barely suffer along.

TG There's more a sense of placement and simplicity, and space, and quiet in Japanese gardens.

GB They are more secluded, where our gardens open out. And that's the way with English gardens. Whenever you see a Japanese garden, its usually got screens or divisions around it, bamboo fences or something.

TG Yes, it's more private and enclosed, the Japanese sense of space.

GB They're dealing with smaller spaces than we have here, and smaller plants, too. I have a lot of space.

TG The Japanese word for garden is *niwa*, which means "pure place." There's a feeling of sacredness in this concept of the garden. Do you have that at all?

GB Yes. I think that it's a pure place, all right. That's a good name for it. What is that phrase again?

TG It's one word, *niwa*, and it means "pure place."

GB Pure place. Well, I think that's a good name for a garden.

TG In what sense would it be pure? What would that mean to you?

GB Well, it would mean the same as anything that's pure. It's not contaminated with people's ideas.

TG So the garden is a place to get away from human troubles and memory. And maybe memory is a kind of contamination. At least troubled memory. So the garden is a place where you go to shed trouble. I wonder what relationship musing, or dreaming, has to your garden?

GB I don't have time to dream. I have so much to do that I sort of go real fast. A lick today and a better one tomorrow.

TG I see I had not imagined you in the garden correctly, because I imagined some relaxation—some time your mind could just range about, reel out, and drift a bit.

GB When you live alone, your life is different. You spend your time differently than most people.

TG OK, tell me the difference. I live alone, too. Is there a way to describe what your mind is doing while you're going about your gardening?

GB You don't have words to describe it. There are days when I go out and I don't do anything. Only just walk around and see what needs to be done.

TG I guess I'm trying to understand what relationship the garden has to your life, besides just a do-this, do-that kind of thing. When there are problems in the family, do you find yourself having little in-between spaces where those things occur to you?

GB I don't mix that up in the garden. When I get in the house, I think about things like that.

TG So in the garden, the doing actually frees you from those kinds of considerations?

GB That's the reason you have a garden, really. To have something that takes you away from all your problems. I don't think about them when I'm outside. When you get in the house, you have photographs and all these memories—your problems and troubles are present.

TG Is there any area of the garden you've purposely left wild or undeveloped?

GB Well, yes. Where I planted the rhodies on the western border of the property. I don't bother them. They sort of grow like wild rhodies do in the forest. I didn't intend to create a wild garden, but you often get what you don't intend when you set out plants you aren't familiar with. I planted those rhododendrons in the early 1960s, and I had no idea they would grow so big that they would grow over into each other. You can't even walk in there.

TG Is there any place on the property that invites you more than any other?

GB I think the vegetable garden invites me more during the growing season. Don't you think it would?

TG Yes, and then you spend a lot of time down in those irises. I look forward to their blooming every year in May. I wanted everyone to know the pleasure they gave me. That's why I wrote about them.

Iris Garden in May

for Georgia Morris Bond

Seen from the road, a herd of sea horses
spoils toward night under the cherry trees.
Like the mind of their gardener, they swim

sun-shadowed continents in place. Each bloom's
aperture rules an unruly cathedral, love
clowning the sword hilt. Chalice-like
the standard cups after-rain, casques of impulse
eager to shake us wet with vigilante droplets

as we follow her cautiously. Unlike St. Teresa
she won't be bribed toward affection
with a sardine. She beheads her Decoration Day
bouquet, prefers hybrids which stretch the rainbow
past color to the under-language of hues and scents.
Heaped with moonlight or plucked suddenly
from the icy spine of winter, they stab into earth
like ardor. If the Rainbow Goddess sent this cavalry

to heaven, the message would be flag-handsome
with new-moon audacity. Ask the gardener if she
has anything to do with their Renaissance velvet,
she answers an imbecile: "Why sure!"
She admires their not being gradual, sidereal,
digressive as she—for to open all at once
surpasses mere beauty by infinities of welcome.
Where we step, the bulb, chicken-footed, shows

through soil as if to taunt joy with sinister
origins. So long a widow, her litany recognizes
black as congratulatory: Hello Darkness, its obsidian
purple-black, Houdini's cherry undertones, dark burgundy
of Black Tornado, or the falls of Tabriz tantalizing
like moths' wings. And there—her tallest black, coveted
by the visitor, never to be cut: Black Out.[5]

GB   That's the first time so many people heard about my garden. The
     poem turned out better than I thought it would.
TG   I was lucky.
         You seem to have more help in your garden than I do in my writ-
     ing. You have a kind of invisible partner in nature. Also, since you
     garden, you're more involved with that invisible growing energy
     than, say, people who don't have gardens.

GB Oh, I think that's true!

TG I would say over the years you've become rather devoted to this garden.

GB Well, as time goes on, the garden grows, and grows, and it needs more care. It's sort of outlived me. It's still growing, and I'm eighty-one and getting to where I can't keep up with it.

TG So you've gotten pulled along by your garden, in a way. Your garden is getting younger, more and more vigorous, and you're getting older.

GB Exactly.

TG Maybe this larger love of gardens belongs to women of your generation, those born in 1914 on into the 1920s, who weren't a part of the workforce for many, many years, except as the Second World War demanded in the early 1940s.

GB I think that's true. Now, there's your Aunt Fay; she had quite a garden.[6] She didn't work out of the home either. Stevie, your sister, even though she works all the time, is a lot like me, and you, too—you like gardens. You like to go out and stay in the garden.

TG Very much. Gardening seems to be handed down among the women in our family. But none of the grandchildren seem to have it, except maybe Rijl.[7]

GB Rijl probably will when she gets older. She'll want to have flowers.

TG Was there anyone in your experience who was like you in preferring the garden to the house?

GB I think Mother was. She didn't care about the house. Of course she didn't have much to stay in the house for, only to cook. She was more or less an outside person in her younger days. She helped in the hay fields and in the big truck patches. In wintertime she'd stay in the house and quilt, but otherwise during summer she stayed outside. That's kind of the way I do, too.

TG Have you ever seen a garden you wished was yours?

GB No. I wouldn't trade mine for anybody's because I have a lot planted that most people don't have. And my ground is level; it's not hilly or sloping, or anything. I have a view from the garden, too.

TG You can see the Olympic Mountains from the south end and the water toward Canada at the north end. Obstacle and invitation.

Maybe we could consider what the inner view or concept of a

garden might be. It's been said that private gardens constitute our efforts to evoke paradise in the world. Does making your garden have anything to do with creating your own form of paradise where you live?

GB Well, what do you consider paradise? If you think of paradise as a place where it's kind of solitary, where nothing bothers and things can just grow at their own speed, well that's the kind of paradise my garden is. It can do what it wants to. It's more or less a paradise for the shrubs and rhodies I've planted there. They can do as nature provides for them.

TG You don't have, in other words, any ideal of the garden as the perfect place where no weeds grow. Your garden can have some weeds, right?

GB It can have some weeds. It's natural for weeds to grow where plants grow. If the weeds wouldn't grow there, nothing would.

TG What has your garden taught you about life, about nature?

GB Well, I don't know if you can separate the garden from life. As you live, nature certainly teaches you. If you don't take care of your garden, you won't have it. That's the first and most important lesson.

TG Do you think it's allowed you some peace of mind, maybe, you wouldn't have had?

GB It's given me something to think about other than myself. You can get out amongst the flowers and see if they have any problems. Most of them do. They want you to stay down with them and weed them. And water them, fertilize them.

TG So there's the sense that whatever else the world is doing, you're needed in your garden. I don't have that sense with my writing a lot of times, that it's needed or that I am strictly needed, so this is really an important difference. As a writer I get the sense that the literary world—my literary garden—can go on quite well without my poems or my stories. So I have to go on for my own pure necessity.

GB Well, no garden gives you back directly. It gives you back indirectly because it gives you something else to think about besides yourself. It makes you feel like you're worth something. It lets you know you're needed when you go out and see the flowers maybe wilted and wanting water. The garden would not flourish without you taking care of it.

TG So in a way it starts to represent you. That is, when somebody goes to your garden, they also go to you.

GB Well, they think about me anyway. They think how crazy I was to plant all this stuff!

TG The garden holds you in the moment, that moment. My writing's like that, too.

GB Yes. You're just dealing right there, getting that one thing done. If you want to have peas, you have to go down there and plant your peas, and when they come up, you have to weed, then pretty soon you can gather them. I bet you there's nothing growing to eat clear down this bluff. I don't know whether they don't know how, or they don't have room or time. But everybody in Missouri around where I grew up in the Ozarks planted a garden.

TG What are your first memories of a garden as a child in Missouri?

GB My mother, hoeing up the beds and planting the seeds for vegetables on the north side of the house.

TG So that garden in Windyville, near Buffalo, Missouri, where you grew up, was the first garden you really knew, the garden of your mother?

GB Yes, the garden of my childhood.

TG Did you see any other gardens when you were a child, that you remember?

GB All of our neighbors had a vegetable garden like we did. They'd all get out in the spring and put out their onions and their potatoes, to grow food. If you didn't get out and plant it, you didn't have it. It was a necessity.

TG From what age were you involved in gardening?

GB From five or six on. My grandmother Morris was a great flower woman. I remember when the cosmos came into the catalogs, she wrote me she had discovered this new flower and its name was cosmos, and she said, "I have ordered some seed." This was my father's mother, at Mack's Creek, Missouri. She knew every flower. She also knew that I liked and planted flowers. Every time I see a cosmos plant, I think about her.

TG What flowers do you have in the Northwest you didn't have in Missouri?

GB I didn't have any rhodies in Missouri, or azaleas. You couldn't grow them in Missouri. Because of the heat. They like moist soil. People had just started planting them in Port Angeles about the time we moved here in 1963. There were wild ones, and the nursery people hybridized them, so there were a lot of different colors coming onto the market. Of course that attracted everybody, not only me. The nurseries portrayed them as being very delicate. You couldn't move them—you couldn't do this, you couldn't do that.

TG So you initially took rhododendrons on as a kind of challenge?

GB Yes. I found you could prune them and do just about what you wanted to with them. They come in so many different colors. "Christmas Cheer" blooms at Christmas. So you're never without blooms if you have a variety. I have some blooming now in October. They will, if they're taken real good care of, bloom out of season. They're also green all year, since they don't shed their leaves.

TG What do you remember when you think about your first garden on Caroline Street?

GB Well, I remember that I started out by planting some little trees and shrubs. Then I planted seeds. I didn't have much for quite a few years because I had too many kids. Five kids. I couldn't get outside. Gradually I worked at it. I had a pretty yard. A pretty garden.

TG I remember when anybody came to visit, we'd walk around the yard, and you'd recite the names of the flowers. I remember being amazed you had learned their Latin names.

GB I was just quoting from the seed books. They give the Latin name and also the common name.

TG For instance, you knew baby's breath was *gypsophila.* I remember thinking what a beautiful word it was. It occurred to me that I had a mother who knew a language beyond everyday English. I'm wondering now, why you bothered to learn those Latin names. Did you have to know the Latin to order them?

GB Not necessarily. It all depended on what name they were listed under.

TG So you just took pleasure in knowing the Latin name.

GB Yes. I had a book here that told the Latin and common name of every flower.

TG Well, I like that idea of things' having two names, an informal name and a formal, exact scientific designation. This reminds me of poets and poetry—the importance of naming that Rilke speaks about. Two literary men who also garden, Stanley Kunitz and Peter Davison, each visited your garden at various times and were struck with the naturalness of it, I recall. It isn't formal, in other words.

GB No, not formal. It just has a rightness of where things are, what is growing next to what. I planted a *Metasequoia glyptostroboides,* commonly known as the dawn redwood, next to my bristlecone pine. Stanley Kunitz gave me that metasequoia after your father died.[8] Those two trees belonged side by side because of our friendly argument about which was the oldest tree on earth.

TG We were talking at one point about how private gardens are sometimes opened up and become public.

GB I wouldn't like a lot of people tramping through my garden. Because even though they might get some enjoyment out of it, it wouldn't do the garden any good. I'm not sure it would do me any good, either. If they like gardens, they can go home and make their own.

TG So it is your garden mainly for your pleasure and the occasional visitor?

GB Yes, anybody that wants to visit me; they can enjoy my garden. But it wouldn't take very many people until your garden would be stomped under.

TG So you have the sense of the garden as ultimately being fragile.

GB Yes, they are.

TG Do you think about people who don't have homes or gardens at all?

GB I often sit and think of people living in those nursing homes who don't have a garden. Sitting up there day after day in their chairs.

TG Do you think that there are healing properties to gardens?

GB I think so, especially for people like those elderly people, there's hundreds of them in rest homes right here. Going up and down the hall in wheelchairs, and some of them walking. They don't even get any sunshine. They never see the sun.

TG Your ideal rest home would have a garden attached to it.

GB It would *have* to have a garden. A big vegetable garden. Wouldn't that be nice? And a lot of flowers—roses, a big rose garden. They shouldn't be allowed to build convalescent homes in the city. They should be out in the country, where there's lots of space.

TG Well, the budget will always include a parking lot, but they wouldn't think to provide land for planting.

GB I guess the people who design those places think of it as a retirement place. But that's not the kind of retirement people really want or need.

TG You think of retirement as an active state.

GB Yes. It should be a time when people can do what they *like* to do. You can't find anything you would like to do sitting in a little six-by-nine room. What could you do in there?

TG Well, unless you're a writer. I might find something to do.

GB You wouldn't have any place to put your books. You'd have to put them under the bed.

Notes

1. Mary Minerva Kirk Morris is my maternal grandmother.

2. The Strait of Juan de Fuca is a wide body of salt water that separates the United States and Canada, with the Pacific at its mouth. It leads into Puget Sound on the east and is anywhere from fifteen to over twenty miles across from shore to shore.

3. Georgia's husband, Leslie Bond, died in 1982 of lung cancer.

4. Stevie is Georgia's youngest daughter, who lives four hours away from her, in Bellingham, Washington.

5. The poem "Iris Garden in May" appeared in *Mirabella,* May 1995.

6. Aunt Fay is Mrs. Cecil Bond.

7. Rijl is my niece, daughter of my sister, Stephanie Barber. Rijl was fourteen at the time of this interview.

8. See my essay "To Work and Keep Kind" in my collection *A Concert of Tenses: Essays on Poetry* (Ann Arbor: University of Michigan Press, 1986) for more on this gift.

Why Write?

AMY LING

As a girl in the pretelevision era, I always loved to read but never gave much thought to writing. From the Victorian novels I devoured, I had learned that girls could only aspire to be the inspiration for male authors and artists, never themselves be authors or artists. But one day, when I was in the ninth grade, in Brooklyn, my English teacher gave me an A+ on a paragraph I had dashed off in class, "The Joys of Spring," which reveled in daffodils, tulips, robins, and the welcome warmth. I'd recycled certain phrases I'd read or heard elsewhere, but I'd also plumbed, and slightly exaggerated, my pleasure at earth's return to life. After reading my paper to the class, the teacher returned it with a smile and a new look of admiration. I was astounded but also delighted because my father gave me a dollar for A's in those days. Busy in the kitchen, my mother, the English major, made no comment.

From ages six through ten, I was the only Chinese girl in Allentown, Pennsylvania, and Mexico, Missouri. When we moved to East New York, I became one of a handful in my junior high and high school; and even at Queens College, there were very few Asians. We did not seek each other out, as though for us to be more than one would call too much attention to our alien presence. Not only did I live in a world that idolized long-legged, blue-eyed blondes, but, having skipped two grades, I was two years younger than everyone else and socially immature. Thus, feeling isolated and estranged, I became a diligent student with a painfully insecure sense of self.

Never seeing myself reflected in anything I ever read was another reason that writing never occurred to me. Writing seemed to require confidence, imagination, and experience—none of which I had in any appreciable quantity. So I gazed with awe and envy at my classmate and friend Toni Cade (Bambara), who had lots of all three of these qualities and who later became justly famous. Her mother encouraged her; my mother silenced me: "If you don't have something nice to say, don't say anything." My father only picked out the flaws in my drawings, never mentioned the good points.

Several decades later, after the Civil Rights and Feminist movements, after Maxine Hong Kingston, Mitsuye Yamada, and Nellie Wong had blazoned the way, and after I had been invited to join a supportive women's writing group, I explored my own self-censorship and self-suppression in a poem:

Questions

Of what am I compounded that I simmer,
do not boil; lid clamped tight against the light,
smolder but never erupt to cast rivers
of scorching, hellish red making new lands,
sputter but never soar to explode ruby
emerald magic against night skies
to craning necks and gasping ohs? What
element too much, what too little or in fatal
combination so that nothing has been,
ever is the catalyst? Why like the caterpillar
do I crawl, dragging butterfly's wings?
And worst of all, if ignorance be bliss
why am I punished by consciousness of this?

Finding the right imagery and polishing this poem with the help of others in the group were pleasures so delicious that I couldn't believe it was not forbidden fruit. I had discovered a cool, clear, crystal spring bubbling up inside me—a secret and wonderful source.

After writing a series of poems exploring my between-worlds identity, I moved outward to other members of my family—other sources of deep love and deep pain. Like most daughters, I had/have a difficult relationship with my mother. Nothing I do pleases her, and yet, because she is my mother, I keep trying. She once had me drive her back to Allentown because there were no trustworthy dentists in New York, only to have the dentist in Pennsylvania tell her that she should find someone closer to home. I told her that, but would she listen to me? A concert pianist in China, she hinted strongly, after I began to bring home a salary, that she would like a grand piano. Unable to afford a new one, I looked in Buy Lines and drove her from Queens to Brooklyn to look at a used baby grand. She liked it; I paid for it and had it sent to her house. There it sat for years, untouched. She refused to play and would make lame excuses. Her rejection of my gift hurt and angered me for years until I sat down and wrote:

Mother's Piano

One Christmas mother asked for a grand piano.
She would have studied at Juilliard,
been a concert pianist had it not been for
his daily letters flying visions of love around
the world to entice her back from
America, its golden gate wonders,
satin and lace underwear, new sights all
across the continent, and being a sight herself
at church meetings. "My foster daughter,
everyone, a Chinese orphan, whom I took in
when she was two, now a college graduate,
product of our mission schools, a living
example of the fine use we've made of your
generous dollars, faithful friends, cheerful givers."

Back she went to her own country,
into the arms of a husband, ten months later
in her arms, a child, crying, needing, developing
sores all over its body, running
sores that had to be bathed one by one, raw
sores that came from the bad combination of
their blood, she said; back to a land cratered
by bombs, raped by gun-bearing Japanese; a land
where an egg was a luxury, an orange a celebration.
She had to cut up her chiffon dresses

to make clothes for her daughter.
There was no money for a piano;
this was no time for music.

Thirty years later, with her own house in Queens,
her husband ejected for the accumulated bad blood
between them, her children grown, unnested,
she asked her daughter for a concert grand,
would not hear her house was too small, grands too dear.
The daughter took her all over town for a used baby grand;
mother chose one with a good tone, a Christman.
A tuner checked it over, a mover moved it in,
her friend admired it, but mother said,
"Oh, that thing? It takes up too much room.
Do you know anyone who wants a third-hand piano?"
would not touch it for years,
"I am too tired after work; my fingers will not
move as they used to; they are too old."

One day last summer, she received a letter
from her teacher of fifty years ago.
Rose Waldron, now eighty-three, wanted to bus from Seattle
to see New York and her favorite piano student.
Then mother opened the Christman and began to play.

In writing this poem, I realized more than the usual exhilaration of
transforming an experience into shapeable words and images on a page.
Unexpectedly, I had arrived at a deeper understanding of my mother and
the quality of her life.

The foster daughter of an unmarried missionary nurse to China from
Pennsylvania, Mother, too, had been brought up between worlds. For the
missionary children, she was always "that Chinese girl," while the Chinese referred to her as "that missionary child." Being shown off as a
curiosity in the United States had to have been alienating. So she married
for love but returned after a year of material luxuries to a China in the
throes of war. After we immigrated to the United States, Father, despite
his prestigious ceramic engineering degree, was always the last hired and
first fired. Her teaching credentials from China dismissed in New York,

Mother took up secretarial work. In China she had had servants; here, she had to make coffee for her boss—a task that was, for her, a daily humiliation. I had been the baby with all the sores that she had to bathe one by one; no wonder she was demanding, resentful, and bitter.

In the process of reviewing her story and setting it down, I was able to step outside my own emotions and to regard her through a different perspective. No longer was I the hurt daughter angered by my mother's selfish demands. Instead, I was a woman feeling the justifiable disappointment and anguish of another woman. I was happy that the right catalyst had come back into her life to galvanize her to making music, delighted the piano was being used. She was like a child again, eager to please her teacher. Suddenly, I understood that all her life, she too has been seeking praise from a mother-figure. How much alike we are!

From this experience, I learned that writing can be a great catharsis, a means of untangling knots of gut-deep emotion, sometimes buried for years. The process begins with an inner Geiger counter, surveying my emotional landscape until it discovers a particularly profound knot. I take it out and examine it. It then becomes a subject that poses an intellectual and aesthetic challenge as I work to craft it into a finished object: poem, story, essay. And if I am lucky, the careful word-smithing magically transmutes this personal tangle of emotion into something that moves others. There can be no more satisfying alchemy than this.

However, life goes on. Yesterday, I asked my eighty-four-year-old mother if she liked the intricately beaded garnet necklace I sent her for her birthday. She seemed annoyed: "I don't wear costume jewelry anymore. It's too much trouble to put on and take off." She left the blooming gardenia I gave her for Mother's Day at my sister's house: "Too difficult to care for." And as for the sewing box I gave her at Christmas: "I don't sew much these days."

It's time to write more poems.

Earning Virginia Woolf's Room

EILEEN TABIOS

the places you get
through inwardness take time
MEI-MEI BERSSENBRUGGE

When I left an international banking career in June 1995 to become a full-time writer, I fully anticipated the joys of no longer "putting on the face" with makeup most mornings. But I had not expected the immense pleasure of avoiding pantyhose once I began spending my days in an otherwise empty bedroom that became my writing studio. It is, I romanticize, another form of constriction I gladly threw off to become a poet and fiction writer: I have never felt so free as when I am lost in a world of my own making. But first I had to free myself from the worldly diversions before entering this inner world that I call *Home*. And having found this *Home*, I have had to redefine the meaning of survival in order to earn my version of Virginia Woolf's room.

I have always loved words, a fact resulting in my first career as a journalist. After graduating from Barnard College in 1982, I worked at the *New York Times*, beginning as a copy person. I also concocted story ideas and pitched them to the *Times's* editors. When one of my ideas was accepted, I would research and write the story on my own time since, as a copy person, I had a full day's workload of tedious administrative duties. I became a copy person for access to the *Times* and the possibility of becoming one of their staff reporters after having proven my talents with freelance articles. Two years later, however, I decided to look for a job that did not involve journalism. In addition to my freelance efforts' co-opting time that I would have wished to spend writing my version of the Great American Novel, I thought the journalistic style was constraining my creative writing attempts. The reporter's focus is on reporting the facts related to a news event and I was seeking a more imaginative scope with my writing. I left the *Times* to become the assistant to the president of a private money management firm.

Having eliminated what I had considered the "cannibalizing effect" of journalism on my creative writing, I began to come home to my type-writer after work, ready to begin my stories. However, my Muse had disappeared. This time I didn't have the excuse of not wanting to write when I had been writing all day, albeit in a journalistic vein. Perhaps I would have overcome this "writer's block" had I not become enmeshed in a year-long attempt to end a mad love affair.

With nothing to fall back on during my evenings over the typewriter, I began to pay more attention to my daytime career. My employers of-fered to send me to New York University's graduate school of business. Three years later, I received my M.B.A. in economics and international business and commenced what became a nine-year career as a project finance banker for three of the world's most powerful banks: England's National Westminster Bank PLC, Japan's Sumitomo Bank Ltd., and Swit-zerland's Union Bank of Switzerland (UBS).

Project finance involves a complex set of activities related to construct-ing and operating huge, capital-intensive "projects" around the world, such as power plants, mining complexes, oil and gas production sys-tems, and manufacturing facilities. The projects utilize loans typically in the hundreds of millions, sometimes in the billions, of dollars, and the project finance banker is required to possess sophisticated credit analysis skills and be highly adept at negotiating. I believe I met the challenges of this industry partly because of an ability to conceptualize and be creative in devising solutions to potential risks faced in the project finance trans-action—the type of prowess similar to the creativity required of a fiction writer. Indeed, part of my job was to envision risks that were possible but might never materialize to harm the transaction. Unexpectedly, I flourished in banking, finding it as "interesting" as T. S. Eliot said he once found his banking career to be.

Thus, in the early days of writing full-time, I comforted myself with the notion that if my writing career failed, at least I had enjoyed a successful career elsewhere. Similarly, to cushion the blows of early rejection letters, I reverted to recalling that I was still a worthwhile, intelligent human being—as proven by my banking career.

Project finance, however, also involved many seven-day work weeks and frequent business trips. After four years of its crushing work schedule, I began to reassess whether I was doing what I really wanted to do. I remembered my old dream to work as a creative writer and began to write in my spare time, beginning with some short stories, which are best never to be revealed to the world but which encouraged me as I sensed that, this time, I at least was successful in producing words.

To increase the time I could give to my writing, I also began to explore other careers that would require fewer hours than project finance and offered a more "artistic" environment. I thought, for example, of working for an art gallery. My husband, too, was supportive of my attempts to become a creative writer. But we ran up against a concern that afflicts working artists and the yuppies that some of us were: paying the bills. By this time, I had been married for nearly five years. Though we both earned a reasonable amount of money, Manhattan offered one of the world's highest cost-of-living standards. Although my husband was a lawyer, we needed my income to meet our mortgage's demands. We could have moved to a less expensive neighborhood, but I was unwilling to ask my husband for this "sacrifice." When he first met me, I already was working on Wall Street. In my mind, my husband did not "bargain" for being married to an artist, with all that such a vocation would entail, including the inability to contribute significantly to the family income. If I was to become a writer, I felt I must do so without harming our lifestyle. I felt no compunction about becoming what I wanted to be, but I could not bear the guilt of someone else's "suffering" from that decision. I refused to rely on my husband's observation that suffering takes many forms—such as the anxiety and concern he felt to see my increasing dissatisfaction with my life.

Thus I decided to continue my project finance career while continuing to develop my creative writing efforts. But after another year it became clear to both of us that this juggling act was making me desperately unhappy. The more I worked on my writing, the more I wanted to devote more time to it. Fortunately, my husband's income also increased during that year so that the loss of my income would not require us to give up our home.

I left Sumitomo in June 1993. Finally, I had all the time in the world to write! Instead of feeling ecstatic, however, I felt tortured. Not yet confident that I had the talent to be a writer, I felt as if I were pretending to be someone I was not. It was also the first time in years that we had to live on a budget. I exaggerated the financial pressure's constraints on us because of an unexpected factor: shame at not earning any type of paycheck.

But my insecurity as a writer and the increased financial pressure were nothing compared to the guilt I felt over losing financial independence. For the first time since graduating college, I was not a career woman paying her own way. I was mooching off someone else's efforts. It was 1993, a time when independent-minded women were no longer unusual; and I was thirty-three years old, not a mother and not a "Trust Fund Baby"—I felt I had no business not to be earning my own way.

In the midst of second-guessing my decision to have left Sumitomo, UBS contacted me about an opening in their project finance department. What intrigued me about UBS's offer was that their position involved no marketing for new business; I simply would manage an existing portfolio of project finance loans. This type of position meant that I would not have to travel as much or work long hours. I returned to the project finance industry, rationalizing that the UBS position would not be as intrusive on my creative writing efforts. I had spent only three months at my first attempt to be a full-time writer.

Though I was relieved at again "earning my own way," I also was determined not to lose sight of my writing goals. Coinciding with beginning my new position at UBS, I started a new novel. I decided to write a murder mystery based—where else?—in a bank. I worked on the novel during most evenings and weekends while maintaining my position with UBS. Three months later, I typed "The End" on a completed draft. It was 107 pages long, and the adjective *egregious* would understate its quality. But I treasured that novel—or novella—because it was the longest fiction work I had ever written.

I began my second novel, a book involving my birthland, the Philippines. Two and a half years after beginning my job with UBS, I finished a first draft of that novel. Almost as soon as I finished the manuscript,

I notified UBS of my resignation and publicly proclaimed I planned to work as a full-time writer. This time I felt no reservations. During my years with UBS, I consistently wrote during my spare time, thereby proving to myself that I *am* a writer. I also had received my first acceptance from a literary journal (for a poem and a short story), a success that I felt helped validate my existence as a writer.

To fortify my resolve to be a writer, I had begun to look for a way to become more involved with the literary community. I volunteered to work at the *Asian Pacific American Journal* as an associate editor, a position involving primarily typesetting and copyediting. My stint as associate editor coincided with my last year at UBS and symbolized clearly the double life I then was leading. By day, I held a prestigious vice presidency at a leading global institution; by night I would go to the *APA Journal's* basement office in New York's East Village to type works accepted by other editors for publication. From the office, I would go home, where I would switch from a business suit to jeans and take off my jewelry in order to fit in with the rest of the younger and/or "starving" writers who worked at the *APA Journal.* My project finance colleagues would have been in stitches had they known that I was reporting to editors ten years younger than I and typesetting copy at night. I didn't mind because the *APA Journal* was my only link to the literary world.

I still was conscious of mooching off my husband, but this time I tried to use my self-consciousness about it in a positive manner. I deliberately used the knowledge of surviving on my husband's income to exhort myself to write diligently during a minimum period of the stereotypical banker's hours of 9:00 A.M. to 5:00 P.M. Unaccustomed to working at home and to working on my own, I self-consciously woke up each morning as if I had an office, rather than a room elsewhere in the apartment waiting for me. Fairly quickly my fears about being productive went away as I began to work hours that came to mirror those I had put in during the peak of my career as a project finance banker. The difference is that now I don't notice the passage of time, nor do I begrudge the effort. I have a lot of material that I feel compelled to write. So far, I see no signs of my pace ebbing during my second year as a full-time writer.

When I first announced to business colleagues that I was planning to work full-time as a writer, I did not expect some of their reactions. Some were relieved to learn that I was married to a lawyer who could support me, as if it offered them an excuse for not taking a similar step with their lives. To some, I became a reminder of dreams they once had before ending up "locked" into their careers, whether because of financial pressures or the need to ensure that they could provide for their children. I remain sympathetic with their constraints—I think that one misses what one has known, which partly explains my initial problems with losing financial independence.

Similarly, perhaps one doesn't miss what one does not know. *Children.* There's the rub; I accept that childlessness might become the price I pay for my decision to become a writer. I was nearly thirty-five years old when I switched careers to become a full-time writer. Writing, I believe, is a process, and I need finally to allow myself the time to begin this process, which I felt I had deferred for too long. This need has translated into a reluctance to bear children in the foreseeable future. I do not believe that I can "have it all"—that is, that I can be effective both as a mother and as a writer. I don't know how long it will take for me to become comfortable with the notion that I have put in enough time "catching up" with my late start in writing so that I can turn to other matters, like parenthood. This conflict makes me respect even more those women who have combined motherhood and writing. I feel I would not be able to manage the combination as adeptly as others have.

I am thirty-six years old as I write this essay. Perhaps the parenthood issue may end up resolving itself happily. But its potential for causing regret—that maybe I will wish one day to have a child and it will be too late—has only enhanced my resolve to write well and, in my mind, thereby deserve the joys of the writer's life.

❧

By "writing well," I don't just mean literally writing well. I also believe in "living well." For me, this means living as a responsible member of the literary community. Thus I have targeted the encouragement of young writers as a primary concern and volunteer my efforts with the Asian American Writers' Workshop (AAWW). AAWW's activities include publishing a biannual literary and arts publication, the *APA Journal*; running a reading series that introduces Asian-American writers and poets to students at universities nationwide; managing the country's largest bookstore that sells Asian-American literature; sponsoring writing workshops; and publishing a select number of books.

Within a year after first volunteering for the *APA Journal*, I became coeditor of the publication along with poet and novelist Eric Gamalinda. Though past issues of the *APA Journal* had featured established writers, it was considered at the time to be a journal primarily for young, emerging writers. We wanted to enhance the *APA Journal's* reputation and make it competitive with more established journals. We saw no reason why the *APA Journal's* ethnic orientation should preclude it from also being a top literary forum. In turn, we thought that the best way to encourage emerging writers was to publish them in as well-renowned a publication as possible.

As part of this effort, I thought in December 1995 of asking Guggenheim awardee Arthur Sze if he would be interested in being the subject of a poetry-in-progress article. I confess I didn't know anything about Arthur (whose major collection, *The Redshifting Web: Poems 1970–1998*, was released in 1998 by Copper Canyon Press). However, I had seen a manuscript of his poems floating around the AAWW offices; that manuscript later became *Archipelago*, his 1995 book that won an American Book Award from the Before Columbus Foundation. I liked the poems in his manuscript and thought it would be interesting to interview the poet himself.

Generously, Arthur agreed to share some early drafts of the title poem, "Archipelago," and, since he lived in Santa Fe, to be interviewed over the phone. Literally hours after our phone interview, it was announced that Arthur had received a Lannan Foundation Literary Award for poetry. Thus Eric asked if I could write my article for the issue then under preparation, instead of for the subsequent issue. To meet the deadline, I was forced to write a first draft in three days before faxing it to Arthur for his perusal. Much to my surprise, Arthur made almost no changes to my piece, which discussed his multilayered, nine-part poem. Subsequently we learned that the article was being used in a number of universities' creative writing courses. The response to the piece on Arthur has been gratifying since I continued to fret—for months after the article's publication—that surely I must have done a disservice to Arthur's work. In addition to being quickly written, the article included some of my own reactions to his poem, and prior to interviewing Arthur, I had not thought once about poetics. Only much later would I treasure that experience specifically for exemplifying the joy that can occur from reading a poem when the reader is simply open-minded and open-hearted.

After positive feedback to Arthur's article, AAWW asked me to put together similar interviews/essays with enough of the leading poets in the Asian-American community to comprise a book-length collection. This book became *Black Lightning: Poetry-in-Progress*, released in the spring of 1998 by AAWW's publishing division; its subjects (besides Arthur) include such renowned poets as Garrett Hongo, Li-Young Lee, John Yau, Mei-mei Berssenbrugge, and Marilyn Chin, among other distinguished artists. By offering a collection of poetry-in-progress articles (including first, intermediate, and final drafts of poems), *Black Lightning* is believed to be the first anthology of its type in poetry literature, and it is certainly the first such featuring Asian-American poets. For its innovative approach to poetry, it was awarded a 1997 poetry grant by the Witter Bynner Foundation.

I firmly believe that I might not have had the courage to approach Arthur Sze—or the fortitude to embark on the *Black Lightning* book—had I been in my twenties. Bolstering my courage with memories of my earlier banking successes and being conscious of having started the writing life belatedly, I try not to be bothered by the possibilities of rejection; I focus instead on consistently making the writing efforts and performing related activities as a responsible member of the literary community. Meanwhile, I believe the response to the poetry-in-progress discussions (now a regular offering) helped achieve our goal of enhancing the *APA Journal's* reputation. With the help of the journal's poetry editor, Christian Langworthy, the spring 1996 issue featured poems by Yusef Kumonyakaa alongside works by writers being published for the first time—as an editor, I consider this type of mix to be ideal.

❧

Poetry—over all other forms of creative writing—has become my passion. I began writing poetry seriously only after leaving UBS because I thought the process would improve my fiction. I spent the summer of 1995 focused primarily on poetry. Certainly, poetry has improved my prose writing, but something else happened to me—the joy of feeling I have written a poem is indescribable. I am now addicted to writing poetry. For me, the genre embodies language on its purest level—harking back to my love of words, which first manifested itself in journalism.

Equally important, I came to love poetry because I have discovered that the writing and reading of it works best if the person does not bring to the experience such negative characteristics that the external world sometimes engenders. As a banker, for instance, it was healthy for me to be a bit skeptical of things (sometimes even cynical) in order to penetrate the marketing bluffs underlying requests to borrow hundreds of millions of dollars from my employers. It was also healthy for me to feel a certain level of competitiveness in order to win the mandates for transactions. Unlike some of the activities in banking, poetry requires me to open my heart in addition to my mind and to respond emotionally instead of dispassionately. As a result, I believe poetry has made me a psychologically healthier person—a person I would rather be.

&

I also have begun to use my fiction and poetry to explore my cultural roots. In *Black Lightning* Garrett Hongo says, "To be without history, to be without an emotional life, to be without the ability even to imagine the emotional lives of the people who came before you, is an incredibly damaging thing, an ache that hurts in a way that you don't even realize hurts." Though I was born in the Philippines, I emigrated to the United States when I was ten years old. Thus I grew up "Americanized" and failed to keep up my knowledge about the Philippines. I began to remedy this when I became a writer because I believe that the writer's "inner world" is enhanced by self-knowledge. My attempt to explore my cultural roots is linked with self-exploration. This attempt has resulted in what I consider to be my most meaningful accomplishment to date as a writer: the publication of a short story in the *Evening Paper* in Manila, whose publisher, Alfred A. Yuson, is one of the Philippines' leading poets and fictionists.

When I became interested in knowing more about the Filipino culture, I began by asking questions of my parents. I learned that in the early 1950s my mother was a student of Edilberto and Edith Tiempo, writers who created the Philippines' renowned Siliman Writers' Workshop, partly based on the model provided by the Iowa Writers' Workshop. Starting in 1962, the couple went on to nurture a number of Filipino writers who now are at the forefront of the country's vibrant literature in English. Edilberto, too, was one of the country's leading novelists; his first novel, *Cry Slaughter*, was published in hardcover in London and went through several Avon paperback printings with translations in French, German, Spanish, Dutch, Danish, and Norwegian.

Another of his works, *They Called Us Outlaws,* was used by American prosecutors in the trial of Japanese war criminals after World War II. Edith is one of the Philippines' most highly regarded poets; her textbook written under Ford Foundation and Asia Foundation grants, *Poetry Through Image and Statement,* was critical in the training of numerous Filipino poets.

As a child and teenager, I had not seen much evidence of my mother's literary interests; like my father, she was forced to be more focused on earning a decent livelihood. As immigrants who had both been teachers in the Philippines, my parents were forced to develop new careers in the United States to support a family that included me and my three brothers. In response to my mother's revelation that, once, she too had focused on poetry and that she knew the Tiempos, I wrote a short story titled "The Naming of My Child." Intended partly to honor the Tiempos for their kindness to my mother, the story presents a female protagonist whose discovery about the Tiempos' tutelage of her mother inspires her to plan on naming her unborn child after the Tiempos: "If a girl, Edith; if a boy, Edilberto."

About a year after I finished the story, the Filipino-American poet Luis Cabalquinto (whom I met through *Black Lightning*) suggested that I send some of my works to publications based in Manila. Among other writings, I sent "The Naming of My Child" to the *Evening Paper.* Alfred Yuson immediately expressed interest in it. But I was stunned to learn later that he was so touched by what I wrote that he mentioned me and my story during a eulogy he delivered during the funeral services for Edilberto Tiempo. Unknown to me, Edilberto had died September 19, 1996. Two weeks later, my story was published by the *Evening Paper.* Though it was too late for Edilberto Tiempo to read the story, it was read by Edith Tiempo and their daughter, Rowena Tiempo Torrevilas, currently the Program Administrator of the International Writing Program at the University of Iowa. The following is an excerpt from Rowena's e-mail to Alfred Yuson:

> Thank you very much for the clipping of the Tabios story, which we received a few days ago. Mom figured out that the author must be the daughter of a student they'd had in the 1950's, Beatriz Tilan. I'm astonished and humbled, over and over again, at the regard in which Dad was held—at least its evidences in the messages of love and comfort we continue to receive—and so

the fact (or even the fictional fact) that this girl who's unknown to me would want to name her unborn child after my parents just leaves me speechless. There should be a word somewhere for the gratitude that the halting tongue cannot pronounce.

Subsequently, I also would come to know Rowena, whose first letter to me begins:

> I'm so glad I have this opportunity to thank you for the honor you've done my family in writing the story. Alfred Yuson sent us a copy of your story, and my mom identified your mother at once, and remembers her vividly. As I told him, whether or not the premise was fictitious, I still find it quite astonishing (and humbling) that the influence of my parents' lives and teaching would be so pervasive that the daughter of one of their students would care enough to name her own child (a third generation!) after them.

I remember, too, that when I first showed my mother "The Naming of My Child," I gave it to her as published by a newspaper in our birthland, along with a copy of the e-mail from the Tiempos' daughter. I can only imagine the fullness of her heart matching mine.

~

Shortly after I began writing full-time, I remember thinking that if I did not succeed as a writer, I still would have achieved the accomplishment of avoiding thinking on my deathbed, "What if I had become a writer . . . ?" Nowadays, I prefer to think about life itself—the ways of writing well and doing so by also living well. Many of the best moments in my writing career have stemmed from the incentive to help or promote other writers.

Living as a responsible citizen—I cannot afford not to do so. It is my way of earning the privilege of Virginia Woolf's room, where makeup and pantyhose are the least of my concerns.

Rescue from Within

Do You Wish to Save?

LINDA PARSONS MARION

As a good Baptist girl growing up in Nashville, I was well-versed in the vocabulary of being saved. Every Sunday school lesson, every dime knotted in my handkerchief, every sword drill with Bible in trembling hand, every hymn repeated until the last weeping woman stood at the altar was all meant to set me on the path of salvation. *Are you saved?* the preacher asked like a bell tolling on the hour. *Are you washed in the blood? Do you know Jesus as your personal Savior?* It was cleansing, filing out of the pew with the other sniffling girls, drawn by a force we could not name or explain. We marched down the aisle to Brother Clyde, who placed his moist hand on top of our heads and sent us into the world to rededicate our lives to Christ. I left feeling washed indeed, wrung out, my heart exhausted but gleaming like a new penny.

Recently I met with my financial advisor to rethink some of my meager investments. He worked out pie charts, standard deviations, and percentages on his notebook computer and, voilà, a restructured portfolio. As he exited the program, a message appeared on the screen: *Do you wish to save Linda Parsons?* I laughed out loud at the question but have since considered its truth and irony. The idea of rescue has always been with me. From my childhood of the 1950s and 1960s, the words *and they lived happily ever after* are as ingrained in my psyche as the memory of my grandmother's fried chicken after church.

Because my parents divorced when I was three, I do not remember ever seeing them together as *parents* who might discuss my welfare and future. They spoke briefly at the door when my father came to pick me up, and they have spoken at weddings and funerals over the years, but it has not been in my experience to "have parents" as most people do. My father was a salesman who traveled the Southeast. He would come into town and take me to lunch or visit me in school, neither of us quite sure what to say, but happy and proud to see each other. The time always seemed so short; then he was on the road again, off to "make the beans," as he said. My mother worked as a secretary, so I stayed with baby-sitters until I began school at six. There are photographs of me in a succession of old ladies' homes, perhaps a small toy in my hand; the rooms perfect and orderly—starched doilies on the chair backs, glass figurines on the shelves. I sometimes wonder if the women played with me, if they even knew how to play. I do remember Mrs. Jones; she was younger than the others and her daughter was so jealous she teased me every chance she got and threatened to run away from home.

My mother was young as well and often went out on Friday or Saturday nights. I spent those nights with my grandmother, and she, not Jesus, became my savior of choice. I was the first grandchild and knew I was her favorite. Not in her words or actions, but in my bones I knew. My mother had three sisters, and before they had their own children, we were great friends. I think they were especially attentive in my early years because, as people used to say, I was from a "broken home." Even as other grandchildren appeared on the scene, the times with my grandmother never changed. She worked at a garment factory, cutting buttonholes in men's shirts for nearly thirty years. There was no union, and when she was "laid off" at sixty-five, she had no pension. She enjoyed her work, her days with "the girls," rising at five, taking the bus uptown. She never mentioned the hump that thickened between her shoulders from hunching over the machine all week and half-days on Saturdays. The foreman chose her to finish the buyers' samples, and she always made her quota from the mountain of dress shirts piled at her feet, the blade dropping down as her long fingers flew safely away. I have idealized her over the years: the star buttonholer, the deliverer of Jell-O and popcorn, the soft presence next to me in bed whose teeth soaked in a glass on the bureau, the one who plaited my hair when my mother wouldn't and who let me watch Frankenstein on late-night *Shock Theatre*, the strong woman who willingly took me in, shepherdess to my lost lamb.

At the same time, my mother was beginning her nomadic career, moving from apartment to apartment, house to house, husband to husband. All told, I attended nine schools in twelve years. My memory developed a selective power during those years, which continues today. I remember lines and details from movies and books I escaped into more clearly than the words and actions of real people in my life. It wasn't until I reached my thirties that I began piecing together my family's past. My grandmother, who was abandoned by her father and had to find work early on, was then similarly abandoned by her husband, an alcoholic. My grandfather was a barber working at Nashville's Maxwell House Hotel when he began slipping love notes to a girl sixteen years his junior as she walked home from work each day. He became a disappointed man whose wife left his bed after four daughters, who got drunk and pulled their young bodies next to him when my grandmother was working. In his better moments, he played the harmonica and drew pictures for me—he even built beautiful clocks from scrap wood in his later years. Still, in my childhood, he was little more to me than the wallpaper or the furniture.

I was vaguely aware of the shame that lived in their house like a third person. The shame of my grandfather, who moved his bottle to the other side of the chair whenever anyone walked by. The shame of my grandmother, who faithfully took "glads" to the altar every Sunday and just as faithfully ignored the true weight of her problems by "giving it to the Lord." The shame of my aunts, whose father was a secret to be swept under the rug, along with the memory of his stinking slop jar, his crayon scribbles on the wall, his blackouts. The shame of my mother, whose search for a strong father frequently dead-ended with the wrong man. As this drama played itself out all around me, my grandparents' house was the only unchanging place I knew. I was there to be rescued, to feel secure and rooted, no matter what storm was brewing.

One face of the coin dark, the other light. As a child, I chose to see more of the light because only then would I be lifted into love and rescue. I offered up my life week after week at the altar, rededicating myself to finding goodness in the world; I sought an earthly angel in the form of my grandmother, whose flesh and blood were real and smelled of Emeraude. But my awareness of the dark face was not entirely obscured, and I believe that my writing benefits from the knowledge of this double: the realization that white is the absence of color and that knowing darkness intimately makes it possible to create light within.

The instinct for survival is strong, even in a child, so it was natural for me to seek out my grandmother's light, despite the prevailing storm. At that time my mother had gone from a quickly failed marriage number-two to being involved with a man who left his wife and children to marry her. Richard was deeply handsome, a James Garner look-alike, fiery, possessive. We moved to an apartment over an Esso station he operated outside Nashville. The atmosphere of my stepfather and his workers reeked of vulgarity and sexuality. I can only think of Stanley Kowalski, dragging Stella down into the mire of his baseness; I also think my mother, like Stella, adored the electricity, the danger, the flame in her soul that flared as never before. Soon they were drinking and he was hitting her, blacking her eyes, splitting her lips. And I was watching, those images frozen in my memory. I became a little mother to their first baby, keeping him clear and covering his eyes when the fighting started. Richard got angry when my mother wore slacks, when she rode the bus, when she talked to the neighbors, when she made any move to join the outside world. He gambled away the rent and my father's child-support check. Yet at night and in the afternoon, they made love as if nothing else mattered on heaven or earth.

Then another light broke through. My father remarried, a woman nine years younger who loved life and seemed to find joy and music everywhere. The first time I saw Judie she was wearing black ski pants, so unlike my mother! She took my wrists, clasped them to hers, and swung me around until we were spinning on our toes. As we spun in circles, I felt my other life melting away. Whenever I was with her and my father, usually on the weekends, I felt on top of the world, but I always had to return to my mother and Richard. The difference between the two worlds kept me yearning for greener grass that always seemed just out of reach. On the weekend I was with a woman who laughed, who read me fairy tales, who played Monopoly and crazy eights. During the week I never knew what might happen — or when. Richard would not let my mother take me to the dentist, so Judie took me. He did not let my mother attend school functions, so Judie and my father went. He did not let my mother take me for my booster shots, so Judie did.

Looking back, I see how determined he was, however unconsciously, to break the bond between mother and daughter, and how powerless—or unwilling—my mother was to fight it. One summer afternoon she was sunbathing in the yard, and I was in the house with Richard. I had heard dirty jokes at school and decided to ask him where babies came from. I was eight years old. Even at that age, I realized I was in a highly charged environment and was strangely drawn to the power of this man even as I feared him. He answered my question by exposing himself. He was erect and was prepared to jack off, to show me the "white stuff," but my mother stirred outside and he stopped, saying not to "tell."

Through the years my anger over this incident was sharp and keen; I showed those sharp edges to my former husband and the men I met. Once a friend pointed out to me the number of "knife" and "cutting" images in my poems. I thought she was exaggerating, but there they were, in poem after poem. I had been using language to slice through my pain and laying it out for all to see—a patient not etherized but bloody and raw upon the world's table. Now my sense of being a woman who is loved from within and without has softened and dulled the old anger. The blood in my poems has been transfigured into woman's wine flowing month after month, carrying me into healing and middle age. For many years I resented my mother for not protecting me, essentially for not being my mother. I have come to understand that she could not save herself, so how could she rescue me?

I luxuriated in the time I spent with my father and stepmother—especially Judie. She became a beacon for me, a way to find my way home. I loved my father, but she and I talked like long-lost sisters. Even with a new son of her own, we played on. In the ring of her laughter, I was able to feel, briefly, like the child I was. She read me the story of Snow White and Rose Red. When we were together, I was Snow White, prized and held to the light; with my mother, I was Rose Red, unfavored and kept apart from the one I loved, a shadow casting itself over the world. She read me "The Princess and the Pea." I knew that somewhere inside I too was of royal blood and, no matter how many bumpy trials I faced, the prince would find me worthy in the end. And we would live happily ever after in a land of laughter and light.

Then my father moved his family to Knoxville. I thought my heart would break. I was heartsick, homesick, every way sick. When I was eleven, I decided I had to live with them. I had to be in a world with *mother*, which meant safe harbor, wholeness. Over the years my friends have asked how I knew I had to change my life at that young age. As I approached puberty, perhaps I sensed the danger from Richard coming closer. Was there an argument? A specific event that hurtled things along? I only remember it happened quickly. My mother was hurt and angry, throwing clothes in the suitcase, shouting, "Good! One less mouth to feed!" My father drove from Knoxville to pick me up. All the way back we were quiet, the reflectors glinting like silver dollars in the night. I ticked them off in my head to fill the silence. When I told my grandmother my decision, she said, "You'll be back." I said, "No, I won't." And except to visit, I never went back.

Even at eleven, I knew this change was larger than simply moving to another house. It was more than making a public declaration of faith that might fade like the shine on my shoes. I was seeking an angel of mercy who would enfold me as my grandmother had and whisk me away to safe ground. More importantly, I had chosen one mother over another. *I had left my mother*. This realization, this breaking of a blood bond, has followed me these many years. Our relationship has never completely healed. True, I gained a place on safe ground, but I diminished the ties with my mother's family—aunts, uncles, cousins. Fortunately, whenever I visited, my grandmother stayed as kind and accepting as ever. However, my old feelings of being alone, figuratively orphaned as such, increased as I straddled two families. I began my journey with my new mother, and we had our own difficulties—as mother, daughter, sisters. I continued to see Judie as my rescuer, essentially the prince(ss) on a white stallion who changed my future by showing me joy and hope and play.

Living with my mother, I was expected to be seen and not heard. Except with my grandmother and stepmother, my stories played only in my head. I climbed to the top of an Osage orange next to the Esso station, above the trash heap and the rats that came out at dusk, and created worlds of happily-ever-afters. But I always had to come down to earth. I married young, at nineteen, and tried to create one of those worlds, hoping again for rescue. Several years into my marriage, the voice so long suppressed began to speak—in anger, amazement, and volume. It spoke in stories, poems, plays, and it hasn't stopped. The quiet child who stood waist-high in uncertainty is still learning the sound and source of her own voice. It comes with attention to and awareness of the natural world and the turning seasons. It comes as my daughters grow up and flutter out of the nest. And this voice comes finally from love and acceptance of the self.

These days, I'm writing mostly poems and personal essays. Now, in my forties and living alone, I understand that rescue, like prayer, comes from within. The poem, in particular, has become a source of strength and light and sanctuary. This does not mean that my poetry is purely sugar and spice—on the contrary. Like the altar awaiting the tears of repentant girls, each line leads me to tread the double edges of darkness and brightness, to consider the complexities of salvation, even as I stood blinking in the eye of my grandparents' storm. The poem embodies the order and safe ground I so craved in my mother's and stepmother's houses, the loved rooms I thought would save me. The following is a poem of such rooms and the weight of their memory—a third-floor apartment my mother and I once lived in.

Rocker

Sweeping today as I do every day,
I moved the chair that was mine as a child.
Forty years of dusting the seat, the laughing
clowns, the blob of petrified gum—and the music
box broke off in my hand. It was mine at four
or five, rocking my bride doll, the metal box
making carnival sounds as I reared forward
and back.

My mother and I were alone
in that attic apartment. I skated round
and round the cedar chest my father
had given for their wedding, their hopes
and creased linens locked inside.
It was where I got over my tonsillectomy
and the lie of all the ice cream I could eat,
dreaming each night of the ether mask

coming down like an ax. It was next door
to the house with goldfish in a pond,
where I pedaled my first two-wheeler.
Where I lay me down in the heat
of red measles, the blinds drawn
to save my eyes, the dark like a kiss
on my forehead.

My mother and I remember it
differently. She says the place had roaches
and on Saturdays the landlord chased her
up three flights. She won't even drive
on that street, it takes her all the way
back. I must've rocked through it,
humming to snatches of a child's music,
wanting our lives to swim gently on,
to be nothing less than beautiful
as a pool of orange fantails.

I wrote this poem in a burst of energy triggered when the music box
broke off in my hand. It is a poem of contradictions, the reality of events
and surroundings versus the hoped-for life. As a child, I did not know
the significance of a "hope chest," only that the chest was my father's
gift and it stored things we never used. I did not fully understand our
aloneness without him in those rooms. The poem's promise of endless
ice cream is countered by the very real pain of swallowing, the sickening-
sweet ether, and the five men who, I am told, held me down for surgery.
The darkness and the act of looking away become saviors as such, shield-
ing my eyes from more difficult vision. I travel from my mother's hard
story of those years to the peace of watching the fantails in the pond. Yet
rocking forward and back through the poem, I know that both stories—
hers and mine—contain the truth of our time together.

My poems are the rooms I have sought all my life. I can enter them at
will to examine my flesh-and-blood saviors as well as my inner saving
graces. There the dark is as welcome as the light, both like a blessing on
top of my head. On this solid ground of my own making, I cast into memory—restless waters sometimes murky, sometimes clear. The losses re-

main and sometimes cut like a blade into shirt collars, but each word I write brings me closer to the mother home of body and soul. I sleep every night on a smooth mattress, knowing my blood is as blue as a princess's and common as dirt. By retelling my personal *once upon a time*, I join the women whose fingers are pricked on stories that have brought them through the fire and washed them clean on the other side.

My Father's Legacy, or Why I Write

JANICE EIDUS

Radical politics, dark sexuality, premature death: these three things are, for me, forever connected and intertwined with images of books; and images of books, themselves, are forever connected and intertwined with images of my father.

I grew up in the 1950s, the youngest child of three, in a lower-middle-class housing project in the northeast Bronx, in a predominantly Italian Catholic, working-class, politically conservative neighborhood. My parents—Jews, atheists, and leftists—were marginalized even within this community that was, itself, marginalized from much of the rest of New York City. My father, the dominant figure in our family, was a large man, with bright blue eyes and dark hair—both of which I, alone of the children, inherited. He also was a rage-filled man, frequently irrational and violent. When I was a small child, I drew a picture of a scowling, fierce-looking man entering a room as three frail females clung in terror to the walls. The females in the picture—an adult and two children—represented my mother, my sister, and me; for some reason, I'd left out my brother, although he was, in fact, also frequently the victim of my father's rage. I titled the drawing "The Tyrant Comes Home." My mother was passive around my volatile father, as well as given to frequent debilitating migraines, and she drilled into me from an early age that my father was "a big baby" and that, in order for me to survive in their household, it was my responsibility to learn how to please him. It was difficult, though, for me ever to get it quite right, what pleased or displeased him at any given moment. A loose knob could send him into a violent rage, or a dirty sponge left in the bathroom.

Luckily for me, however, there was one thing I learned to do that never failed to please him. And that was to take down from the shelves of the many bookcases in our two-bedroom apartment—most of which he'd designed and built himself—his beautiful, dusty, hardbound books. He loved books of all sorts: nonfiction, poetry, plays, short stories, novels, even cartoon collections. He loved the very *idea* of writing, of taking the raw material of language, of manipulating and controlling it until something original, complete, and beautiful on its own terms emerged. He also loved to *own* books. Although we were always short of money, he never minded spending what little money we did have on books. So it pleased him enormously when I memorized passages and poems from these books—from *his* books—and recited them aloud to him. And since pleasing my father was so intertwined with my own survival, I was deeply grateful to books and grew to love them.

Among my father's books were the collected works of Edgar Allan Poe. I fell in love with Poe, whose poems, in particular, seemed to please my father. And so I learned to recite them by heart: "Annabel Lee," "Lenore," "The Raven," and "The Bells." While my father sat in his easy chair in the living room, I stood before him and recited, my childish, high-pitched voice throbbing with emotion, my face turned heavenward, and my eyelashes fluttering dramatically. I identified strongly with the heroines of Poe's poems, those frail young girls who died so young, and so romantically. I sometimes longed for a similar escape.

My father also took great pleasure in telling me tales—some real, some imagined—of Poe's own wanton life and premature death. When my teacher took my class on a trip to "Poe's Cottage"—the cottage in Poe Park in the West Bronx where Poe had lived for a while—I eagerly let her know that I knew all about Poe's alcohol and drug addictions as well as his emotional problems. She was shocked and quickly changed the subject. (Before the trip, my father—always mischievous and always eager to subvert the authority of others—had urged me to demand that my teacher show us Poe's liquor bottles and opium pipes, but I had stopped short of that.)

Books pleased my father in another way, too: my brother, sister, and I would sit on the rug before him while he read aloud to us sections of his political books, educating us about class and race issues, and any other issues he deemed important. A great favorite was *The Atheist Manifesto*, a slim hardback. He would read from it so beautifully—with so much passion and force—that I was completely won over to the book's argument. I felt especially united with him at those moments because I, too, understood (even if I was only five years old) that religion was the opiate of the masses. And I also knew that it pleased him greatly that I'd taken his side against the oppressors. Another favorite work of his was *The Green Pastures,* by Mark Connolly—a play that, for liberals of my parents' generation, was innovative and groundbreaking. It takes place in a sunny outdoors Heaven—located in the deep South—where a festive fish fry is in progress and where God and the Angels are all poor and black. My father would have us perform it with him, and naturally, during these performances—despite his atheism—he always assigned himself the role of the powerful, but benign, God. My brother, sister, and I were the Angels. We would sit at God's feet, rapt and adoring, as he read his lines. And then, in unison, we would happily sing out our scripted angelic praise of His wise and mighty proclamations.

My father was a pharmacist. He'd gone to college on the GI Bill after he'd fought in World War II. He'd gone into pharmacy because it was one of the fields then open to Jewish men without money or connections. He had written short stories and poems in college, however, and he frequently lamented not having gone on to write professionally. For a while, he'd thought about teaching English in the public school system—another career then open to Jewish men—in order, I suppose, to instill his own love of books in the hearts of countless worshipful pupils. My mother told me years later how happy she'd been that he decided not to go into teaching, however, since with his temper, she said, "he would have killed someone." And, after all, he had me—his *most* worshipful pupil. My father frequently told me stories about his own childhood. To me, these anecdotes simply sounded like tales from another of his wonderful, dramatic books, not much different from Poe's tales or the tragic narratives of "The Highwayman," "The Rime of the Ancient Mariner," and "The Solitude of Alexander Selkirk"—the other poems I loved to recite to him. He would tell me about his violent mother and father, who had fistfights in front of him, and how he would run away from home, sleeping on park benches, until his father found him and hit him over the head with a violin (his father was a vaudevillian violinist) and then drag him home by his hair. My mother frequently said that

I was like the members of *his* family—hot-tempered and stubborn—whereas my sister and brother, she would say, were like the members of *her* own, much calmer, nicer family. Whatever my mother's intentions, I felt flattered to be included among my father's family, these colorful, fictional-seeming characters, none of whom (with the exception of my father's older brother, who lived in a nearby suburb) I had ever met. They all lived in California, and for some reason—perhaps financial, perhaps emotional—there were no visits back and forth. It was only as I grew up that I began to hear the subtext, the pain in my father's stories, and came to understand what a sad book it was that his life would have made.

When I was very small, my father worked at a pharmacy in the South Bronx, a rough Latino neighborhood. His dream, however, was to own his own pharmacy. Despite his leftist politics, he had a fervent desire to become a capitalist, to *own* something, just as he loved to *own* books, to see great numbers of them displayed in his bookcases. He and his brother decided to go into partnership together, starting up a pharmacy in the West Bronx, near Yankee Stadium. My uncle, an affluent lawyer, was the silent, moneyed partner, while my father worked in the store with a third partner, also a pharmacist. Eventually my father and my uncle had an explosive falling out and never spoke to each other again. Years after that, my father and his other partner, too, had a dispute and also never spoke again. And eventually the pharmacy went bankrupt.

But what had fascinated me most about my father's pharmacy when I was a child hadn't been his volatile dealings with his partners. It was, rather, the pharmacy's paperback book rack. Again, he seemed especially proud that he sold not merely pharmaceuticals and cosmetics but *books* too. From age ten or eleven, I would go over and pick books off the shelves, as many as I could load up in my arms. They were less beautiful, true, than my father's big, dusty tomes, but they were so much lighter, and in a way, they were still *his*. My father was too busy working around the clock, trying to make his store into a success, to take any notice of *which* books I was grabbing from the shelves. He never knew that among my new books were a group of soft-porn novels. My favorite was *Awake, Monique*, about a woman who learns true sexual happiness after a number of false starts. He also never knew that I was discovering formalist and "experimental" novels like *The Floating Opera* and *The End of the Road,* by John Barth, books that were a far cry from his own favorites, the political, social realists—Steinbeck, Hemingway, Odets, Sinclair Lewis. Since he never did find out, though, he remained genuinely pleased by my continued interest in *his* books, from *his* very own store.

Only once do I remember a book displeasing my father. I was fourteen or fifteen, in my room, lying in bed, reading *Another Country*, by James Baldwin. My father came into my room—for what reason I can't remember—saw what I was reading, and flew into a rage. He didn't strike me, although I waited for it. But I was shocked. He had always been irrational, true, but never about *books*. Books were our great bond; we shared reverence for books. "Garbage, trash! I forbid you to read this!" he kept shouting. It was inexplicable, but I didn't question him or try to defend myself, since I had learned by then that those things were to no avail. Instead, I agreed not to finish reading it, although I didn't have a clue what had so enraged my father. I knew it couldn't be because Baldwin was black; my father, the leftist, had more black friends than white friends. And it certainly couldn't be Baldwin's politics. I figured I would understand soon enough, though, since I intended to finish it in secret anyway, despite my promise. (I had learned, too, by then that secrecy within my family was a great help to survival.) But still, even after I'd finished reading *Another Country*, I couldn't see what had so enraged my father. It was a beautifully written book about marginalized people, and it dealt boldly with issues of class and race. In other words, it was exactly the kind of book, as a leftist Jew in a Bronx housing project, my father had brought me up to love. It was only years later that I understood, after I'd left home, when as an adult I would casually mention things to my father about my gay friends, male and female. Because only then did I learn that my father—despite his liberalism—was homophobic. And I realized that, back when I was a teenager, he'd been frightened that Baldwin's beautifully rendered, powerful scenes of homosexual sex would win me over to "the love that dare not speak its name," as perhaps my father himself had once won me over—also through the power of a book—to his atheism.

Still, despite that disappointment, most of my happy memories of childhood *are* about books. And I like to think that this holds true for my brother as well, who grew up to be a labor organizer and who's as passionate and fierce about books and politics as my father. My sister—who died young of a rare, particularly brutal form of cancer, with nothing at all romantic or Poe-like about her premature death—also loved books. And for me, writing has come to be synonymous with my very survival. When I'm not writing—creating my *own* stories and books—I don't feel alive. It's clear to me that, like my father, I must have something that I can claim ownership of, something that I can control fully. When I'm writing, I feel, always, as though I've entered a very safe place—a place of "green pastures," a place where, through the power of even just one book, three frightened little children can be transformed into Angels and an angry father into a most benign and loving God.

Contributors

Sandra Benítez, Puerto Rican and Midwestern by heritage, grew up in Mexico, El Salvador, and Missouri. She is the author of *A Place Where the Sea Remembers* (Coffee House Press, 1993; Scribner's, 1995), which won the Minnesota Book Award and the Barnes and Noble Discover Award and was a finalist for the *Los Angeles Times's* Art Seidenbaum Award for First Fiction. A second novel, *Bitter Grounds*, was published by Hyperion in 1997 and won an American Book Award. Benítez was the Keller-Edelstein Distinguished Writer in Residence at the University of Minnesota in 1997.

Julie Checkoway's books include *Little Sister: Searching for the Shadow World of Chinese Women* (Viking, 1996) and *Creating Fiction* (Story Press, 1999). She is the recipient of a fellowship from the National Endowment for the Arts and currently is director of the Creative Writing Program at the University of Georgia as well as president of the Associated Writing Programs. Her fiction has appeared in literary journals and is listed in *The Best American Short Stories 1991*. At present she is at work on a novel. A native of Massachusetts, she lives in Athens, Georgia, with her husband and daughter.

Patricia Clark's *North of Wondering* won the first-book award from Women-in-Literature, Inc., and will be published in 1999. Clark is associate professor of English at Grand Valley State University in Michigan and is the university's first poet-in-residence. Her poetry won the 1997 *Mississippi Review* Prize, and she has also won the Lucille Medwick Memorial Award from the Poetry Society of America. Clark is coeditor of *Worlds in Our Words: Contemporary American Women Writers*.

Lucille Clifton's most recent books of poems are *the terrible stories* (BOA, 1996) and *the book of light* (Copper Canyon Press, 1993). She is the only author to have had two books selected as finalists for the Pulitzer Prize in the same year—*good woman: poems and a memoir 1969–80* and *next: new poems*, both published by BOA in 1988. Her many volumes for children include the award-winning series of Everett Anderson stories and *Three Wishes* (1992). Clifton has won an Emmy Award for her children's programming on Public Television. Her honors include the Shelley Memorial Prize, the Juniper Prize, and two fellowships from the National Endowment for the Arts. She served as Poet Laureate of Maryland from 1979 to 1985 and is Distinguished Professor of Humanities at St. Mary's College in Maryland.

Judith Ortiz Cofer, coeditor of this volume, is a poet, essayist, novelist, and short story writer. Her many volumes include the novel *The Line of the Sun* (1989), *The Latin Deli: Poetry and Prose* (1993), which won the Anisfield Wolf Book Award, and a memoir, *Silent Dancing* (1990). Her most recent books are *An Island like You: Stories of the Barrio* (1995) and *The Year of Our Revolution* (1998). Her stories have won both the Pushcart Prize and the O. Henry Prize. She is professor of English at the University of Georgia.

Janice Eidus is twice winner of the O. Henry Prize as well as a recipient of the Pushcart Prize. She is the author of two volumes of short stories, *The Celibacy Club* (1997) and *Vito Loves Geraldine* (1990), as well as two novels, *Faithful Rebecca* (1987) and *Urban Bliss* (1998). Her writing has appeared in many anthologies including *The Oxford Book of Jewish Short Stories* and *Worlds in Our Words: Contemporary American Women Writers*.

Lucy Ferriss is the author of four novels, including *The Misconceiver*, published by Simon and Schuster in 1997. She is also the author of a work of literary criticism, *Sleeping with the Boss: Female Subjectivity and Narrative Pattern in Robert Penn Warren* (1997). Her essays and short stories have appeared in the *New York Times*, the *Missouri Review*, and other publications. She teaches English and creative writing at Hamilton College in New York and was awarded a Fulbright lectureship to Brussels in 1999.

Amy Friedman Fraser writes a weekly children's feature, *Tell Me a Story*, which is syndicated by Universal Press Syndicate and runs in twenty newspapers worldwide. She is the author of several books—two works of nonfiction and two children's story collections—and she teaches college writing. She and her husband, dogs, and cats live on the edge of the St. Lawrence River in Gananogue, Ontario.

Alice Friman won the 1998 Ezra Pound Poetry Award from Truman State University for her book *Zoo*, forthcoming from the University of Arkansas Press. Her most recent poetry collection is *Inverted Fire* (BkMk Press, 1997). Published in ten countries, Friman's poems have appeared recently in the *Ohio Review, Boulevard, Prairie Schooner, Gettysburg Review*, and *Field*. Among her honors are first prize in the *Akibo Quarterly* International Poetry Contest (1994), three prizes from the Poetry Society of America, and an Individual Artist Fellowship from the Indiana Arts Commission (1996–97).

Tess Gallagher is a poet, short story writer, essayist, and translator who lives in Port Angeles, Washington. Her most recent book of fiction is *At the Owl Woman Saloon* (Simon and Schuster, 1997). Recent volumes of her poems include *Portable Kisses* (1996), *My Black Horse: New and Selected Poems* (1995), and *Moon Crossing Bridge* (1992). She was the Edward F. Arnold Visiting Professor of English at Whitman College in 1996–97 and Stadtler Poet-in-Residence at Bucknell in 1998. In May 1998 she received an honorary Doctorate of Humane Letters from Whitman College.

Barbara Goldberg is the author of five books of poetry—most recently, *Marvelous Pursuits* (Snake Nation Press, 1995), winner of the Violet Reed Haas Award. Goldberg coedited, with the Israeli poet Moshe Dor, *After the First Rain: Israeli Poems on War and Peace* (Syracuse University Press, 1998). She is the recipient of two fellowships from the National Endowment for the Arts and three grants from the Maryland State Arts Council, and she has received a Translation Award from Columbia University. Her work has appeared in the *Paris Review, Harvard Review*, and *Poetry*. Goldberg is currently an executive speechwriter for AARP.

Joy Harjo is an enrolled member of the Muskogee tribe. Her most recent books of poems are *The Woman Who Fell from the Sky* (1994) and *In Mad Love and War* (1990), which won the William Carlos Williams Award from the Poetry Society of America in 1991. With Gloria Bird, Harjo coedited an anthology of native women's writing, *Reinvent-*

ing the Enemy's Language (Norton, 1997). She and her band, Poetic Justice, have released a CD titled *Letters from the End of the 20th Century*.

Colette Inez has authored eight books of poetry, the most recent of which, *Clemency*, was published by Carnegie Mellon University Press in 1998. She has received fellowships from the Guggenheim and Rockefeller foundations, as well as two fellowships from the National Endowment for the Arts. Widely published in literary journals, Inez has taught poetry at Cornell, Ohio, and Bucknell universities, the New School, and other institutions. She is currently an associate professor in the Writing Program at Columbia University.

Marilyn Kallet, coeditor of this volume, is director of the Creative Writing Program and professor of English at the University of Tennessee, Knoxville. She is the author of eight books, including three volumes of poetry, as well as anthologies, essays, criticism, and translations. Her most recent books are *How to Get Heat Without Fire* (New Messenger/New Millennium Writings, 1996) and *Worlds in Our Words: Contemporary American Women Writers* (Blair Press/Prentice-Hall, 1996). Kallet has received numerous fellowships from the Virginia Center for the Creative Arts and the Mary Anderson Center for the Arts. She is also a recipient of the Tennessee Arts Commission's Literary Fellowship in poetry.

Denise Levertov was born in England and emigrated to America after World War II. Her citizenship and her poetry were American. She published more than thirty books of poetry as well as translations and essays during her lifetime. Her last published works are *The Life Around Us: Selected Poems on Nature* and *The Stream & the Sapphire: Selected Poems on Religious Themes* (New Directions, 1997). *This Great Unknowing: Last Poems* will be published by New Directions in 1999. Among Levertov's numerous honors is an Academy of American Poets Fellowship for distinguished poetic achievement.

Mary C. Lewis is the author of *Herstory: Black Female Rites of Passage,* a study on teenage girls, published by African American Images. She has received a grant from the Chicago Department of Cultural Affairs (1997) and two prose fellowships from the Illinois Arts Council (1995 and 1999). She has been a Fellow at the Virginia Center for the Creative Arts, Ox-Bow, Ragdale, and Hedgebrook. Lewis has also taught creative writing at Columbia College in Chicago, the city where she resides.

Amy Ling was born in Beijing and came to the United States when she was six. She received her undergraduate degree from Queens College of the City University of New York, her M.A. from the University of California at Davis, and her Ph.D. from New York University. Ling is currently professor of English and Asian American Studies at the University of Wisconsin at Madison. She has published a volume of poetry and paintings, *Chinamerican Reflections* (1984), and a work of groundbreaking scholarship, *Between Worlds: Women Writers of Chinese Ancestry* (1990), and she has coedited several volumes of multicultural literature. Her most recent anthology is *Yellow Light: The Flowering of Asian American Arts* (1999).

Linda Parsons Marion is poetry editor of *Now & Then: The Magazine of Appalachia*. Her most recent volume of poetry is *Home Fires* (Sow's Ear Press, 1997), and her poems have been published in the *Georgia Review* and the *Iowa Review,* among other national magazines. Her honors include the Tennessee Arts Commission's Literary Fellowship in poetry (1998–99) and the Tennessee Writers Alliance Poetry Award (1996). She is coeditor of *All Around Us: Poems from the Valley* (Blue Ridge Publishing, 1996).

Colleen J. McElroy is professor of English and creative writing at the University of Washington. Among her six poetry collections are *Lie and Say You Love Me, Queen of the Ebony Isles, Bone Flames,* and the most recent, *Travelling Music.* She has also written two volumes of short fiction, a textbook on language and the preschool child, two films on language acquisition, a collection of travel memoirs, and plays and screenplays for Public Television; a volume of her translations of folktales is forthcoming. She is editor in chief of the *Seattle Review.* Among her honors are the Before Columbus Foundation's American Book Award for *Queen of the Ebony Isles,* a Pushcart Prize for poetry, and two fellowships from the National Endowment for the Arts.

Tillie Olsen, born in Omaha in 1912 or 1913, was largely self-educated through what she has called "the college of life, the college of work, and the college of motherhood." *Tell Me a Riddle* (1961, 1995) won the Rea Award for the Short Story. Her published fiction also includes *Yonnondio: From the Thirties* (1974) and *Silences* (1978). Olsen's groundbreaking essay on silences in writers' lives remains a classic in feminist studies. Olsen composed *Mother to Daughter, Daughter to Mother, Mothers on Mothering: A Daybook and Reader* (1984) and, with her daughter, Julie, published *Mothers and Daughters: That Special Quality: An Exploration in Photographs* (1987, 1995). She received the O. Henry Award for her story "Tell Me a Riddle," a Guggenheim Foundation Fellowship, and grants from the Ford Foundation and the National Endowment for the Arts.

Hilda Raz's most recent books are *Divine Honors* (Wesleyan Poetry Series, University Press of New England, 1997) and *Living in the Margins: Women Writers on Breast Cancer* (Persea Books, 1999). She is editor in chief of *Prairie Schooner* and professor of English at the University of Nebraska.

Aleida Rodríguez was selected by Marilyn Hacker to win the Kathryn A. Morton Poetry Prize for her book *Garden of Exile* (Sarabande Books, 1999). Her work has appeared in many journals, textbooks, and anthologies since 1973, including *Not for the Academy* (Onlywomen Press, England, 1999), *In Short: A Collection of Brief Creative Nonfiction* (W. W. Norton, 1996), the *Spoon River Poetry Review* (Editors' Prize winner 1996), the *Kenyon Review, Prairie Schooner, Ploughshares,* and ZYZZYVA. Among her awards are fellowships from the National Endowment for the Arts, the California Arts Council, and the California Community Foundation.

Katherine Smith's poetry has appeared in many literary journals including *New Millennium Writings, Berkeley Poetry Review, Clockwatch Review, Many Mountains Moving,* and *Now & Then.* Among the honors she has received are an Academy of American Poets Award, the Knoxville Writers' Guild Libba Moore Gray Award in Poetry, and two fellowships from the Virginia Center for the Creative Arts.

Eileen Tabios is the author of a poetry collection, *Beyond Life Sentences* (Anvil, 1998), and *Black Lightning: Poetry-in-Progress,* a collection of essays about Asian-American poets (Asian American Writers' Workshop, 1998), for which she received a 1997 Witter Bynner Poetry Foundation grant. She is currently editing *The Anchored Angel: The Selected Works of José García Villa,* a volume devoted to the most important contemporary English-language poet of the Philippines. Tabios is editor of the *Asian Pacific American Journal.*

Pamela Walker received her M.F.A. in fiction from the University of Iowa Writers' Workshop, and she earned an M.Ed. in learning disabilities from Bank Street College in New York City. With two other women, Walker opened the Bronx Dance Academy, a New York public school of choice in which academics are integrated with the arts. Her publications include a novel, *Twyla,* and short fiction that has appeared in *Hawaii Review* and *Iowa Woman.* She has been awarded fellowships from the Virginia Center for the Creative Arts and from Yaddo.

Lynna Williams was formerly a political reporter and speech writer in Texas and Minnesota and is now an associate professor of English at Emory University in Atlanta. Her short fiction has been published in the *Atlantic, Lears,* and a number of literary magazines. *Things Not Seen and Other Stories,* her first collection, was named a Notable Book of the Year by the *New York Times.* She is at work on a novel, *The Faith of Gazelles.*

Elaine Zimmerman is executive director of the Connecticut Commission on Children. Known for community organizing and crafting national policy agendas, she has written numerous articles on policy-making. Most recently her poetry has appeared in *Worlds in Our Words: Contemporary American Women Writers.* During the summer Zimmerman teaches a course titled "Policy as Democracy" at the Transregional Center for Democratic Studies in Krakow, Poland, under the cosponsorship of the New School for Social Research. Her poetry on the Holocaust is currently being translated into Polish.

DATE DUE

MAR 2 1 2002			
APR 2 7 2004			